The Contemporary Western

The Contemporary Western
An American Genre Post-9/11

John White

EDINBURGH
University Press

Edinburgh University Press is one of the leading university presses in the UK. We publish academic books and journals in our selected subject areas across the humanities and social sciences, combining cutting-edge scholarship with high editorial and production values to produce academic works of lasting importance. For more information visit our website: edinburghuniversitypress.com

© John White, 2019, 2021

Edinburgh University Press Ltd
The Tun – Holyrood Road
12 (2f) Jackson's Entry
Edinburgh EH8 8PJ

First published in hardback by Edinburgh University Press 2019

Typeset in Monotype Ehrhardt by
IDSUK (DataConnection) Ltd

A CIP record for this book is available from the British Library

ISBN 978 1 4744 2792 0 (hardback)
ISBN 978 1 4744 2793 7 (paperback)
ISBN 978 1 4744 2794 4 (webready PDF)
ISBN 978 1 4744 2795 1 (epub)

The right of John White to be identified as author of this work has been asserted in accordance with the Copyright, Designs and Patents Act 1988 and the Copyright and Related Rights Regulations 2003 (SI No. 2498).

Contents

List of Figures vi
Acknowledgements vii

1. Introduction 1

Part I The Cinema of Heroes and Heroic Action
2. Reclaiming the Heroes and Heroic Attitudes of
   Classic Westerns: *Open Range* (2003) 21
3. Restoring the Western Hero and Reclaiming the
   Classic Hollywood Experience: *True Grit* (2010) 36
4. Defending Home, Defending Homeland: *Jane Got a Gun*
   (2016) 54

Part II The Cinematic Big Screen, Surround Sound, Ride
5. Updating the Escapism of the Western:
   The Lone Ranger (2013) 73
6. Affect and the Immersive Experience of Bodily Excess:
   The Revenant (2015) 91
7. The Anchorless Postmodern Experience within an Ahistorical
   Filmic Space: *Django Unchained* (2012) 109

Part III The Cinema of Contemplative Reflection
8. Employing Religious Concepts to Address the
   Political Situation Post-9/11: *The Three Burials of
   Melquiades Estrada* (2005) 133
9. Living in a World of Fear and Inexplicable Evil: *The
   Assassination of Jesse James by the Coward Robert Ford* (2007) 152
10. Conclusion 168

Bibliography 179
Index 194

Figures

1.1	The role, purpose and usefulness of 'gun work' and those who are able to perform it, visually emphasised in *Appaloosa*	10
2.1	The trail boss revered by the cinematography in *Open Range*	22
2.2	Charley demonstrating the 'ability' when necessary to execute declared enemies in *Open Range*	30
3.1	Mattie with her father's handgun viewed in close-up in *True Grit*	39
3.2	LaBoeuf intervenes to kill Pepper from distance in *True Grit*	46
4.1	Jane professionally loading her handgun in *Jane Got a Gun*	57
4.2	Jane, dominant and empowered, as she is about to execute Bishop in *Jane Got a Gun*	60
5.1	Tonto gazing at us as spectators watching the film, in *The Lone Ranger*	76
5.2	'For God and for country!': the US Army in *The Lone Ranger*	85
6.1	The lynched body of Hikuc in *The Revenant*	94
6.2	Hawk viewed alongside an image of the crucified Christ in *The Revenant*	104
7.1	Immediate visual representation of the brutality of the African American experience, in *Django Unchained*	112
7.2	Schultz shows his distress at Beethoven being played in the Candieland mansion, in *Django Unchained*	119
8.1	For the first time in the film Mike shows signs of empathy with another person: *The Three Burials of Melquiades Estrada*	140
8.2	Mike is required, highly symbolically, to drink from Melquiades's cup: *The Three Burials of Melquiades Estrada*	142
9.1	Jesse boxed and framed in relation to 'the cross' in *The Assassination of Jesse James by the Coward Robert Ford*	154
9.2	Jesse dressed in black and standing in darkness in *The Assassination of Jesse James by the Coward Robert Ford*	156
10.1	Warpaint erasing any sense of shared humanity in *Hostiles*	174

Acknowledgements

Thanks are due to Matthew Carter and Marek Paryz for allowing me to work through ideas for Chapter 3, which first appeared as 'Defending Home, Defending Homeland, Post-9/11: *Jane Got a Gun*', in their edited special issue, 'The Visual Language of Gender and Family in the Western', for *Papers on Language & Literature*, 54: 1 (2018).

I would also like to thank Lee Broughton for his help and advice in ordering the material in Chapter 8, much of which first appeared as 'Contemporary Obsession with the Inexplicable Nature of Evil as Expressed in *The Assassination of Jesse James by the Coward Robert Ford*' in his edited collection *Critical Perspectives on the Western: From A Fistful of Dollars to Django Unchained* (2016), published by Rowman & Littlefield.

CHAPTER 1

Introduction

I

As George W. Bush concluded his presidential victory speech on 13 December 2000, he set out America's view of the world and its place within it as he (and his speechwriters) saw it:

> I have faith that with God's help we, as a nation, will move forward together as one nation, indivisible. And together we will create an America that is open, so every citizen has access to the American dream; an America that is educated, so every child has the keys to realize that dream; and an America that is united in our diversity and our shared American values...[1]

In its emphasis on 'God', 'nation', 'the American dream' and 'American values', and in its fusing of these elements, this speech expressed the essence of the dominant American ideology and revealed the backbone to that world view to be an implicit belief in the destiny of America as a world leader. The image given is of a country rooted in its religious belief and confident in its relationship with God. This is a country that is united: 'indivisible' picks up the words of the 'Pledge of Allegiance', 'one Nation under God, indivisible, with liberty and justice for all'. The nature of 'the American dream' does not need to be spelled out because it is a mantra that has been chanted an infinite number of times. 'American values' do not need to be listed because they are embedded within this very speech: faith, unity, openness, equality, education, diversity, reason, freedom. A moment's consideration, of course, reveals the papering over the cracks that has been necessary for the speechwriters in crafting, for the president in delivering, and for audiences in applauding these words.

Less than twelve months after his victory speech, on 20 September 2001, Bush addressed Congress following the al-Qaeda attacks of 11 September 2001 on the World Trade Center and the Pentagon, events that came to be referred to as 9/11:

> Tonight we are a country ... called to defend freedom ... Whether we bring our enemies to justice, or, bring justice to our enemies, justice will be done.

> On September the 11th, enemies of freedom committed an act of war against our country. Americans have known wars, but for the past 136 years they have been wars on foreign soil, except for one Sunday in 1941 . . .
> Americans are asking, why do they hate us? . . . They hate our freedoms – our freedom of religion, our freedom of speech, our freedom to vote and assemble and disagree with each other.
> . . . I ask you to live your lives, and hug your children . . . I ask you to be calm and resolute, even in the face of a continuing threat. I ask you to uphold the values of America, and remember why so many have come here. We are in a fight for our principles, and our first responsibility is to live by them. No one should be singled out for unfair treatment or unkind words because of their ethnic background or religious faith.
> Great harm has been done to us. We have suffered great loss. And in our grief and anger we have found our mission and our moment. Freedom and fear are at war. The advance of human freedom – the great achievement of our time, and the great hope of every time – now depends on us. Our nation, this generation will lift a dark threat of violence from our people and our future . . . Freedom and fear, justice and cruelty, have always been at war, and we know that God is not neutral between them.[2]

It is not just in the obvious use of words such as 'freedom' and 'justice' that the full spectrum of an American ideology is being brought to bear here: a small phrase like 'hug your children', for example, activates a whole hinterland of associated meanings, essentially clustering around certain idealised concepts of 'home' and 'family'.[3] The magnitude of the events of 9/11 for America can be seen in the way Bush evokes the experience of Pearl Harbor through his use of the phrase 'one Sunday in 1941' (and the use of 'Sunday' is not insignificant). Again, what we can see is a series of words put together in a certain way so as to be impregnated with a culturally known (and now activated) ideological conception of America and with the perceived relationship of that country to the rest of the world. Again, what we can see is a papering over of the cracks. For example, America is seen as hated for the fact that it has 'a democratically elected government', but in the presidential election of November 2000 in which Bush was elected only 55% of the voting-age population exercised their right to vote;[4] and while around 70% of those earning the highest salaries voted, only 40% or less of those in the lowest wage brackets went to the polling stations.[5] We could go on to investigate the exact nature of 'freedom of speech' in America, or indeed the concept of 'freedom' itself. And if we did what we would find would be huge contradictions, multiple ambiguities and massive gulfs between various groups within the United States that would be divided one from another in particular by gender, ethnicity and economic disparity.

In a speech at West Point in the following year, Robert Denton quotes Bush as saying:

> There can be no neutrality between justice and cruelty, between the innocent and the guilty. We are in a conflict between good and evil, and America will call evil by its name. By confronting evil and lawless regimes, we do not create a problem; we reveal a problem. And we will lead the world in opposing it.[6]

As in the primary surface display of values to be found in Hollywood Westerns, there is no middle ground, the binary split between good and evil is definite and absolute; and, as in the narrative trajectory of such Westerns, there comes a moment when confrontation becomes inevitable, unavoidable and necessary. As the US and its allies prepared to invade Iraq in 2003, Bush made a further speech addressing the 'terrorist threat':

> We are a peaceful people, yet we're not a fragile people, and we will not be intimidated by thugs and killers. If our enemies dare to strike us, they and all who have aided them will face fearful consequences.
> We are now acting because the risks of inaction would be far greater . . . responding to such enemies only after they have struck first is not self-defense, it is suicide.[7]

Underpinning each of these speeches is a focus on the individual as the central determining reality of existence. Even the concept of 'the nation' is conceived as a coming together of autonomous individuals united in a shared set of values. The primacy of the individual is implicit in the emphasis that is placed on choice, free will and moral responsibility. Conspicuous by its absence is any attempt to investigate deeper structural explanations for events that have taken place: the expansionist policies of global (American) corporate capital, the paternalism of Western (American) foreign policies, the subordination of developing countries to Western (American) diktat brought about by international financial institutions and organisations, etc. The 'America' which is being evoked is, like the hero of a Hollywood Western, peace-loving and slow to anger but ultimately, if necessary, able to bring down 'fearful consequences' on its enemies. This narrative arc will be found in several Westerns to be considered in this book. America's perceived exceptionalism will be seen to be embodied in a range of central characters. America's destiny will be seen to be similarly expressed through the paths that have to be walked by these characters.

Inevitably, the cultural product expresses the central concepts of the culture. Each of these speeches (and others by US politicians made during the post-9/11 period)[8] bear re-reading in relation to the films being dealt with in this book. Frequently, protagonists are called on to defend not only themselves but also their values and sacred spaces attaching to those values. Often, characters find themselves having to confront personifications of evil, and are faced by the necessity of having to respond to the actions of evil people. Events are continually pushing characters within these narratives to decide how far they will go to right a wrong or to bring about justice. The nature of world as a place of confrontation between good and evil, and within which soft liberal values simply will not be sufficient for good to win out over evil, is constantly brought home to characters. Recognition of the need to fight back, to be resolute and to use overwhelming force if necessary: this is the position to which protagonists in post-9/11 Westerns frequently have to be brought during the course of the narrative.

II

It was, of course, inevitable that fears and uncertainties brought about for the United States by the events of 9/11 would be reflected in the films that emerged from that country in the early years of the twenty-first century.[9] How could this not be the case? With this in mind, and aware of the fact that, as Ralph Lamar Turner suggests, Westerns are 'often employed, to examine current problems through the lens of past dilemmas',[10] this book will examine a range of contemporary US Westerns. What draws the pieces of analysis together is an emphasis on the paramount importance of ideology in understanding how each film sits in relation to the society that has produced it. In an article in 2003, Mark Cousins spoke of 'the ideological aims' of *The Alamo* (John Wayne, 1960). The historical event of the Battle of the Alamo in 1836, he said, 'will always, for conservative America, be a reminder to be vigilant and, if necessary, fight'.[11] Cousins argued that both Wayne's film and John Lee Hancock's remake in 2004 asked the same two questions that were relevant to the current period: 'Who hates us?' and 'How can we stand against them?'[12] The basic approach on offer in this book therefore follows a line of inquiry that, as the quotes from Turner and Cousins suggest, has been pursued by a variety of writers in relation to the Western. Discussing *Brokeback Mountain* (2005) and *The Three Burials of Melquiades Estrada* (2005),[13] Camilla Fojas describes the way in which the Western 'is continually being reimagined and redeployed to explore the most salient issues of contemporary culture'.[14] These films, she argues, 'put both U.S. culture and its major media industry on the line' and force 'an examination of the myths of the West and Southwest and their role in national self-definition'.[15] Rita Keresztesi sees the Western as 'the quintessential visual vehicle of American imperialist myth-making and rugged individualism'.[16] Taking a slightly different tack but still interested in placing the films she is looking at within an ideological framework, Carolina Rueda suggests, 'The Western helps people to get away from the complexities of modern life and back to the "restful absolutes" of the past';[17] in other words, back to a more comforting (imagined) position of ideological certainty. Flagging up the crucial linkage of all of this to historical context, Scott Stoddart suggests the Western tends to decline during relatively quiet periods of history and re-emerge at times of crisis.[18] Stephen McVeigh suggests the current 'vitality' of the Western derives from its 'resonance with the political culture of the United States'.[19] And, seemingly inadvertently, David Lusted illustrates for us the role, power and place of ideology within social and cultural formation:

> Playing 'Cowboys and Indians' was a regular feature of my childhood ... The individual and the collective imagination was fed by Westerns on the screens of cinemas and television sets, in the context of a wider culture which included novels, comic strips and advertising ... The idea of the West in Western fiction has been central to the global imaginary for over two hundred years.[20]

In explorations of the genre then, discussions around the Western's connection to history and to belief systems is frequently, as it will be here, the very currency of the debate. At the same time, as Janet Walker explains in great detail in *Westerns: Films through History*, the relationship to be found in Westerns between the historical and the fictional is complex and varies across the range of films generally classified as Westerns. She describes the genre as a 'melange of history, fiction, and historiographic metafiction'.[21] That is to say, not only do these films to varying degrees mash up history and fiction, but they also demonstrate an increasing awareness of their own constructed nature and a preparedness to present this fabrication to the audience.

With this in mind, it is still the case that in this study the contemporary Westerns under examination will, unashamedly, be considered as expressions of ideology and primarily as articulations of a dominant American ideology. Although it may be important to remind ourselves that the concept of ideology does not suggest the operation of some form of conscious and deliberate manipulation of texts in order to shape public consciousness. In fact, a key element in the functioning of any ideology is generally seen to be that its operation is not immediately apparent to those agents and agencies giving it cultural expression. In other words, ways of seeing the world that have been historically determined within a culture are viewed from within that culture as natural, obvious, incontestably apparent to anyone and everyone. This is what Slavoj Žižek is getting at in his assessment of the current, post-9/11 state of the world when he says that 'Ideology does not reside primarily in stories invented (by those in power) to deceive others, it resides in stories invented by subjects to deceive themselves'.[22] As John Mepham expressed it, several decades ago: 'Ideology is not a collection of discrete falsehoods but a matrix of thought firmly grounded in the forms of our social life.'[23]

For the purposes of this investigation, it is also considered important to place this view of ideology within the framework of what Noam Chomsky has described as 'Cartesian common sense'. The baseline for each analysis to be found here will be the belief that every member of an audience watching a film is constrained within a pattern of pressures exerted by the ideological framework of their society, but equally every member of the audience has the capacity to produce their own individual reading of any film. Chomsky believes, and I concur, that 'The social sciences generally, and above all the analysis of contemporary affairs, are accessible to anyone who wants to take an interest in these matters.'[24] In a PBS television interview, Chomsky expressed his position in simple, direct terms: 'I believe in Cartesian common sense. I think people have the capacities to see through the deceit in which they are ensnared, but they have got to make the effort.'[25]

The presidential speeches quoted above seek to affirm a very particular way of seeing and understanding the world. Certain keynotes are repeatedly emphasised. In their response to 9/11, Americans are being brought together as Americans, as members of the same nation, believing in the same foundational principles. Differences are subsumed in a patriotic call to arms that, because it is grounded in consistent representational configurations expressed over a long period via a spectrum of cultural expressions, has the appearance of the obvious and (to use the same phrase in a different sense to that being activated by Chomsky) common sense. A range of possible political, economic and historical contexts for the events of 9/11 are side-stepped by a call to a myth-laden, collective consciousness.

Of course, it is not this simple because, as post-Marxism highlights, subject positions are multiple, in process and in dynamic interplay and flux. That is to say, those hearing the 'message' will come from a range of divergent backgrounds. Collective consciousness of any sort is in tension with the lived experience of differences of gender and sexuality, ethnicity and nationality, not to mention economic class.

As with films, the speeches quoted above exist in complex relation to both history and something which, not to call it fiction, might be described as the collective cultural imaginary. However, having recognised all of this, when we consider such oration it remains the case that the intended direction of travel is clear. Furthermore, the dominant fictions that underpin these presidential speeches are those that are inscribed within the culture as a whole, and as such they are to be found inscribed within the full range of cultural artefacts produced out of that ideological base.

Considering films and looking at the full scope of those produced in Hollywood in the early years of the twenty-first century, Douglas Kellner sums up the situation by saying that 'culture is a social construct that reproduces dominant ideology and its contestations, intrinsically linked to the vicissitudes of the socially and historically specific milieu in which it is conceived'.[26] That is to say, in these films the dominant ideology is clear but at the same time we can also see those places where that ideology is uncertain of itself and those positions on which that dominant ideology is finding itself subject to challenge. As Matthew Carter explains in examining *Shane* (George Stevens, 1953) as a 'so-called classical Western', such films exhibit 'an ambiguous textual relationship with dominant ideologies'[27] so that ultimately they might best be seen to highlight 'ideological contradictions'.[28] Carter sees the character of Shane, for example, as the defender of 'the family' but also as a force that threatens the stability of that institution.[29]

III

Before providing an overview of what you can expect to find in each chapter of this book, it may be useful to address two further questions. Firstly, why investigate contemporary Westerns when, although they were clearly at one time a massively popular genre, they are now only of marginal interest? And, secondly, if you are going to look at Westerns why not study them as a global phenomenon rather than perpetuating an outdated focus on them as an American product?

There can be little doubt the Western declined in importance as a Hollywood product after 1960. Richard Aquila puts the number of Westerns made in the United States between 1929 and 1959 at more than 3,700 but says after 1960 'the number dropped off precipitously'.[30] Some, however, have argued that the Western has seen something of a revival in the twenty-first century. According to Joseph Walker, there have been 'more big-screen Westerns produced since the turn of the century (and, crucially, since the attacks of 9/11) than in the comparable number of years preceding it'.[31] And, Scott Stoddart, in a move that demonstrates the extended hybridity of the genre, concludes his edited book *The New Western: Critical Essays on the Genre Since 9/11* by demonstrating how

Christopher Nolan's Batman trilogy derives its 'ideological underpinnings'[32] from the Western.

However, although discussions around the relative health or otherwise of the Western, the difficulty of defining the boundaries of the genre and increased genre hybridity may be interesting they are not directly relevant to this book. In his investigation into the relationship between Westerns and the Cold War, *Cowboys as Cold Warriors: The Western and U.S. History*, Stanley Corkin sees the Western as having a very particular relationship to US history between 1946 and 1962. This current study aims to view 'War on Terror Westerns' in a somewhat similar light. Corkin is concerned with the ways in which his chosen films 'metaphorically narrate the relationship between the United States and the world'.[33] For him, this is 'the story that is focal to this genre'.[34] For this current study, while we may feel Walker is right to suggest there have been more 'big-screen Westerns' in recent years, this is not essential to the argument. The focus here is not on the number of Westerns being made but the extent to which films that might be classified as belonging to the genre could be seen to express political concerns of the time; and beyond this, how these Westerns might be viewed as a cultural barometer of wider media tendencies. As Corkin points out, 'all historical texts necessarily are marked by the time of their production'.[35] With the substitution of 'post-9/11' for 'Cold War' his statement that 'As products of a particular time and cultural climate, these Cold War films address and express those circumstances'[36] accurately summarises the foundational position of this book. The Western post-9/11 is not doing anything different from that which the genre has always done: it is expressing the current US experience in cinematic terms, reflecting on the current US position with respect to global politics and working to ideologically position the audience in relation to the material being shown.

Turning to our second question: why conceptualise Westerns as American when they are surely best seen as a global phenomenon existing within a globalised marketplace within which the experience is of cultural flows moving in all directions rather than simply as some unidirectional emanation out from the United States to the rest of the world? It is certainly the case that in studying the Western[37] scholars have in recent decades worked to transfer the emphasis away from viewing this as a specifically American genre and towards a transnational perspective. This has allowed acknowledgement of (1) the interventions made by other national cinemas in the genre and (2) the range of films to be found from other cultural backgrounds that essentially deal with similar issues of imperialism. Will Higbee and Song Hwee Lim suggest 'the shift from the national to the transnational within film studies is firmly established and still gaining momentum'.[38] In many ways this is to be applauded, not least because it works to address the notion of American exceptionalism. However, alongside the transnational, it remains important to continue to see specific expressions of the Western coming out of Hollywood in relation to the context of American politics, that is, in relation to that country's handling of both its domestic and its foreign affairs. In other words, such articulations of the genre should continue to be considered as an ideological measurement of the state of this most powerful and influential of nations. Any films emerging out of the Californian economic power-base of a country that is not only the pre-eminent post-war global power, but also (and critically) an imperial superpower in decline and viewing its continued existence in relation to a series of external threats, should continue to come under intense scholarly scrutiny. It is within this context that, at this critical moment for global politics, Westerns should continue to be seen as a specifically American genre.[39] As Andrew Patrick Nelson has it: 'The Western, because of its special relationship with American history and culture, is a vehicle for grappling with the ideological and political tensions of the day.'[40] When Michael Pitts, explaining how he decided on the films to include in his massive *Western Movies: A Guide to 5,105 Feature Films*, says that the crucial factor was 'having the plot take place on the frontier',[41] he makes it clear how the Western is always taking place at the nation's boundaries, always existing within that borderland space between the self and the 'Other', and, therefore, always a likely candidate for the expression of not only national but also transnational tensions. In their book *Ride, Boldly Ride: The Evolution of the American Western* Mary Lea Bandy and Kevin Stoehr propose the idea that the Western has become 'a kind of territory that is defined by borders and boundaries regularly crossed in dialectical fashion',[42] but perhaps it has ever been thus.

IV

Each chapter in this book will offer an analysis of one film, with each successive investigation adding a further dimension to the context within which, it is argued, contemporary Westerns should viewed. A range of alternative ways of reading each of these films would be possible, placing the emphasis on a variety of different thematic and/or stylistic elements. However, for the purposes of this study, in essence these films will be viewed from the following keynote positions:

- reinforcing a particular myth of America: *Open Range* (Kevin Costner, 2003)
- endorsing the use of extreme overwhelming force in dealing with enemies: *True Grit* (Joel and Ethan Coen, 2010)

- highlighting the importance of defending the homeland: *Jane Got a Gun* (Gavin O'Connor, 2016)
- providing audiences with exhilarating escapist entertainment: *The Lone Ranger* (Gore Verbinski, 2013)
- delivering an immersive experience of visceral body abuse: *The Revenant* (Alejandro González Iñárritu, 2015)
- engulfing audiences within an ahistorical postmodern space: *Django Unchained* (Quentin Tarantino, 2012)
- foregrounding religious concepts of forgiveness and redemption: *The Three Burials of Melquiades Estrada* (Tommy Lee Jones, 2005)
- augmenting a contemporary Western culture of fear: *The Assassination of Jesse James by the Coward Robert Ford* (Andrew Dominik, 2007).

Chapters 2 to 4 look, in particular, at the restoration to the forefront of Westerns of heroes and heroic actions. Chapter 2 views *Open Range* as rehearsing key aspects of the classic Western myth of American history, asserting the existence of collectively agreed American values, and reinforcing a corresponding concept of nationhood. We could equally have looked at *Appaloosa* (Ed Harris, 2008), which performs essentially the same functions. In both films, a town has been violently seized by a powerful man and a gang of thugs, the townspeople are running scared, and our two heroes have to step beyond the bounds of current law to restore civilised order. A crucial focus is on the role, purpose and usefulness of 'gun work' and those who are able to perform it (Figure 1.1).[43] Chapter 3 evaluates *True Grit* (Joel and Ethan Coen, 2010), which remakes an earlier version of the same story, as a film that works to restore the concept of the American hero and to endorse the necessity of using overwhelming force

Figure 1.1 The role, purpose and usefulness of 'gun work' and those who are able to perform it, visually emphasised in *Appaloosa* (Ed Harris, 2008).

in order to confront evil in the world. *3:10 to Yuma* (James Mangold, 2007) would have offered another remake of a classic Western that could have been explored. Comparing this film to the original *3:10 to Yuma* (Delmer Daves, 1957), and highlighting our central concern with seeing each film within its contemporary historical context, Stephen Mexal suggests: 'Each generation gets precisely the western it needs.'[44] As director, Mangold complicates the scenarios for a post-millennial world: the nominal hero, Dan Evans (Christian Bale), is the 'vet' who lost his leg to 'friendly fire' and is, therefore (particularly in his own eyes), devoid of heroic status, and Ben Wade (Russell Crowe) is the 'baddie' who is the product of poor/absentee parenting. However, the central plot is in line with a raft of these post-9/11 Westerns – the 'hero' faces an absolutely pitiless force moving inexorably towards him and the only question is how he is going to measure up.[45] Chapter 4 evaluates *Jane Got a Gun* (Gavin O'Connor, 2016) as a film focused on the importance of defending the home against a brutal outside force. *The Keeping Room* (Daniel Barber, 2014) would have offered another possibility for this chapter. In *The Keeping Room*, as with *Jane Got a Gun*, the central characters are in a dark, unforgiving place and at the mercy of an approaching, impending, predator-like and seemingly unstoppable force of evil. The primary interest for the audience is in how these characters will fare in these circumstances? What will they defend? How will they defend it? And, what will they carry with them out of the end of the film and into the future? In its focus on the experience of women and its challenge to the portrayal of 'violent masculinities as heroic'[46] that is usually seen in Westerns, this could (in contrast to *Jane Got a Gun*) be viewed as a 'counter-narrative'.[47]

The following three chapters focus, in particular, on the audience experience. Chapter 5 reflects on *The Lone Ranger* (Gore Verbinski, 2013), which is predominantly seen as providing the audience with fairground-ride entertainment such that the thrill and excitement of the moment deny any space for critical reflection. Had we wished to consider a film employing even more flamboyant spectacle we might have turned to *Cowboys & Aliens* (Jon Favreau, 2011). This hybrid Western imagines a scenario within which, under the leadership of heroic white males (of course), all the classic oppositional groups from the genre – Native Americans, Mexicans and outlaws – have to work together to defeat an alien monster that has appeared in the sky and cast a shadow over the land. This film's key advice seems to be that given to the character of Doc (Sam Rockwell): 'Take some friendly advice? Get yourself a gun and learn how to use it.' In looking at *The Revenant* (Alejandro González Iñárritu, 2015), Chapter 6 mainly considers the display of body abuse found in this film. *Bone Tomahawk* (S. Craig Zahler, 2015) suggests itself as an alternative that might have been given a similar analytical focus. In the most infamous scene from this film a victim is scalped alive, turned upside down, and then bisected with an axe. In best post-9/11 style, white Americans facing a barbaric, uncivilised people have to undertake a rescue mission into hostile territory. Chapter 7 assesses *Django Unchained* (Quentin Tarantino, 2012) as a film existing within an ahistorical space and contributing towards cutting off the virtual, postmodern, media-ever-present from any contact with either the lived present or historical reality. Not unexpectedly, because they have the same director, we could have considered *The Hateful Eight* (Quentin Tarantino, 2015) for this chapter. Both films have critically important (for the US) historical events as their backdrops, slavery in the case of *Django Unchained* and the Civil War in the case of *The Hateful Eight*. Both are to some extent based on careful historical research.[48] Both have a key thematic interest in issues relating to race. And yet, both exist primarily within the virtual reality of Tarantino's oeuvre which itself exists as a matrix of playful, desperate and despairing cinematic references.

Chapters 8 and 9 consider two, more low key, Westerns that provide the audience with rather more space for contemplative reflection. Chapter 8 examines *The Three Burials of Melquiades Estrada* as a film that interrogates issues of race and nationhood in greater depth than usual. Again, there would be other possibilities: we could have considered, for example, either *Meek's Cutoff* (Kelly Reichardt, 2010), or *The Keeping Room* as films that offer a similar depth of investigation; in both these cases, largely though not exclusively in relation to gender. *Meek's Cutoff* exposes a patriarchal society – the men are shown gathering to make decisions, excluding the women and only later telling them what has been decided – and questions white ethnic supremacy but ultimately fails to challenge the foundational myth of westward expansion and empire-building. As with *The Three Burials* the film looks at issues to do with borders and the movement of migrants who are pretty much at the mercy of their guides (or traffickers). Chapter 9 considers *The Assassination of Jesse James by the Coward Robert Ford* (Andrew Dominik, 2007). This is examined as a film that confronts the audience with what is seen as the inexplicable nature of evil in the world. We could also have looked at *No Country for Old Men* (Joel and Ethan Coen, 2007), where this position is, if anything, even clearer. At one point in this latter film as he tries to comprehend the callous brutality of the film's embodiment of evil, Anton Chigurh (Javier Bardem), a sheriff muses, 'Who'd do such a thing? How do you defend against it?' By the end of the film, Chigurh – described by Richard Gilmore as 'an inexorable force'[49] – is still at large, while two key characters in whom the audience has put its trust to cleanse the world of this threat, and who are (significantly) both Vietnam 'vets', are dead.

The eight films chosen for detailed study are not singular examples of the chief line of inquiry posited for each. As suggested above, other films could have been chosen that to some extent would have led down similar avenues of investigation.

This study does not consider TV Westerns made in the period: this would require its own book-length survey. This book does not consider the commercial success of the focus films other than in passing. Several of these films are what are called 'box office flops', others made what the industry would see as very reasonable profits; but this is not of direct interest for this examination. This book simply considers films as texts, each with its own particular content and style, which can be discussed in relation to the context of the period in which the films are made.

Notes

1. George W. Bush, 'Victory speech, 2000', 13 December 2000, *American Rhetoric: Online Speech Bank*. Available at <https://www.americanrhetoric.com/speeches/gwbush2000victoryspeech.htm> (accessed 11 May 2018).
2. George W. Bush, 'Address to joint session of Congress following 9/11 attacks', 20 September 2001, *American Rhetoric: Online Speech Bank*. Available at <http://www.americanrhetoric.com/speeches/gwbush911jointsession-speech.htm> (accessed 11 May 2018).
3. Subjecting Bush's speeches from 2001 to 2003 to linguistic analysis, Antonio Pinna sees them as 'portraying and promoting a specific definition of Americanness'. See Antonio Pinna, 'Evaluation and ideology in political discourse: the use of extended units of meaning centred on modal verbs in G. W. Bush's Presidential speeches', in Giuliana Garzone and Srikant Sarangi (eds), *Discourse, Ideology and Specialized Communication* (Bern: Peter Lang, 2007), p. 449. America is presented, he suggests, 'as a spiritual community whose moral virtues are inspired by a higher authority' (ibid. p. 449). The audience, he proposes, is 'persuasively invited' to share a vision of 'a community that pursues ethical, God-sanctioned ends', and 'the doctrine of American hegemony is established on moral and religious foundations' (ibid. p. 444).
4. Amie Jamieson, Hyon B. Shin and Jennifer Day, 'Voting and registration in the election of November 2000', US Census Bureau, *Current Population Reports*, February 2002. Available at <https://www.census.gov/prod/2002pubs/p20-542.pdf> (accessed 6 June 2018), p. 2.
5. Ibid. p. 5.
6. Robert E. Denton (ed.), *The George W. Bush Presidency: A Rhetorical Perspective* (Lanham, MD: Lexington Books, 2012), p. 44.

7. George W. Bush, 'Address to the nation – ultimatum to Saddam Hussein', 17 March 2003, *American Rhetoric: Online Speech Bank*. Available at <http://www.americanrhetoric.com/speeches/wariniraq/gwbushiraq31703.htm> (accessed 15 August 2018).
8. In 2015, for example, President Barack Obama made a televised speech from the Oval Office in which he said: 'The threat from terrorism is real, but we will overcome it. We will destroy ISIL and any other organization that tries to harm us. Our success won't depend on tough talk, or abandoning our values or giving in to fear . . . we will prevail by being strong and smart, resilient and relentless. And by drawing upon every aspect of American power . . . I am confident we will succeed in this mission because we are on the right side of history. We were founded upon a belief in human dignity that no matter who you are, or where you come from, or what you look like, or what religion you practice, you are equal in the eyes of God and equal in the eyes of the law . . . Let's make sure we never forget what makes us exceptional . . . Let's not forget that freedom is more powerful than fear. That we have always met challenges, whether war or depression, natural disasters or terrorist attacks, by coming together around our common ideals as one nation and one people.' See Barack Obama, 'Address to the nation on foreign and domestic counter-terrorism strategies', 6 December 2015, *American Rhetoric: Online Speech Bank*. Available at <http://www.americanrhetoric.com/speeches/barackobama/barackobamaforeigndomesticterrorismresponseovaloffice.htm> (accessed 15 August 2018).
9. Although the focus here is on films made since 2001, '9/11' could be seen as shorthand for a shift in global politics that has gathered momentum since roughly 1989 and the end of the Cold War, perhaps developing with increasing intensity and certainty of direction since then. George Lawson suggests: 'the failures of Western capitalism, political institutions and cultural mores since 1989 have fostered new forms of opposition to Western order'. See George Lawson, 'Introduction: the "what", "when" and "where" of the global 1989', in George Lawson, Chris Armbruster and Michael Cox (eds), *The Global 1989: Continuity and Change in World Politics* (Cambridge: Cambridge University Press, 2010), p. 10. He identifies key sources of these oppositional forces as being based within Islam, Latin America and China.
10. Ralph Lamar Turner, '"Why do you think I am paying you if not to have my way?" Genre complications in the free-market critiques of fictional and filmed versions of *True Grit*', *Journal of Popular Culture*, 2015, 48(2): 357.
11. Mark Cousins, 'America seeks comfort in Westerns', *Evening Standard*, 16 October 2003. Available at <https://www.standard.co.uk/go/london/film/america-seeks-comfort-in-westerns-6956608.html> (accessed 4 January 2018).
12. See how this echoes Bush's question, 'Americans are asking, Why do they hate us?', in his address to Congress in 2001, given above.
13. *The Three Burials of Melquiades Estrada* (Tommy Lee Jones, 2005) will be discussed in Chapter 8.
14. Camilla Fojas, *Border Bandits: Hollywood on the Southern Frontier* (Austin: University of Texas Press, 2008), p. 187.

15. Ibid. p. 187.
16. Rita Keresztesi, 'Cowboys and West Indians: decolonizing the Western and Perry Henzall's *The Harder They Come*', in MaryEllen Higgins, Rita Keresztesi and Dayna Oscherwitz (eds), *The Western in the Global South* (New York and London: Routledge, 2015), p. 110.
17. Carolina Rueda, 'Carlos Bolado's *Bajo California*: crossing borders and dislocating the Western tradition', in MaryEllen Higgins, Rita Keresztesi and Dayna Oscherwitz (eds), *The Western in the Global South* (New York and London: Routledge, 2015), p. 213.
18. Scott F. Stoddart, '*Epilogue* – new visions/new vistas: Christopher Nolan's *Batman* trilogy and the New Western', in Scott F. Stoddart (ed.), *The New Westerns: Critical Essays on the Genre Since 9/11* (Jefferson, NC: McFarland, 2016), p. 229.
19. Stephen McVeigh, *The American Western* (Edinburgh: Edinburgh University Press, 2007), p. 220.
20. David Lusted, *The Western* (Harlow: Pearson Education, 2003), p. 4.
21. Janet Walker (ed.), *Westerns: Films through History* (New York and London: Routledge, 2001), p. 15.
22. Slavoj Žižek, *Against the Double Blackmail: Refugees, Terror and Other Troubles with the Neighbours* (London and New York: Penguin, 2017), p. 89. (Although, Žižek does muddy the waters by talking of 'stories invented (by those in power) to deceive others' when, because of the suggestion of conscious intervention, this is categorically not what ideology is about.)
23. John Mepham, 'The theory of ideology in *Capital*', *Radical Philosophy*, Summer 1972, 2: 17.
24. James McGilvray, *Chomsky: Language, Mind, Politics*, 2nd edn (Cambridge and Malden, MA: Polity, 2014), p. 162.
25. Mark Achbar (ed.), *Manufacturing Consent: Noam Chomsky and the Media* (Montreal and New York: Black Rose Books, 1994), p. 20.
26. Douglas M. Kellner, *Cinema Wars: Hollywood Film and Politics in the Bush-Cheney Era* (Oxford and Malden, MA: John Wiley, 2010), p. 40.
27. Matthew Carter, *Myth of the Western: New Perspectives on Hollywood's Frontier Narrative* (Edinburgh: Edinburgh University Press, 2014), p. 55.
28. Ibid. pp. 54–5.
29. Ibid. pp. 68–9.
30. Richard Aquila, *The Sagebrush Trail: Western Movies and Twentieth-Century America* (Tucson: University of Arizona Press, 2015), p. 8. Although, Andrew Patrick Nelson suggests, 'Westerns continued to be produced with regularity well into the 1970s', and goes into some detail to support this position. See Andrew Patrick Nelson, *Still in the Saddle: The Hollywood Western, 1969–1980* (Norman: University of Oklahoma Press, 2015), p. 62.
31. Joseph S. Walker, 'Coen, Coen on the range: Rooster Cogburn(s) and domestic space', in Scott F. Stoddart (ed.), *The New Westerns: Critical Essays on the Genre Since 9/11* (Jefferson, NC: McFarland, 2016), p. 64.
32. Stoddart, '*Epilogue* – new visions/new vistas', 2016, p. 242.

33. Stanley Corkin, *Cowboys as Cold Warriors: The Western and U.S. History* (Philadelphia, PA: Temple University Press, 2004), p. 3.
34. Ibid. p. 3.
35. Ibid. p. 3.
36. Ibid. pp. 3–4.
37. Famously described in the 1950s in the title of a book by Jean-Louis Rieupeyrout, with a preface by André Bazin, as 'Le Western: ou, Le cinéma américain par excellence'.
38. Will Higbee and Song Hwee Lim, 'Concepts of transnational cinema: towards a critical transnationalism in film studies', *Transnational Cinemas*, 2010, 1(1): 17.
39. There is a sense in which what is being proposed here *is* 'transnational' in that the effort is to view Westerns produced in the US in the context of global politics. However, it would be possible to further develop this strand of inquiry by putting in place studies to look at (1) thematically related Westerns produced in other parts of the world and (2) the global reception of these films.
40. Andrew Patrick Nelson, *Still in the Saddle: The Hollywood Western, 1969–1980* (Norman: University of Oklahoma Press, 2015), p. 61.
41. Michael R. Pitts, *Western Movies: A Guide to 5,105 Feature Films*, 2nd edn (Jefferson, NC: McFarland, 2013), p. 1.
42. Mary Lea Bandy and Kevin Stoehr, *Ride, Boldly Ride: The Evolution of the American Western* (Berkeley and Los Angeles: University of California Press, 2012), p. 17.
43. *Appaloosa* is also of particular interest for its discussion of gender. One of the final shots of the central female character, Allie French (Renée Zellweger), has her standing in front of a chromolithograph, *The Lion Queen* (c.1874), showing a woman in a cage with a variety of towering big cats. See Gibson & Co., *The Lion Queen*, Library of Congress. Available at<https://www.loc.gov/item/2006678343/> (accessed 25 June 2018).
44. Stephen Mexal, 'Two ways to Yuma: Locke, liberalism, and Western masculinity in *3:10 to Yuma*', in Jennifer L. McMahon and B. Steve Csaki (eds), *The Philosophy of the Western* (Lexington: University of Kentucky Press, 2010), p. 72.
45. The conclusion to this film sees the death of the 'hero' and totally undermines American myth-making. As Thomas Horne explains it: 'Dan Evans has the respect of the audience, his mission seems in the best tradition of American idealism, and the structure of the film deeply invests the audience in the mission's success, yet at the end Dan is shot and killed by a near-psychotic outlaw. It is the mission itself and not Dan's character that this film calls into question.' Thomas A. Horne, 'James Mangold's *3:10 to Yuma* and the mission in Iraq', *Journal of Film and Video*, Fall 2013, 65(3): 47.
46. Matthew Carter, '"I've been looking for you": reconfiguring race, gender, and the family through the female agency of *The Keeping Room*', *Papers on Language and Literature*, Winter 2018, 54(1): 26.

47. Ibid. p. 44.
48. See Gregory J. W. Urwin (ed.), *Black Flag Over Dixie: Racial Atrocities and Reprisals in the Civil War* (Carbondale: Southern Illinois University Press, 2004) for information on the treatment of captured black Union troops, for example.
49. Richard Gilmore, '*No Country for Old Men*: The Coens' tragic Western', in Mark T. Conard (ed.), *The Philosophy of the Coen Brothers* (Lexington: University Press of Kentucky, 2009), p. 60.

PART I

The Cinema of Heroes and Heroic Action

CHAPTER 2

Reclaiming the Heroes and Heroic Attitudes of Classic Westerns: *Open Range* (2003)

I

Why was *Open Range* (Kevin Costner, 2003) given this particular title? What is implied by the choice? The opening certainly reinforces the title's importance since it sets out not only to visually express the concept of open range but also through these visuals allied to the script (and with deferential reference to previous Westerns and to artists who have portrayed the American West[1]) to define the term. What we see is a land without fences, indeed a land without any sign of physical barriers. This is a wide open space with spring flowers in the foreground and green grass stretching into the distance; a land as sweeping, unenclosed and impressive as the monumental skyscape hanging above it. When we cut to a shot from a rise overlooking a valley the rolling countryside continues as far as the eye can see; and, as we pan right in a movement as slow and unhurried as life itself in this Arcadian landscape, the classic image from popular art of a cowboy in the saddle comes into view with an even stronger abundance of prairie flowers in the foreground. A second cowboy on horseback joins the first and following a short conversation moves away, and we are left with a low-angle shot of the original rider (Robert Duvall as 'Boss' Spearman) revered by the cinematography not simply as a character in this film but also as an icon of the heroic American West (Figure 2.1).

When we cut from the trail boss on his horse, we are shown a wagon moving across the screen. Within the film narrative this is simply a wagon accompanying the cowboys and carrying their supplies, but within the iconic images brought to mind by the mutually supportive myths of the West and the American Dream this is the classic image of a pioneering wagon moving into the interior, opening the continent and providing all-comers with the opportunity to determine their own future for themselves, for their families and for generations to come. In overall terms, the shots we are given within

Figure 2.1 The trail boss revered by the cinematography in *Open Range* (Kevin Costner, 2003).

the first minutes present us with *the* American idyll, the environmental embodiment of the quintessence of Americanism, that mythic space offering the promise of individual fulfilment that sits at the heart of the array of expectations supposedly guaranteed for US citizens and embedded within the country's shared national identity. Such expanses – open and inviting, free to be roamed, waiting to be inhabited – are to some extent the truth but more largely the lie intrinsic to white European colonisation of the Americas. This is a determined depiction of 'the big country' at the heart of the United States that provides, offers, indeed guarantees there will be room not only for national expansion but, more importantly, personal freedom. It is the visual representation of the 'manifest destiny'[2] of a nation born to inherit the open expanses of a continent.

Later, as the film develops, the viewer is given a powerful sense of Boss and his right-hand man, Charley Waite (Kevin Costner), being deliberately placed in strongly contrasting outside and inside spaces. Because they are viewed initially in wide open spaces, when the two men are subsequently seen indoors the viewer feels them to be confined. Placed in these circumstances they become restrained, hesitant and unsure of themselves. Despite their desire to cross the threshold into the homely, civilised space of china teacups and domesticity linked to the female presence of Sue Barlow (Annette Bening) they feel themselves to be inadequate, unable to measure up to the demands of feminine delicacy and gentleness. The home, which is such a strong indicator of progress towards the attainment of civilised values in John Ford's Westerns, is resurrected and re-emphasised for contemporary times. The stress, in Charley's body in particular, when placed within a house, arises from the tension between a longing for the peace and contentment the comforts of the home are seen to bring (not least the comforts of a woman within this masculinist view of the world) and a feeling of being trapped and confined by the walls of domesticity. As the film progresses Boss and Charley are increasingly filmed in boxed spaces. To some extent this is an inevitable function of their movement from the prairie and into urban spaces. However, for the firefight with Denton Baxter (Michael Gambon) and his henchmen we might note they choose to fight in the open. Certainly, at this point they are seen to have to leave the appreciated comforts of domesticity and return to the potentially hostile space outside, beyond the walls of home, in order to deal with the threat being offered to civilised values.

In this film, Joseph Walker tells us, the 'complications and ambiguities' to be found in Westerns from the early 1990s such as *Unforgiven* (Clint Eastwood, 1992) and *Dances with Wolves* (Costner, 1990) have 'vanished'. Walker says,

> though Waite is allowed some guilt over his violent actions earlier in life, he and Spearman are essentially the kind of unvarnished, straight-shooting heroes rarely seen in the Western since the stylized, nihilistic films of Sergio Leone and Sam Peckinpah undermined the simplistic conventions of the genre.[3]

Although there are more barely submerged tensions than this assessment initially allows it is fundamentally correct. *Open Range* is an attempt to return to the surface certainties of Westerns made prior to heavy US involvement in the Vietnam War.

II

When the young trailhand, Button (Diego Luna), regains consciousness after being almost killed by Baxter's men Sue is in no doubt that it is God rather than her that Boss and Charley should be thanking. Boss replies respectfully, 'Yes, mam, we'll give that a try', but within the certainties of the Western genre we know (as Boss knows) that the outcome of events will come down to men and the actions of men. Sue, we might notice, understands the role of men in this (mythic) world and is aware not everything can be left to God. When Charley tells her 'Men are going to get killed here today, Sue, and I'm gonna kill 'em, you understand that?', her simple reply is, 'Yes'. In the style of films like *Bad Day at Black Rock* (John Sturges, 1955), or *Westbound* (Budd Boetticher, 1959), this is about a community needing to re-learn how to fight back against evil in the world and needing heroic men to deliver the lessons the community requires.

'I didn't raise my boys just to see 'em killed', says one of the townspeople, to which Charley replies: 'Well, you may not know this but there's things that gnaw at a man worse than dyin'.'

Charley enters the arena of necessary male violence as a man with experience of the requirements of war. As a 'vet' he contains within him a terrible knowledge of the brutality that is unavoidable in these circumstances but the film demands he should place this alongside an awareness of the more measured response to any threat to civilised values that is expected of those upholding liberal American principles. In his role as educator, Boss tells Charley 'We came for justice, not vengeance: now, them is two different things.' This new understanding, which stands alongside (and legitimises) Charley's capability for extreme violence, has been acquired through being prepared to walk in the shadow of Boss and to learn from his balanced, honest, forthright speaking of truth to power. During the final shootout it is the cool, considered capacity for brutality exemplified, for example, by Ethan Edwards (John Wayne), Ford's white guardian enforcer of law and order in *The Searchers* (1956), or by Josey Wales, Eastwood's protector of the weak and vulnerable in *The Outlaw Josey Wales* (1976), that is of necessity required of Charley as the direct genre descendant of these sorts of characters. As with these 'heroes' from past Westerns, Charley embodies the ambiguity of being both the saviour of the nation and a merciless killer. Like them he is capable of being tender and gentle with women (and young people). We might think of Ethan kissing his brother's wife, Martha (Dorothy Jordan), on the forehead in *The Searchers*, or Josey Wales (Eastwood) in delicately lit scenes with Laura Lee (Sondra Locke) in *The Outlaw Josey Wales*. But, ultimately, in saving ordinary people from the bullying attentions of evil, democratic values and civilised norms must be put aside to make way for the force that is necessary if the social framework required by ordinary people wishing to live their lives in peace is to be restored. This is the action of Batman in *The Dark Knight* (Christopher Nolan, 2008) when he is prepared to go beyond regulations bounding the lawful questioning of suspects and move into the realms of Guantánamo-style interrogation in order to attempt to extract information from The Joker (Heath Ledger). What we see in *Open Range* is not unique to Westerns post-9/11.

Such scenes could be viewed as an attempted justification of the more extreme measures taken by the US Department of Defense, the Central Intelligence Agency and the Department of Homeland Security as part of the presidentially declared 'War on Terror'.[4] Such a reading would suggest what is being explained, or explored, is the necessity of a democracy allowing its special services to engage in activities generally proscribed by law. These filmic events become a vindication (or a questioning) of extra-judicial undertakings such as 'enhanced interrogation' involving water-boarding and the use of stress positions, 'extraordinary rendition' and detention in Guantánamo Bay. What may be suggested is the unavoidable necessity of employing the darker 'arts' of military engagement when confronted with a committed enemy. Charley's termination with extreme prejudice of Butler (Kim Coates) at the commencement of the final shootout, when he shoots him suddenly and unexpectedly in the forehead, vividly expresses the implied necessity of actions such as, for example, the extra-legal execution of Osama bin Laden.[5]

Earlier in the film we have been shown the violence of Boss's questioning of three of Baxter's men who are surprised at night while sitting around a campfire and beaten with rifle butts.[6] However, we are quickly shown such relatively low level violence is inadequate. In the absence of Boss and Charley, other members of Baxter's gang have attacked the two trailhands who have been left with the wagon, Mose (Abraham Benrubi) and Button, leaving one of them dead and the other fighting for his life. The two senior figures, who should have known better – like Ethan Edwards in *The Searchers* – have left 'home' and 'family' unguarded. The concept of the unexpected, surprise attack (on the homeland) is a key concern post-9/11 (as it was post-Pearl Harbor).[7] Towards the end of the film we see Boss arrive at the point where he seems ready to execute Baxter in cold blood. However, he draws back, unable because of his liberal values to follow through on 'termination with extreme prejudice'. As Boss turns away from delivering the *coup de grâce* he says he is not going to use a 'good' bullet to ease Baxter's pain; and, if there are 'good' bullets, presumably, there are also 'bad' bullets. The point may be that what makes the bullet 'good' or 'bad' is the person who uses it. We will return to this when discussing *Jane Got a Gun* (Gavin O'Connor, 2016); a key moral standpoint for Westerns is the idea proposed by the hero in *Shane* (George Stevens, 1953) that 'A gun is as good or as bad as the man using it'.

III

Open Range is a homage to a genre that during successive decades embodied an inherent belief in America and American values. It remains the American genre par excellence[8] for recreating history as cultural myth. The historical moment when cowboys under trail bosses drove herds of longhorn cattle huge distances north to railheads in order for them to be shipped to markets along the eastern seaboard and elsewhere was, in reality, very short, extending from the late 1860s to the late 1880s. This film, set in

1882, looks at the latter part of this period when, in an attempt to find further areas for grazing, herds were driven further north through Montana.[9] The film attempts to reinforce, maybe to re-establish, the concept of the open range and its associated values as central to any notion of the nation. The images given of the prairie are not those of a Western such as *Heaven's Gate* (Michael Cimino, 1980) in which the serf-like physical labour of central and east European families attempting, often unsuccessfully, to cultivate the thin soils of the interior is shown. Instead, these images construct a paradise of vibrant colours and man's harmony with the natural world. A heavy thunderstorm is shown that has in some senses to be endured and during which the horses are scattered but afterwards Charley's intense bond with horses means he is easily able to recapture his mount and Boss is able to round up the remaining horses and herd them towards the camera to the strains of epic background music. This is an idyllic world but one that also carries as a central component the importance of honest, hard work, as witnessed by a scene showing the men labouring to dig their wagon out of the mud. The brotherhood of these men is emphasised by their discussions of values; not only 'respect' as discussed by Button and Mose, but also, the importance of 'trust' as emphasised by Boss. When the young, inexperienced Button attempts to cheat at cards it is time for tuition from the father figure of Boss: 'A man's trust is a valuable thing, Button: don't wanta lose it over a handful of cards.'

We are presented with a 'family'. When Mose and Button are playfully wrestling, Boss's comment to Charley makes this clear: 'couple of damn kids' he says paternally. To be sure, the family is not fully rounded in that it lacks the presence of a woman but the love between them, as well as the already discussed 'trust' and 'respect', is clear.[10] It is a 'family' like that of the band that ends up accompanying Josey Wales, that is to say they are a group of misfits; but this is in keeping with the acclaimed founding principles of the US in that this is a country that welcomes all, has a set of clear values and recognises the contributions all-comers bring to the collective group. This liberal Hollywood vision of an America that embraces diversity and sees itself as welcoming the weak and the vulnerable is embodied in the story of Button, the immigrant Boss found 'in a Texas town a few years back living off café garbage' who 'couldn't speak a word of English'.

Both Boss and Charley have a gap in their lives in that they lack being part of a 'normal' family. When they are served tea at the Barlows' house their awkwardness in the face of china teacups and a fancy teapot is made clear for us. At one time Boss had both a wife and child but they died. He sums up, contains and controls within just six words both the traumatic dislocation of his life and the awful reality of the world thus demonstrated:

'They caught the typhus and died', he tells Sue. But, within a few lines, he sets about realising a re-definition of the concept of the home. After his wife and child died, he says, 'home didn't seem a place to spend time'; but now he has changed his mind: 'If Button lives . . . I swear I aim to see to it that there's a home he's sleepin' in, instead of the cold prairie.' Both 'home' and 'family' can appear in a variety of forms but, in keeping with the classic genre position, these things are viewed as fundamental necessities underpinning any correctly functioning society.[11] In the production notes for *Open Range*, Costner reflects on the characters typically found within Westerns:

> In all Westerns you have enigmatic characters; you don't know how they arrived or how they got to where they are. The only possessions they have are on their horse. It's a terribly romantic image, but if you think a bit longer, you wonder, what do they do when it rains? When they run out of food? They've got to go forage for themselves. They had to be very resourceful. We have this romantic view of the West when, in fact, it was terribly difficult.[12]

Often, in reviews and such like, it is the final sentence here that is quoted, and as such it appears an eminently reasonable view implying the need for increased social realism in such portrayals. However, when the longer, fuller quote is considered the most striking element is the way in which Costner conflates fiction and historical reality. He discusses the fantasy of 'Westerns' and the historical 'American West' as if they are one and the same thing. The 'enigmatic characters' of Westerns seem to his mind to be 'real', so that we can consider what they might do when it rains, or when they run out of food. As already mentioned, Costner does show his central cowboy group – Charley, 'Boss', Mose and Button – sitting out a thunderstorm with very little shelter and afterwards struggling to move their wagon out of the mud, but the representation remains nothing more than purely romantic. There is some effort to suggest the physicality of this life – the saddles, for instance, are heavy to carry and when they are put down hit the ground with real weight – but all of this remains locked uncomfortably and unconvincingly within the glossy, high production values of a Hollywood product.

Open Range works towards reclaiming the mythical space of the West(ern) in association with concepts of common human decency overcoming evil, the emergence of community spirit (for which we might read, national unity), and the creation of interlocking social and personal harmony. This is an attempt to return to the comforting spaces and narratives of the genre but it also locks neatly into the post-9/11 necessity for the US military to be able to pursue a determined enemy through a series of means directly at odds with much-heralded American democratic values. The central characters are ordinary, honest, decent folk who, within the moral parameters of this film, know how and when to deploy violence.

IV

The effort in *Open Range* is to move the viewer towards an understanding of a particular interpretation of what it means to be in the middle of a 'hot' war. The world with which we are confronted is one in which, as Charley says to Button, you need to 'keep that rifle close'. The threat is ominous and ever-present. It is expressed not only in the dialogue but also in the way in which a scene such as the one from which this phrase is taken just 20 minutes into the film – Charley and Boss ride off to town, leaving Button alone with the wagon – is concluded by a fade to black. The idyll established over the opening minutes begins to seem fragile. This is a note frequently struck in Westerns throughout the genre's history: a tranquil, peace-loving American way of life comes under threat from forces of evil. Boss's attitude is perhaps that of the gun lobby in America: 'A man's got a right to protect his property and his life', he asserts. In *Guns, Crime and Freedom*, Wayne LaPierre, executive vice president of the National Rifle Association, discusses 'the basic and fundamental right of every citizen to self-defense'.[13] In *Guns, Freedom and Terrorism*, published in the same year *Open Range* was released, LaPierre says:

> With the threat of more terror attacks . . . Americans are looking toward the protection of the Second Amendment. The most basic element of that right goes to the individual citizens' abilities to protect themselves, their families, their homes, their communities, and, if need be, their nation.[14]

What is presented as the common decency and humanity of our central characters is accompanied by knowledge of guns and a comfortableness with the potential necessity of the use of guns. This is the libertarian understanding of freedom frequently found in Hollywood Westerns. As Charley and Boss approach the town of Harmonville, a word and a place with the potential for both 'harm' and 'harmony', we have a shot of the church in the background with Charley in the foreground checking his handgun. Boss describes his weighty gun as a 'damn fine weapon' but remarks knowingly, and in a way that draws the audience into his knowingness, that he has noticed Charley prefers a lightweight gun (that is, he realises Charley has probably been a professional gunslinger).

The potential of Harmonville to be a place of harmony is underlined by shots of a building under construction and mothers with young children and teenagers. This is reinforced when we arrive at the doctor's white painted, weather-boarded house surrounded by a white picket fence enclosing a carefully tended garden containing flowers and washing on a line. The use of a vibrant green together with bright blues, yellows and reds is the only time such a colour palette is employed in the film.[15] The predominant colours in Harmonville are much darker. The gloom is heightened by setting scenes at night and by the use of low key lighting, and is further emphasised by cloud-filled skies. The owner of the livery stable, Percy, expresses the nature of Harmonville in his brief exchange with Boss. 'Can't stay away from our little paradise', he says, exploring a use of dry humour and heavy irony not lost on Boss, who replies, 'Believe Satan says the same at the gates of hell, old-timer.' Adding to the ominous nature of all of this, not only do we have the location as a reminder of 'The Gunfight at the OK Corral', but we also have a shot from behind Percy in the stable loft that resembles one used by Charles Laughton in the equally dark and ominous *Night of the Hunter* (1955). In that film the shot has a young boy in the foreground, but in both films the emphasis is on the tension created by the presence of both innocence and evil within the world, which is, of course, amplified by Boss's reference to Satan. Within the ideology of the film this conundrum can only be dealt with in one way, which is through periodic ritual cleansing. When Charley and Boss shelter from a storm in the town's cafe, not only are they (and we) told that 'The town's been here a long time . . . and it'll be here a lot longer' – i.e. that civilisation (that is, the film's concept of 'the American way of life') will continue and is not ultimately threatened by such momentary expressions of evil – but they are also informed that 'Every once in a while a good storm washes through and leaves Harmonville as clean as a baby's bottom.'

Charley, in particular, like a string of Western 'heroes', has a darker side but like his antecedents he is what is needed in order to secure the democratic freedoms of a civilised country. The extremes to which Batman is pushed by the demonic Joker in *The Dark Knight* could be seen either as necessary transgressions of democratic norms in the face of terrorists who recognise no rules or regulations governing their violence, or as fundamental errors of judgement that mean the upholder of law and order has through his actions destroyed the very foundations of the authority given to him to maintain order;[16] but the actions of Charley in *Open Range* are infused with no such ambiguity. These are the entirely necessary actions of a fundamentally decent man who has the necessary capabilities to deal clinically and efficiently with extreme moments of jeopardy for democracy/civilisation. Boss sums up Charley in his usual efficient way with words when talking to Sue: 'Charley thinks for himself, Mrs Barlow. He's a good man and he knows what has to be done.'[17]

V

This is a film about the defence of democratic freedoms and the necessity of having 'capable' gun-law people who can lead the community towards playing its role in maintaining these freedoms. When the small group of cowboys out on the trail is initially threatened by masked riders attempting to scare them off from free-grazing on the prairie, Boss makes it clear exactly what is at stake in his mind and within the moral framework of the film. In response to Charley asking 'You reckon those cows worth gettin' killed over?' he says: 'Cows is one thing, but one man tellin' another man where he can go in this country's somethin' else.' He is clear that the central issue here has nothing to do with cattle, or sheep or any form of farming; this is about defining this society's central tenet of 'freedom' and asserting it as a sacrosanct point of faith. When, as mentioned earlier, Boss and Charley ambush three of the night-riders and have them disarmed and at their mercy we are shown a glimpse of just how ruthless Charley is capable of being. He cocks his gun ready to execute one of the three men who in a high-angle point-of-view shot taken from Charley's perspective is shown squirming on the ground (Figure 2.2). Boss calls to him and manages to bring him out of the intensity of his moment of near cold-blooded bringing of death to an unarmed man. For the moral purposes of the film Boss and Charley are one entity. They operate as the protector of democratic freedoms, embodying the necessity of calm reason and restraint working in balanced co-existence with the necessary capability for extreme violence if and when the moral values of the community become unacceptably compromised. When they return to their wagon they find Mose is dead having being shot in

Figure 2.2 Charley (Kevin Costner) demonstrating the 'ability' when necessary to execute declared enemies in *Open Range*.

the head. Mose has been executed in exactly the manner Charley has been shown as capable of practising, but as one entity Charley/Boss has been able to pay rigorous attention to the critical line between barbarism and civilised values. Being civilised and maintaining civilised values does not preclude the necessary use of extreme, shocking violence but it does require the full certainty of the requirement to cross the line into violence before such action is taken.

As a single entity operating to enforce democratic freedoms, Boss needs Charley's knowledge of violence as much as Charley needs Boss's mature reason and restraint. When Boss says he plans to wait on his own with the cows and 'kill every son of a bitch that comes to take 'em', Charley's response effectively points out that this strategy will not succeed: 'For one man in open ground you sure gotta lot o' killin' in mind.' At this moment it is Charley's clear reasoning that is needed in order to give shape to Boss's anger and desire for justice. Both men are clear that in certain circumstances killing is both necessary and required. Boss says he aims 'to kill Baxter and those that done this', that is, those that killed Mose and shot Button, both of whom are representations of innocence. Charley's response to Boss's assertion that 'You best get your mind right about what's gotta be done' is in many ways the key message for an audience invested in democratic principles: 'I got no problem with killin', Boss, never have.'

A huge effort is made to portray Charley and Boss as ordinary, everyday people. The key aspects of both are that they have values that lead them to *think* about what is right and wrong, and they care about and feel for others. All of this is made apparent in the funeral scene where Mose and the dog, Tig, that has also been shot, are buried. The beauty of the natural environment is emphasised with Charley digging the grave on a hillside covered in wild flowers. Mose's innocence is highlighted. Charley tells us Mose 'Woke with a smile: seemed to keep it there all day' and was 'The kinda man that would say "Good morning" and mean it'. The lesson is that being good, gentle and innocent is not enough in this world because it places you at the mercy of others. These are attributes to be admired and valued but if they are to flourish they need to be defended when necessary through violence. People such as Boss and Charley, together with their attitudes and preparedness to take action, are necessary alongside the goodness of everyday, common humanity. This is the very essence of the Western narrative as it has been presented through much of cinema history and *Open Range* is a re-assertion of this key underpinning theme of the genre.

After their brief experience of the comforts of home under the Barlows' roof, Boss and Charley have to leave the to-be-protected family space. In particular for Charley this movement out through the door is a movement into *his* space, into the place where he serves the community (and the home), protecting it in the face of brutal outside forces that have no conception of the value of the home and the ordinary, decent people who occupy that space. By the end of the film it remains somewhat unclear as to whether, like Ethan Edwards, he is ultimately unable to return to that space of the home or whether at some stage he will be able to claim the position alongside Sue that the narrative structure has opened for him. When Charley comes into the Barlows' home for a second time he takes off his gun in respect for the place in which he finds himself but he places it on the table. Is this the necessity of the two things going together, the 'table' as the heart of the home and the 'gun' as the thing that protects this critically important social space? Or, does it show how Charley will remain unable to ever take up a place within the home? Or, does it express both of these things?

Charley's backstory is a further assertion of the presence of evil in the world and the need for it to be confronted, if necessary with brutal violence. Like other Western heroes, Charley's first killing occurred when he was a child. After talking about his childhood playing with other children in woods, he says: 'Killed my first man in them woods. Held the paper on our farm and after my pa dies he would come round to get payment from my mom in any way he could. Weren't much older than Button when I shot him in the throat.' We are given an extreme close-up of Charley's face as he tells this story. He is shown as having been brutalised by his participation as a young man in the Civil War: 'Must have been a hundred of 'em lyin' dead after the smoke cleared. Went and shot the rest who weren't. Those of us who had the knack was made into a special squad so we could travel light and on our own into enemy territory.' He tells Boss, 'It wasn't long before we was killin' men that weren't even in uniform', and that after the war he moved west and put his 'skills' to use for men like Baxter. Charley has been a hired killer. He has been on what for this film is morally the wrong side, but his distinguishing feature is that he has a conscience and cannot avoid thinking: 'Every once in a while I almost got through a day without thinking, who I am, what I'd done.' For Boss, this truth-speaking, this facing up to the truth of his life, highlights a further key feature of his character: 'You're a real honest man, Charley.'

Open Range is about the reclamation of both this type of Western 'hero' and classical Western values. It is not, fundamentally, the values of conservative America that are being proclaimed by this film but rather those of liberal America. It is the immigrant, Button, who leads the final assault on Baxter and his embodiment of the threat to American values. The position of the film is that Charley and Boss are to be admired in their ability to marry extreme violence with honesty and decency. After they have sighted the masked night riders for the first time, Boss and Charley have a scene together set within the vast space of the prairie with their herd of cattle grazing in the distance. 'Beautiful country', says Boss. 'A man can get lost out here, forget there's people and things that ain't so simple as this.' They work out they have been riding together for ten years and Boss asserts, 'There's been a lot o' change since then.' With this film said to be set in 1882 in Montana, this statement is true of the historic previous decade. Barbed wire was manufactured from 1873 and from then the open range was increasingly fenced. In terms of the period prior to when the film was made, the past ten years had also been a time of change. Ten years previously, Democrat Bill Clinton had been elected president. The 9/11 attack came eight months into George W. Bush's first term as president. From liberal optimism in the wake of a Democrat victory and the economic prosperity of the 1990s to the post-9/11 experience these ten years could certainly be described as having seen 'a lot o' change'.

The fundamental difficulty for the film is how to contain within the narrative a character like Charley who is seen by Sue as 'gentle and caring' but who is able to kill with impunity as and when the necessity arises. This would not seem possible but within the ideology of the film there is no alternative if the presence of evil and the threat it offers is to be dealt with. The film is driven back to the original Western ethos. It has to re-state and re-assert the original founding themes of the Western in the face of the contemporary threat offered to society.[18]

Notes

1. 'The Trail Boss' (pen and ink) showing a rider on a low rise overlooking the herd, attributed to Charles Marion Russell, was reproduced on postcards as a line drawing during the early twentieth century and used on postage stamps in the 1960s. Also, see the similar positioning of Russell's 'Wagon Boss' (oil on canvas), 1909, Gilcrease Museum, Thomas Gilcrease Institute of American History and Art, University of Tulsa.
2. John O'Sullivan is generally credited with first using the term 'manifest destiny'. He spoke of it being the destiny of the United States 'to overspread the continent allotted by Providence for the free development of our yearly multiplying millions'. See John O'Sullivan, 'Annexation', *United States Magazine and Democratic Review*, 1845, 17(1): 6.
3. Joseph S. Walker, 'Coen, Coen on the range: Rooster Cogburn(s) and domestic space', in Scott F. Stoddart (ed.), *The New Westerns: Critical Essays on the Genre Since 9/11* (Jefferson, NC: McFarland, 2016), p. 65.

4. For an initial discussion of this phrase, see 'What exactly is the War on Terror?', in Mark N. Katz, *Leaving Without Losing: The War on Terror After Iraq and Afghanistan* (Baltimore: Johns Hopkins University Press, 2012), pp. 15–18.
5. Robert O'Neill, the US Navy SEAL who killed bin Laden, claimed to have shot him twice in the forehead. Robert O'Neill, *The Operator: Firing the Shots that Killed Osama Bin Laden and My Years as a Seal Team Warrior* (New York: Scribner, 2017), p. 310.
6. It is not clear why Boss orders these men to put on their 'spook hats' (hoods with eye-holes that the men wear when they are out to terrorize opponents of Baxter's) but the 'hooding' of suspects is widely seen as an element of 'enhanced interrogation' used by US forces. According to James White, in modern times, 'Psychological torture is common and includes prolonged solitary confinement, hooding, stress positions, withholding food and water, sleep deprivation, loud noise, bright light, hot and cold temperatures, nakedness, rape and sexual humiliation, mock executions, water boarding, and the use of dogs.' Boss also orders the men to take off their trousers and lie face down on the ground with their 'peckers in the dirt'. See James E. White, *Contemporary Moral Problems: War, Terrorism, and Torture* (Belmont, CA: Wadsworth, 2011), p. 66. Also, 'The rise of the torture-intelligence nexus', in Vian Bakir, *Torture, Intelligence and Sousveillance in the War on Terror: Agenda-Building Struggles* (London and New York: Routledge, 2016), pp. 61–90.
7. See, for example, Larry Hancock, *Surprise Attack: From Pearl Harbor to 9/11 to Benghazi* (Berkeley, CA: Counterpoint, 2016).
8. Jean-Louis Rieupeyrout's book, with a preface by André Bazin, *Le Western: ou, Le cinéma américain par excellence* (Paris: Éditions du Cerf, 1953), famously employs this phrase in its title.
9. Although the barbed wire fencing of land was already well under way, the drives were perhaps effectively ended by the harsh winter of 1886–7 when '50 to 80 percent of the various herds across the northernmost ranges' died. See Christopher Knowlton, *Cattle Kingdom: The Hidden History of the Cowboy West* (Boston, MA: Eamon Dolan/Houghton Mifflin Harcourt, 2017), p. xxii.
10. The relationship into which this might throw Boss and Charley would be the subject of a whole other book.
11. We might also note how the makeshift male family of Boss, Charley, Mose, and Button replicates the 'family' of Ben Cartwright (Lorne Greene), Adam Cartwright (Pernell Roberts), 'Hoss' Cartwright (Dan Blocker) and 'Little Joe' Cartwright (Michael Landon) that was central to the long-running TV series *Bonanza* (1959–73).
12. Cinema Review, 'OPEN RANGE, Production notes – about the production', *Cinema Review*. Available at <http://cinemareview.com/production.asp?prodid=2177> (accessed 22 June 2018).
13. Wayne LaPierre, *Guns, Crime and Freedom* (Washington, DC: Regnery, 1994), p. 33. LaPierre dedicates his more recent book, *Guns, Freedom and*

Terrorism, to Charlton Heston, 'Who has never lost sight of what is important in life – faith, family, and freedom'. See Wayne LaPierre, *Guns, Freedom and Terrorism* (Nashville, TN: WND Books, 2003).
14. LaPierre, *Guns, Freedom and Terrorism*, 2003, p. 10.
15. The film echoes the use of bright colours around women and domesticity found in other Westerns; for example, see Ben Stride (Randolph Scott) helping Annie Greer (Gail Russell) with her washing in *Seven Men From Now* (Budd Boetticher, 1956).
16. Terence McSweeney, *The 'War on Terror' and American Film: 9/11 Frames Per Second* (Edinburgh: Edinburgh University Press, 2014), pp. 119–22.
17. In that he suffers post-traumatic stress syndrome Charley is linked to the veterans of wars involving American forces stretching back at least to the American Civil War and including, crucially, Vietnam and the Iraq War. Eric Dean suggests, 'To anyone familiar with the American Civil War, the suggestion that Vietnam was unique in producing psychiatric casualties is suspect.' See Eric T. Dean, '"We will all be lost and destroyed": post-traumatic stress disorder and the Civil War', *Civil War History*, 1991, 37(2): 139.
18. Further contradictions, ruptures within the ideational body of the film, clearly remain and could be explored in depth. In particular, the presence of evil is located within the community's current governing forces, the chief exponent of corporate power and the main agent of law enforcement. That which has come to be perceived as a threat is that which has become integrated into the economic and political framework of the community.

CHAPTER 3

Restoring the Western Hero and Reclaiming the Classic Hollywood Experience: *True Grit* (2010)

I

In *Rooster: The Life and Times of the Real Rooster Cogburn, The Man Who Inspired True Grit*, Brett Cogburn encapsulates what John Wayne playing the role of US Marshal 'Rooster' Cogburn in *True Grit* (Henry Hathaway, 1969) represented for many Americans.

> For those of us weaned on Fourth of July flag waving, the image of him as that lovable rogue with a patch over his eye dealing out justice to the bad guys with a gun in each fist is the epitome of manly virtue.[1]

The same response – viewing this character as an American hero – might well hold true for the majority of the domestic audience watching Jeff Bridges tackle the role of 'Rooster' Cogburn, in the Coen brothers' remake of *True Grit* from 2010. There seems little room for an alternative reading. Watching the film we may be able to debate matters around the periphery but the core issue of the unavoidable need for 'good' ultimately to confront 'evil' in physical combat, and for good to win in such a way as to safeguard the future of our shared cultural community, can never be in doubt. According to Richard Aquila:

> the Coen brothers' rendition of *True Grit* is very much a traditional western. Like the heroes in the original, the protagonists in the remake defeat the bad guys and demonstrate courage, determination, and, of course, true grit.[2]

For Aquila this film takes Westerns back to fundamentals of the genre, reflecting the mood of the nation in relation to international affairs but also promoting a set of basic ideological beliefs:

> The film reflects the anxious mood of a nation reeling from 9/11, mired in two wars in Iraq and Afghanistan, and staggered by a Great Recession. But it also mirrors a new sense of optimism in the country . . . showing that individuals could achieve equality and justice as long as they held fast to the values and resolve that had won the Old West.[3]

In *Rooster: The Life and Times of the Real Rooster Cogburn* the author writes about his great-grandfather, John Franklin Cogburn, born in Arkansas just after the Civil War and apparently nicknamed 'Rooster'. This historical rather than fictional Cogburn was very much on the opposing side to US marshals of the time, being involved in a gunfight in which a deputy marshal was killed. However, the attitudes said by Brett Cogburn to be embodied by his great-grandfather seem entirely relevant to the fictional 'Rooster' Cogburn found in both film versions of *True Grit*:

> The only authority the Cogburn clan recognized was God and the gun. Governments didn't build your home, make your clothes, hunt your meat or defend your life. When it came to the Law, a man rolled his own from the makings of his individual ideas of right and wrong.[4]

John G. Cawelti suggests, 'the hero's code' found in Westerns 'rests primarily on a personal sense of honor and rightness, which is outside both law and conventional morality'.[5] In other words, like Franklin, the heroes in Westerns 'roll their own'. Cawelti proposes there is something at work in Westerns he describes as 'the Code'. This is 'a stringent set of moral rules concerning, above all, the proper uses of individual violence'.[6] He adds that 'the Code'

> assumes that neither written law nor the conventional standards of society are adequate guides to moral conduct. True morality can only be decided by a man who is prepared to face extremely violent situations with trust in his own individual judgment.[7]

This is the position embodied for the audience by both Wayne in the original film and Bridges in the recent remake; and it is, therefore, the moral compass presented to the audience.

The Coen brothers received the backing to produce their version of *True Grit* some forty years after the original was produced. Part of the interest in this chapter is in why 2010 was seen as a good time for this narrative to be revisited. The suggestion is that it may have felt an appropriate time to redefine, or restate, the meaning of 'true grit' for a new post-9/11 era. The titles of films are important. If a film is called 'True Grit' it is likely it will attempt to define that term in some way. It is also to be assumed that it is felt this character trait is, in some way, significant and to be valued. And, in this particular case, in re-defining 'true grit' one further vital thing is achieved: that iconic American star, John Wayne, is invoked, or re-imagined, for the present time. In doing this, the complex, compound structure of 'the American hero' is reconceived for the contemporary audience. In effect, because of the nature of the character of Cogburn, a range of longstanding conservative values and perspectives are re-asserted in a reminted form.

II

In essence, the narrative of *True Grit* is a simple one of outlaws being pursued by law enforcement officers. The crucial concept at stake here is that of justice; and, although the importance of setting up and maintaining a system of law and order has always been a crucial theme within Westerns, the dynamics of how that would work in practice in a wild frontier territory have always been heavily debated within the genre. David T. Ritchie states that in the Western 'the inability of the law and the judicial system to maintain order and to bring about justice is a recurrent motif'.[8] For Ritchie, 'the tension between this ineffectiveness on the part of legal institutions and the desire for justice on the part of principal characters is absolutely central to many of these movies'.[9] This clearly expresses the scenario under investigation in *True Grit* (2010). Both Mattie Ross (Hailee Steinfeld), a fourteen-year-old girl determined to obtain 'justice' for her murdered father, and 'Rooster' Cogburn (Jeff Bridges), the marshal she hires to track down her father's killer, embody this tension.

Considering an earlier film, Ritchie observes that the central character in *The Man Who Shot Liberty Valance* (John Ford, 1962) has to come to the realisation that on the frontier he has to 'put down his law books and pick up the gun'.[10] These ideas, firstly, of living on the frontier at the edge of civilisation and needing at times to cross the divide into lawless, barbarous territory, and, secondly, of necessity within this space having to 'pick up the gun', are central to the Western. In *True Grit* special (almost reverential) attention is given to Mattie's father's handgun as, after his death, she picks it up from amongst his few possessions and we view it in close-up (Figure 3.1). Although the contexts are different, Mattie is like Jane (Natalie Portman) in *Jane Got a Gun* (Gavin O'Connor, 2016)[11] in that she is prepared as a woman to take up the gun and to use it. It is she who eventually shoots and kills her father's killer,

Figure 3.1 Mattie (Hailee Steinfeld) with her father's handgun viewed in close-up in *True Grit* (Joel and Ethan Coen, 2010).

Tom Chaney (Josh Brolin). Again, in this she is like Jane, who is also (within the constructed narrative) permitted to kill her nemesis, John Bishop (Ewan McGregor). In a new era, those members of society often seen in earlier Westerns as in need of male protection are both willing and able to join with men in righting wrongs.[12]

The original movie, based on the book *True Grit* by Charles Portis that had been published a year earlier in 1968, was made at a time of increased social unrest: there was strong opposition, particularly by young people, to American involvement in the Vietnam War; there was an increasingly militant African American Civil Rights Movement; and there was forceful feminist agitation taking place on issues from abortion to beauty pageants. In this film, as in the later version, Cogburn (Wayne) sees the society around him as going soft. His outlook on the world is that of John Franklin Cogburn outlined above. He tells Mattie (Kim Darby): 'You can't serve papers on a rat, baby sister: you gotta kill him, or let him be.' In other words, there are good people and bad people in the world, and the only way to deal with the bad people is through employing the ultimate sanction. As a US deputy marshal, Cogburn is operating inside the law, but he feels hamstrung by the formal processes of the courts. The phrase 'you can't serve papers on a rat' is an especially powerful statement for a genre often seen as being in negotiation with the concept of law and order.[13]

The suggestion from Cogburn is that at a certain point, when dealing with extreme wrongdoers, the law becomes inadequate and it becomes necessary to step outside of the law if 'order' is to be restored. He is angry his methods are not fully appreciated by the society within which he is operating. As he sees it, the dominant perspective he finds himself up against is one that believes, as he explains it, that you can be 'too tough on the rats' and that you should 'give them rats a fair show'. This is the position taken by the character of Cogburn in both film versions of *True Grit*, as well as in the novel. It is also the position taken by Mattie Ross, a fourteen-year-old with definite views on the world. When she is told there are several marshals she could hire to pursue her father's killer she pointedly does not choose the one who is said to believe that 'even the worst of men is entitled to a fair shake'. She is sure who killed her father, certain there are no further circumstances to consider and definite about the form of 'justice' she expects to get. Mattie is determined to appoint 'Rooster' Cogburn, the man who is described as the 'meanest' of the deputy marshals, because the 'justice' in which she is interested is 'vengeance'. Some critics have seen the film as, in this respect, appropriate to the current period in US history. Richard Brody, for example, has described it as a movie 'for the post-9/11 age of devil-may-care vengeance'.[14] And, some of the taglines used to promote the film – 'Punishment comes one way or another' and 'Retribution', for example – would suggest a similar emphasis was placed on the production by the filmmakers.[15]

III

Like Cogburn, Mattie is less than enamoured with her society. Her father has been murdered in the street in Fort Smith, Arkansas; but, as she describes it, the killer who fled on horseback could have walked out of town 'for not a soul in that city could be bothered to give chase'. In fact, historically Fort Smith is (in)famous during the period this film is set for the number of executions in the town. Judge Isaac C. Parker returned death sentences on 160 people between 1875 and 1896. More than forty of these sentences were commuted to life in prison or lesser terms, and more than thirty convictions were overturned on appeal, but seventy-nine people were hanged during the period, with up to six being hanged on one day.[16]

This was a violently dangerous region of the country for those on both sides of the law in the late nineteenth century. Various figures are given, but as many as 100 deputy US marshals may have been killed in western Arkansas and Indian Territory between 1872 and 1896.[17] This part of Arkansas was on the edge of Indian Territory, an area outlaws would frequently attempt to disappear into in order to evade capture.

In line with this history, when Mattie arrives in Fort Smith intending 'to avenge her father's blood' she joins a crowd watching three men being hanged. She is looking for the sheriff and when she finds him she states very clearly the outcome she is determined to achieve: 'I intend to see Papa's killer hanged', she says.

Executions from the period are documented as drawing large crowds. Here one writer describes the walk to the gallows of three men in Fort Smith in 1874:

> At one o'clock the three men were led from the guardhouse with the ministers in the lead singing hymns ... The whole procession was surrounded by an armed guard who had difficulty keeping back the immense crowd ... At the scaffold thousands of spectators were kept back by a stout rope and deputy U.S. marshals.[18]

Describing a mass hanging of six men in 1875, Roger H. Tuller says:

> Whole families from forty and fifty miles distance converged on the little city, their numbers augmented by newspaper reporters from Little Rock, Kansas City, and St. Louis. By 9.00 A.M. over five thousand people jammed the jail yard around the gallows.[19]

The film is set in a violent time and place where the struggle to establish the dominance of a set of values and beliefs interpreted as being at the heart of American society was actively taking place and this context is quickly established for the audience. In the 2010 film, within a few minutes we have been confronted with the crumpled dead body of Mattie's father lying in the street, his embalmed body in its coffin, three men dropping through gallows trapdoors to their deaths, and Mattie entering a darkened funeral parlour where these men's bodies are stored and where she is to sleep the night. The darkness of the night of the killing (and the way in which the body is only slowly revealed to us), the noir lighting of the funeral parlour, and the brilliant sunlight of the gallows scene, each work in their own way to confront us with the harsh realities of the period in Arkansas.

IV

However, although it is possible to read these opening scenes in the way described, is this the way a younger contemporary, cinemagoing audience is likely to see things? In the film, the crowd watching the execution of the three men first of all gasp as the trapdoor is opened and they drop to their deaths, and then they break into applause. But, how does a modern audience react to seeing these things represented on the screen? And, how do the filmmakers expect the audience to react? If we return for a moment to the idea of Mattie sleeping amongst the coffins in the funeral parlour/undertaker's workshop, this is something the Coens added to the narrative that was not in the novel. It could be said this scene helps to give a further sense of Mattie's character (in particular, perhaps, her grit); but, from the filmmakers' perspective, it also allows for a moment of gothic horror as Mattie walks past the dead bodies of the men who have just been executed.

As postmodern filmmakers, the Coens see this scene as a moment of dark comedy, a cinephile moment they are able to share with their knowing postmodern audience that is alert to the nuances of genre. The filmmakers even go to the elaborate process of setting up a joke within the dialogue for this moment of Mattie's entry into the funeral parlour. When Mattie first comes to see her father laid out in his coffin, the undertaker is given an idiosyncratic tic of language use (taken from the novel): he repeats the phrase 'If you would like to kiss him, it would be alright' twice. This means when she returns to sleep the night and the undertaker says 'If you would like to sleep in a coffin, it would be alright' we can be sure we have been cued for a comic moment. All of this suggests those people who have commented on the YouTube clip of the execution scene that they have found various parts of this to be darkly humorous may be correct in their reading.[20] Denying the Native American the chance to deliver any final words to the crowd by having a sack pulled over his head to prevent him speaking could be seen as a moment of social commentary, and in a way it is, but it is social commentary reduced to comedy. It is the political position sidestepped by knowingly clever, postmodernist humour.

In addition to Mattie sleeping amongst the dead bodies in the undertaker's workroom/funeral parlour, the filmmakers add various other scenes not found in the original novel. For example, they include a scene with Cogburn and Mattie coming across a dead body hanging in a tree, and another bizarre scene following on from the body in the tree in which the two central characters meet a nomadic doctor-cum-dentist wearing a bearskin. Each of these scenes is episodic and, as such, intrudes into and dislocates the flow of the narrative. In postmodern terms, the audience is invited to step outside of the storytelling world, to look in on that realm from a knowing distance, and to become complicit with the filmmakers in an extra-narrative percipience. This aspect of the filmmaking creates some difficulty for any reading of the film. On the one hand, in line with the style of their overall body of work, the Coens seem in places to invite spectators to adopt an ironic, detached perspective on events. On the other hand, they have chosen to remake a particular Western and, outside of such postmodernist moments, to stick quite closely to the events of the original narrative, genuinely it would seem inviting our admiration for the attitudes and outlooks of particular characters.

V

The star of the original movie, John Wayne, was of course well known for his right-wing politics, and became especially closely associated with the character of 'Rooster' Cogburn after taking up the role again in a sequel, *Rooster Cogburn* (Stuart Millar, 1975). Ron Briley highlights, not only the way in which Wayne's politics remained consistent through the 1960s, but also the way in which his position remained in line with the thinking of a sizeable proportion of American voters.

> Of course, the events of the 1960s, such as assassination, racial violence, student unrest, the war in Indochina, and political corruption, laid bare the thin fabric of the postwar consensus . . . Nevertheless, one figure from the 1950s continued to cast a giant shadow well into the 1960s . . . And, like many Americans, Wayne's politics did not change during the turbulent 1960s.[21]

Supporting his assertion that Wayne was actually in line with a good percentage of American voters, Briley reminds us Wayne's representation of the Vietnam War, *The Green Berets* (Wayne and Ray Kellogg, 1968), 'found an appreciative audience' and was 'one of the most lucrative Warner Brothers releases of the 1960s'.[22] From its reception among critics, Robert Eberwein may justifiably describe this film as 'probably the most despised American war movie ever made because of its pro-war stance at a time when protests against the war had become increasingly intense',[23] but this does not take account of the popular response to the film. One of the issues at stake in *The Green Berets*, as with *True Grit* and Westerns in general, is the concept of the administration of justice. At one point in *The Green Berets*, newspaper reporter George Beckworth (David Janssen), appalled at the brutal interrogation of a suspected Việt Cộng soldier he has just witnessed, says: 'There's still such a thing as due process'. To which Wayne's character, Colonel Mike Kirby, replies: 'Out here due process is a bullet'. To all intents and purposes, this is the preferred option of Cogburn in both filmed versions of *True Grit*, the argument being the 'rules' do not apply, and cannot apply, in 'Indian territory'.[24]

Noah Gittell argues that throughout their careers the Coens, in contrast to Wayne's conservatism, have been 'quietly, perhaps unconsciously, preaching' what he calls 'apolitical populism'.[25] He argues their position is one of rejecting the in-place political structures. However, when Donald Trump was elected president in 2016, Ethan Coen openly attacked all those who he saw as having allowed this to happen. In a satirical piece for the *New York Times* he criticised various sets of voters, assorted public figures, and the media for their roles in facilitating Trump's victory.[26]

However, despite the differences between the overt Republican leanings of Wayne and the much less publicly pronounced political inclinations of the Coen brothers, there is little difference between the political positions occupied by the two versions of *True Grit*. Despite their body of work frequently being seen as apolitical, the Coens' rendering of *True Grit* would seem when push-comes-to-shove to assent fairly easily to a position that fully endorses the necessity of unhampered military action when dealing with unrepentant opposition. Leaving aside for a moment the elements of postmodernism we find in the Coen brothers' *True Grit*, their film would seem to be just as conservative in outlook as Wayne's original star-driven version.[27]

Jenna Hunnef claims both the 1969 film and the 2010 remake 'actively support and even exceed the novel's conservative ideology'.[28] This political positioning, she says, was 'in response to their respective contexts of national crisis that shook the foundations of what it meant to be a man in America'.[29] She views both the late 1960s and the period leading up to 2010 as moments of 'national crisis' in the United States, and sees both periods as creating severe challenges to previous conceptions of masculinity and manhood. These two versions of *True Grit*, she says, championed '*white* heroic individualism'.[30]

In line with others who have written about the film,[31] Hunnef struggles to understand the fairly traditional filmmaking style employed by the Coen brothers on this film when it is seen against the postmodernism found in the rest of their body of work. 'For a filmmaking duo known for its quirkiness and subversion of generic and cultural conventions (cf. *Fargo*, 1996; *No Country for Old Men*, 2007),' she says, 'their vision of *True Grit* is staunchly conservative'.[32] But, returning us to one of the basic functions of the genre, Joseph S. Walker puts this in perspective and reminds us what is happening here is in fact nothing new. He highlights the way Westerns have often attempted 'to come to terms with a new global reality, where America is confronted by enemies who are difficult to identify and successfully confront'.[33] Walker draws attention to the fact that the Western 'has always been an allegorical representation of America's understanding of itself' and how in the period post-9/11 'America has struggled to achieve any such understanding'.[34]

VI

The climax to *True Grit* (2010) occurs near the end of the film when Cogburn (Jeff Bridges) singlehandedly confronts 'Lucky' Ned Pepper (Barry Pepper) and three members of his gang in a shootout in which the protagonists charge towards each other on horseback firing their weapons. This is the scene in the original 1969 movie referred to by Brett Cogburn in the opening to this chapter. Although the narrative details remain the same the Coen brothers shoot this scene slightly differently to Henry Hathaway, who directed the 1969 version. They employ close action shots from cameras in amongst the participants in this cavalry charge-style gunfight but intersperse this material with long shots. For the viewer this detracts from the intensity of the drama. The experience of being 'in the moment' as the fighting develops is broken four or five times by long shots placing us at a detached, observational distance. On each occasion, cutting to a long shot means we are suddenly pulled out of the chaos of the firefight and placed in a moment of calm distanciation that is at the opposite end of the spectrum of spectatorial engagement. This highlights the fact that warfare is not (especially, perhaps, since the advent of high technology modern weapon systems) only about the warm-blooded passion of hand-to-hand combat. It is also about cold-blooded, detached calculation. The long shots are taken from the perspective of fourteen-year-old Mattie Ross (Hailee Steinfeld) and Texas Ranger LaBoeuf (Matt Damon) watching events unfold from a rocky cliff overlooking the battle. And it is LaBoeuf who at this point through his actions embodies for the viewer this second more clinical and dispassionate aspect of warfare.

Because Cogburn is outnumbered, because he is on the side of 'the law', and because we identify with him through having followed his story for much of the film, we are given a very clear sense of who we should be rooting for in the melee unfolding on the arid floodplain below Mattie and LaBoeuf. In this sense, even in the Coen brothers' version, this is old-style Western filmmaking, presenting us with a clear understanding of 'goodies' and 'baddies'. Cogburn has his limitations – he has what might by some be seen to be questionable morals – but he remains essentially the classical hero. He confronts evil in a direct and courageous manner, and he successfully defeats his adversaries. However, as suggested above, he cannot manage entirely on his own. At the end of the battle, he has to be saved by his colleague, the younger man, LaBoeuf. In both versions of the film and in the novel, Cogburn is old and one-eyed. He has limited vision and is not omnipotent; but, crucially, at an important level, he also represents the past and brings with him the experience and knowledge of what to do within the sphere of violent confrontation. Richard Slotkin has described the heroes of Westerns as 'mediators' who 'can teach civilized men how to defeat savagery on its native grounds'.[35] This, in essence, is Cogburn's role in both filmed versions of *True Grit*.

Figure 3.2 LaBoeuf (Matt Damon) intervenes to kill Pepper (Barry Pepper) from distance in *True Grit*.

In this climactic gunfight Cogburn is about to be killed by the leader of the 'baddies', Pepper, who is 'shot to pieces' but has his gun trained on Cogburn and seems to have sufficient strength to pull the trigger and kill Cogburn before he himself dies. Cogburn is only saved by LaBoeuf who, from his vantage point on the bluff above the battle, uses his Sharps carbine to shoot Pepper. This is a weapon known for its long range accuracy and the Coen brothers emphasise the distance at which the shot is taken through careful use of camera set-ups and editing (Figure 3.2). In his relationship to the heat of battle, LaBoeuf takes on the role of a sniper (or, perhaps, a drone-operative capable of killing with clinical precision from a great distance). He is not taking part in open warfare but he is a vital part of the 'operation', able to deliver unseen, unexpected, long-range death. More than that, his ability to be able to kill from a distance with calculated accuracy is applauded by the admiring public. 'Some bully shot', Mattie whoops in delight, when he dispatches Pepper.

In the end, what we see played out is a curious combination of inputs from our three main protagonists, and, in particular from Cogburn and Mattie. Cogburn is the ageing and flawed hero: he knows about warfare and how to go about bloody battlefield fighting. He is able to shoot a man at such point blank range that the man's blood splatters his face. If he can, he will arrange the circumstances of the 'battlefield' so that he has all the advantages he can manage over his enemy. When he is expecting Pepper and his gang to arrive at a cabin he sets himself on the high ground with a rifle and waits for them to arrive. 'What we want is to get them all in the dugout . . . I'll kill the last one that goes in; then we'll have them in a barrel', he tells Mattie. Her response is to ask if Cogburn means he will shoot this man in the back. 'It will give them to know our intentions are serious', he responds. 'Then I'll call down – see if they'll be taken alive. If they won't, I'll shoot them as they come out.' Mattie's verdict on this is not to decry it as an unfair approach lacking chivalry but to compliment Cogburn. 'You display great poise', she tells him. She accepts both the proposed shooting of a man in the back and the tactic of seeking as great an advantage as possible over the enemy.

Cogburn himself dismisses the whole planned venture as 'just a turkey shoot' and is certainly not troubled by attaching such a description to what he plans to do. He goes on to recount being pursued by seven men in New Mexico and how he took his horse's reins in his teeth and 'rode right at them boys'. His conclusion is that: 'You go for a man hard enough and fast enough, he don't have time to think about how many is with him. He thinks about hisself, how he might get clear of that wrath that's about to set down on him.' His attitude here echoes that of Dan Frost (Joel Edgerton) in *Jane Got a Gun* who, as the experienced soldier who fought in the Civil War, tells Jane that if you have 'will and purpose' when you are facing an enemy, then 'the numbers ain't shit'. When Mattie asks why Cogburn was being pursued by seven men it emerges this was a posse who were chasing him after he had 'robbed a high-interest bank'. Demonstrating just the sort of home-grown attitude towards right and wrong and law and order seen by Brett Cogburn as attaching to his great-grandfather at the start of this chapter, Bridges as the fictional Cogburn says, 'You can't rob a thief, can you. Never robbed a citizen. Never took a man's watch.' In this he links himself to Jesse James – both the historical figure and the character in *The Assassination of Jesse James by the Coward Robert Ford* (Andrew Dominik, 2007) – whose hero status accorded him in newspapers of the time and pretty much ever since was largely attributable to the fact that this sort of attitude towards banks was shared by a large percentage of the public.[36]

VII

Mattie is an intense, doggedly determined representative of this wider public who drives Cogburn and LaBoeuf on towards their confrontation with the depraved and the nefarious. She is also our narrator, a much older woman looking back at the most momentous event of her life. In keeping with the descriptions of many who have had wartime experiences, this was a defining moment in her life, and would never be matched by anything else she might undergo. In the story, Mattie is a Presbyterian Christian and Confederate sympathiser living in Arkansas during the Reconstruction era after the Civil War. She believes, 'You must pay for everything in this world one way or another. There is nothing free except the Grace of God.'[37] These words from the novel are used in the 2010 film, although they are positioned differently within the narrative. Portis has Mattie employ this clear statement in relation to two wagon-loads of prisoners arriving in Fort Smith, whereas the Coens use the words in relation to Tom Chaney: 'No doubt Chaney fancied himself scott-free, but he was wrong. You must pay for everything in this world, one way or another. There is nothing free except the grace of God.' The Coens also omit a further qualifying sentence that is used in Portis's novel: 'You cannot earn that or deserve it.' In the novel, this comes immediately after the sentence, 'There is nothing free except the Grace of God'. The Mattie of the novel believes in the Calvinist doctrine of the 'elect'. She does not believe entering heaven depends on performing good deeds and thereby coming to a point of deserving to be saved but, instead, that your fate is predestined. Later in the novel, she says:

> I too am now a member of the Southern Church. I say nothing against the Cumberlands. They broke with the Presbyterian Church because they did not believe a preacher needed a lot of formal education. That is all right but they are not sound on Election. They do not fully accept it. I confess it is a hard doctrine, running contrary to our earthly ideas of fair play, but I can see no way around it. Read, I Corinthians 6: 13 and II Timothy 1: 9, 10. Also, I Peter 1: 2, 19, 20 and Romans 11: 7. There you have it.[38]

So, although this filmed version of *True Grit* retains Mattie's Christian stance, it omits the Calvinist basis to her belief system. At first sight, the apparently fickle aspect of fate and the arbitrary nature of events to be found in the notion of there being an elected band of people who are destined to go to heaven come what may, might seem to appeal to a postmodern sensibility. However, this dimension to Mattie's faith, as embodied in the novel's use of this crucial caveat, 'You cannot earn that or deserve it', is glossed over by this film. Instead, the emphasis is left on the fact that 'You must pay for everything in this world, one way or another'. In other words, a complete reversal of meaning is achieved. Mattie's words in the film suggest a deity weighing your thoughts and deeds upon some divine equivalent of the scales of justice, whereas her words in the novel suggest the divine will is ultimately unknowable.

In *Unforgiven* (Clint Eastwood, 1992), as William Munny (Eastwood) is about to shoot him at point blank range as he lies helpless on the ground, Little Bill Daggett (Gene Hackman) says 'I don't deserve this . . . to die like this'. To which Eastwood's character replies 'Deserve's got nothing to do with it'. In our 2010 version of *True Grit* 'deserve' has everything to do with your eventual fate. Chaney 'deserves' to be pursued and executed. He embodies evil. No reason is given for him being as he is: he is simply malevolent. Brolin plays the role as if Chaney is, at least, slightly demented; and the filmmakers employ camera angles to accentuate this aspect of the performance. After the title and before the story begins a single phrase is placed on its own on the screen: 'The wicked flee when none pursueth. *Proverbs 28: 1.*' Without being chased the wicked flee, because they are struck by the awful reality of what they have done, because their conscience tells them they have committed sin, and because they are scared of the wrath of God. However, as the second part of this sentence in Proverbs tells us, on the other side of this equation, 'the righteous are bold as a lion'. In other words, right and wrong, wicked and righteous, are clear and apparent.

In line with the original film from 1969, the Coen brothers' remake of *True Grit* forty-plus years later successfully works to remind the audience that, according to the 'best' traditions of the Western, 'baddies' need to be confronted head on. They need to be pursued into Indian Territory,[39] hunted down and then 'taken down' by whatever means necessary. 'Lucky' Ned Pepper is the leader of an outlaw group living in the desert-like Badlands of Indian Territory. He is a man people escaping the law go to in order to join his terrorising band. He is a man who is capable of killing children in cold blood. At one point, with Mattie captured and on lying the ground, and with his gun pointing at her, he calls out to Cogburn, 'You answer me, Rooster. I will kill this girl. You know I will do it.' This is the person who is 'taken out' by LaBoeuf, somebody he does not even see, from an unbelievable distance. As LaBoeuf takes his shot he quietly calls for divine help muttering 'Oh, Lord' to himself, thereby drawing God in on his side in the action and in the fight against the outlaw band. The requirement in a fight such as this is to be able to deliver a form of 'justice' that involves 'termination with extreme prejudice'.

The Coen brothers' penchant for postmodernist filmmaking means the post-9/11 message is accompanied by a dark, sideways glance at human experience. However, at its heart this film lays out one of the most consistently expounded 'lessons' of the genre, namely that in a clash between value systems there is no alternative other than to pursue the enemy into his home territory and confront him on his own violent terms. For the filmmakers, their tendency to view the world from a perspective of detached irony and to revel in interjected scenes of surrealism perhaps means they never have to fully commit themselves within the messy realms of politics.[40] And, the distance they are able to achieve from the messiness of the blunt instrument actually being advocated is further enhanced by the comedy they find in the original novel and exploit on the screen.

Andrew Moss has analysed the Coen brothers' oeuvre in connection with the idea of schizophrenia, describing these filmmakers as '*agents of schizophrenia*'.[41] Within this context he claims the postmodernism of their filmmaking becomes a way of thinking rather than a method of approach to filmmaking. He suggests the filmmakers are 'more interested in the viewer's affective rather than intellectual engagement' and aim 'to create not coherence but incoherence, to produce in the mind of the viewer a state of schizophrenia that ultimately frustrates a single, unified reading'[42] Moss is talking specifically about the earlier films, *Raising Arizona* (1987) and *Barton Fink* (1991), but his approach is insightful. The Coens' revision of *True Grit* is schizophrenic but not in the same way. Here the split within the mind of the film comes in the effort to incorporate postmodernism's detached awareness of 'multiple and irreconcilable realities'[43] with the demand to demonstrate political commitment during a time constructed as a 'War on Terror'. In a book written six years before *True Grit* was made, R. Barton Palmer discusses the Coens' 'unsatisfied protagonists' living in an America where everyone is on their own, and the 'loner protagonists' in their more comic films as sometimes managing to 'become reconciled to dissatisfaction'.[44] In terms of the final outcomes for both Mattie and Cogburn, *True Grit* enables the Coens to hold to this basic postmodern position of the lonely isolation of the human condition, while at the same time both harking back to and lionizing a time of heroic confrontation.

Notes

1. Brett Cogburn, *Rooster: The Life and Times of the Real Rooster Cogburn, The Man Who Inspired True Grit* (New York: Kensington Books, 2012), p. viii.
2. Richard Aquila, *The Sagebrush Trail: Western Movies and Twentieth-Century America* (Tucson: University of Arizona Press, 2015), p. 335.
3. Ibid. p. 335.
4. Brett Cogburn, 'The real Rooster Cogburn: remembering my great-grandfather's role in the creation of a classic Western character', *True West: History of the American Frontier*, 19 March 2011. Available at <https://truewest-magazine.com/the-real-rooster-cogburn/> (accessed 3 January 2018).
5. John G. Cawelti, *Mystery, Violence, and Popular Culture* (Madison: University of Wisconsin Press, 2004), p. 187.
6. Ibid. p. 167.
7. Ibid. p. 167.
8. David T. Ritchie, '"Western" notions of justice: legal outsiders in American cinema', *Suffolk University Law Review*, 2009, 42(4): 849–68. Available at

<http://suffolklawreview.org/ritchie-justice/> (accessed 15 January 2018). Quote on p. 850.
9. Ibid. p. 850.
10. Ibid. p. 855.
11. See Chapter 4.
12. When she accompanies the men, LaBoeuf and Cogburn, into Indian Territory, Mattie adopts male clothing, wearing her father's trousers and overcoat.
13. As always, in the final analysis this comes down to any particular group's definition of the key terms employed, in this case, perhaps, essentially 'law', 'order' and 'justice'. In other words, the issue becomes one of ideological positioning.
14. Richard Brody, 'Hits and misses: *True Grit* vs. *The Social Network*', *The New Yorker*. Available at <https://www.newyorker.com/culture/richard-brody/hits-and-misses-true-grit-vs-the-social-network> (accessed 8 January 2018).
15. Although some might reflect Mattie too is punished in that after having achieved her revenge she is bitten by a rattlesnake and has her arm amputated.
16. Six people were hanged in one day at Fort Smith on 3 September 1875 and the same number on 16 January 1890. See National Park Service, Fort Smith, 'Men executed at Fort Smith: 1873 to 1896'. Available at <https://www.nps.gov/fosm/learn/historyculture/executions-at-fort-smith-1873-to-1896.htm> (accessed 16 January 2018).
17. Jeffrey B. Bumgarner, *Federal Agents: The Growth of Federal Law Enforcement in America* (Westport, CT: Praeger, 2006), p. 41 – outlines the role of deputy US marshals in western Arkansas and Indian Territory in the late 1800s. Also see Ron Owens, *Oklahoma Heroes: The Oklahoma Peace Officers Memorial* (Nashville, TN: Turner Publishing, 2000), pp. 25–6, for the number of deaths amongst law enforcement officers. This second book summarizes the role of the Indian Police in the area, pp. 22–3.
18. Jerry Akins, *Hangin' Times in Fort Smith: A History of Executions in Judge Parker's Court* (Little Rock, AR: Butler Center Books, 2012), p. 19.
19. Roger H. Tuller, *'Let No Guilty Man Escape:' A Judicial Biography of 'Hanging Judge' Isaac C. Parker* (Norman: University of Oklahoma Press, 2001), p. 57.
20. See <https://www.youtube.com/watch?v=AlSjBAQixGI> (accessed 17 August 2018), for example.
21. Ron Briley, 'John Wayne and *Big Jim McLain* (1952): the Duke's Cold War legacy', *Film & History: An Interdisciplinary Journal of Film and Television Studies*, 2001, 31(1): 28–33; quote on p. 30.
22. Ibid. p. 31.
23. Robert Eberwein (ed.), *The War Film* (New Brunswick, NJ: Rutgers University Press, 2005), p. 8.
24. John Pilger recounts a story of going to the cinema to see *The Green Berets* in 1968: 'I had just come back from Vietnam, and I couldn't believe how absurd this movie was . . . I laughed and laughed. And it wasn't long before the atmosphere around me grew very cold. My companion said, "Let's get

the hell out of here and run like hell." We were chased all the way back to our hotel ...'; John Pilger, 'The invisible government', johnpilger.com, 16 June 2007. Available at <http://johnpilger.com/articles/the-invisible-government> (accessed 30 January 2018).

25. Noah Gittell, 'The Coen brothers' subtle politics', *The Atlantic*, 20 December 2013. Available at <https://www.theatlantic.com/entertainment/archive/2013/12/the-coen-brothers-subtle-politics/282501/> (accessed 30 January 2018).
26. Ethan Coen, '2016 Election thank you notes', *New York Times*, 11 November 2016. Available at <https://www.nytimes.com/2016/11/13/opinion/sunday/2016-election-thank-you-notes.html?_r=1&register=facebook> (accessed 30 January 2018).
27. Although things are always slightly more complex than we might like them to be. Marguerite Roberts, the screenwriter in 1969, was blacklisted by Hollywood for her Communist sympathies. And, she undoubtedly, for example, had pleasure placing Wayne in the backroom of a Chinese shop.
28. Jenna Hunnef, '"Fooling around with Papa's pistol": avenging patriarchy in *True Grit*', in Scott F. Stoddart (ed.), *The New Westerns: Critical Essays on the Genre Since 9/11* (Jefferson, NC: McFarland, 2016), p. 59.
29. Ibid. p. 59.
30. Ibid. p. 60.
31. For example, Thomas Caldwell said 'What makes *True Grit* such a unique Coen Brothers film is how conventional it is in the way it conforms so closely to a traditional western.' See Thomas Caldwell, 'Film review – *True Grit* (2010)', *Cinema Autopsy*, 2011. Available at <https://blog.cinemaautopsy.com/2011/01/24/film-review-true-grit-2010/> (accessed 8 January 2018). And Christopher Orr suggested *True Grit* 'may be the most conventional and least Coens-y of the Coens' pictures'. See Christopher Orr, '30 years of Coens: *True Grit*', *The Atlantic*, 26 September 2014. Available at <https://www.theatlantic.com/entertainment/archive/2014/09/30-years-of-coens-true-grit/380776/> (accessed 8 January 2018).
32. Hunnef, 'Fooling around with Papa's pistol', p. 46.
33. Joseph S. Walker, 'Coen, Coen on the range: Rooster Cogburn(s) and domestic space', in Scott F. Stoddart (ed.), *The New Westerns: Critical Essays on the Genre Since 9/11* (Jefferson, NC: McFarland, 2016), pp. 62–80; quote on p. 64.
34. Ibid. p. 64
35. Richard Slotkin, *Gunfighter Nation: The Myth of the Frontier in Twentieth-Century America* (Norman: University of Oklahoma Press, 1998), p. 14.
36. He also, of course, links himself to Ethan Edwards (John Wayne) in *The Searchers* (John Ford, 1956), who is found to have newly minted coins in his possession when he arrives at his brother's farmstead after the Civil War.
37. Charles Portis, *True Grit* (London: Bloomsbury, [1968] 2005), p. 37.
38. Ibid. pp. 109–10.

39. The Indian Territory was seen as 'a notoriously lawless land'. Michael J. Brodhead, *Isaac C. Parker: Federal Justice on the Frontier* (Norman: University of Oklahoma Press, 2003), p. xv.
40. Ryan Gilbey is correct in his identification of the nature of the filmmaking at work here. See Ryan Gilbey, 'Sultans of smug: the Coen brothers are the most conservative of directors', *New Statesman*, 14 February 2011: 42.
41. See Andrew Moss, 'Schizophrenia and postmodernism: *Raising Arizona*, *Barton Fink*, and "The Coen Brothers"', *Post Script: Essays in Film and the Humanities*, 2008, 27(2): 23–37; quote on p. 24.
42. Ibid. p. 27.
43. Ibid. p. 36.
44. R. Barton Palmer, *Joel and Ethan Coen* (Urbana: University of Illinois Press, 2004), p. 39.

CHAPTER 4

Defending Home, Defending Homeland: *Jane Got a Gun* (2016)

I

> . . . as Americans and as a nation, we will not be terrorized. We will not cower in fear. We will not be intimidated. We will be vigilant, and we will work together. And we will protect and defend the country we love to ensure a safe and prosperous future for our people.[1]
>
> Barack Obama, *Public Papers of the Presidents of the United States 2010*

Towards the end of *Jane Got a Gun* (Gavin O'Connor, 2016), just before the concluding act is played out in the form of the genre-required final showdown, Natalie Portman as Jane Ballard delivers the most significant line in the film. Speaking moments before her home comes under sustained attack from a band of outlaws, she asserts in effect that she 'will not be terrorized' and 'will not cower in fear'. She states defiantly, 'They come to my house, I'm gonna protect it.' The line reproduces the tone of Barack Obama's statement above, and echoes the attitude expressed by countless American politicians since 9/11. Not only do these words summarise the storyline, they also succinctly express the central theme of this Western. The home, both as encapsulating dominant American values and as an image for the homeland, is a place under threat and in need of resolute defence post 9/11. *Jane Got a Gun* operates as a post-9/11 expression of that traditional Western trope of the need to defend the home and all it stands for in American national mythology.

In terms of the development of Jane's character within the narrative, the statement 'They come to my house, I'm gonna protect it' can be viewed in two ways. It might be seen as an expression of a position Jane has held from the outset, that is to say, from the first moment we see her in the film. If this is the case, her character has not really developed but rather has been consistent throughout. However, this declaration of intent might also be seen as the putting into words of an understanding Jane has been led towards during the course of the film, something that for the ideational shape of the film she needs to verbalise before the final showdown can begin. Despite the fact that within any form of storytelling we would more generally expect to see the central character undertaking a journey of some sort, evidence from within the film could be put forward for both positions, And, the fact that these two potential interpretations of the key moment of succinct expression of the central attitude of the film exist alongside each other emphasises a critically important uncertainty at the heart of *Jane Got A Gun*. There is an ambivalence over how Jane should be presented and, therefore, viewed by the audience. Since the title would indicate this is to be her story and that she is the central character it is crucial the film should be clear about who she is, what she is like, and how she develops. However, as consideration of this critical moment in the film shows, as viewers our understanding of Jane remains equivocal. To restate the position. Why does she tell us at this point 'They come to my house, I'm gonna protect it' when every action she has taken pretty much since the start of the film has been in preparation for the defence of her home?

Certainly, with respect to this central idea of defending the home, this film is in line with a whole series of Westerns produced by Hollywood over the years. This is what Westerns do: they defend the bastion of American values. That which is to be protected may take the outward form of something like the Alamo Mission in San Antonio in *The Alamo* (John Wayne, 1960), or more commonly the home, as in *Shane* (George Stevens, 1953) or *The Searchers* (John Ford, 1956), but the central concept of defending an ideological expression of 'America' in the face of an external threat remains consistent. The main character in *The Searchers*, Ethan Edwards (Wayne), knows the home has to be guarded. As he departs with a posse to track down cattle rustlers, leaving the home dangerously undefended and exposed, he tells his brother, 'Stay close, Aaron', that is, close to the homestead and alert to the possibility of an attack. Ethan patently fails to safeguard the home (and the values there enshrined) and the consequences are played out through the remainder of the film. In *Shane* the central character, Shane (Alan Ladd), has to leave the homestead and move into enemy territory in order to protect the home, leaving behind the expansive Technicolor countryside to enter an altogether darker, shadow-filled space, inside a bar in town. This idea of the home as a space which embodies the values that have to be defended is at the core of *Jane Got a Gun*.

As if to emphasise the issue at stake, Jane follows the line of script we have been considering with a supplementary line, which further highlights both the sense of a decision having been made and her determination to follow through – 'Whatever happens I gotta put my face to it.' But, again, within the moral compass of the film and given the context of contemporary Hollywood portrayals of the woman of action, has there ever been any doubt that a 'kickass' woman like Jane would do anything other than face up to whatever comes her way? The problem is the film seemingly wishes to allow two versions of Jane to coexist within its fantasy. She should be a 'girl power' female action hero full of inner strength and independence but she should also be a rather weaker woman who needs to be brought by a man to an understanding of the true nature of the world.[2]

II

We certainly see Jane presented as a strong woman from the start. When her husband, Bill 'Ham' Hammond (Noah Emmerich), returns home riddled with bullets after a gunfight with 'the Bishop boys' and announces this gang of notorious outlaws are on their way to the little homestead where the couple live with their young daughter, Jane is quietly, and lovingly, furious. 'If the bullets don't kill you and the storm you somehow brought upon us don't kill you,' she says, 'it goes without saying, I will kill you.' Within this reading of Jane's character, she is already tough and capable, as further evidenced by the way she is able to dig bullets from her husband's back with a knife. Seen from this perspective, the story shows her setting about the defence of her house and home immediately she knows the 'baddies' are riding her way. She is already a fully formed character who knows where she stands in relation to the presence of good and evil in the world,[3] and knows that there comes a point at which there is no alternative other than to defiantly confront evil.[4] From being the classic woman of the house found in countless Westerns in her pale blue, buttoned to the neck dress and tied back hair, she transforms herself. She professionally loads her handgun, puts on a long black frock coat, dons a black cowboy hat and pulls on leather working-man's gloves (Figure 4.1). Talking tenderly to her child, bridging the loving mother–action woman duality, she takes her daughter to a place of safety before riding off on a long and sustained feat of horsemanship in order to attempt to find hired help to defend the house and to visit a gunsmith to buy extra arms. Under this reading, throughout the film and not simply from the start of the final act, Jane is determined that, 'They come to my house, I'm gonna protect it.' She does not arrive at this position as a result of a moral journey she undertakes within the narrative. This is a woman who can kill an attacker from close range with a heavy Colt Walker 1847 less than a quarter of the way into the film. And, as her backstory unfolds through flashbacks it becomes clear Jane has had enough experiences of treachery and brutality

Figure 4.1 Jane (Natalie Portman) professionally loading her handgun in *Jane Got a Gun* (Gavin O'Connor, 2016).

in her life for her to have come to this very clear conclusion about defending her home by the time we see her at the start of the film.

However, as suggested above, there is another way of looking at the statement made by Jane before the assault on her home begins. From this perspective, the assertion that 'They come to my house, I'm gonna protect it' amounts to the succinctly expressed culmination of an educational journey undertaken through the course of the film. Within this reading, we see Jane coming to an understanding she has had to work her way towards under the tutorship of the man who has come to help her to defend her house, her former lover, Dan Frost (Joel Edgerton). This point in the film, deliberately positioned before the final act, becomes the moment of formal intellectual recognition of the necessity of employing violence at certain moments in life. This version of Jane needs to be brought to a realisation of the requirement for gunplay, to an appreciation of the fact that the civilised, safe space of the home only exists if at some point you are prepared to defend it against those who would destroy it.[5]

The uncertainty over exactly how this key idea of the need to defend the home should be read in relation to the character of Jane is at the heart of some critics' difficulties with the film. Referring to the oddness of the film title with its girl-power assertiveness, in relation to what we actually see on screen, Peter Bradshaw in *The Guardian* begins his review: 'Actually, Jane is demurely reliant on old-fashioned menfolk getting their guns to protect her.'[6] If the central character is not logically developed in such a way as to be in keeping with the intended key idea of the film confusions are inevitable. If we cannot clearly see how Jane moves from uncertainty over violence and the place of violence within society to an understanding of how crucial violence is as a bedrock to the establishment and maintenance of a democratic society,[7] the film has failed to communicate its central premise with sufficient lucidity. We can still find the presence of the idea but the film loses clarity of purpose and vision. If the character development of Jane carries an ambivalence, then the whole film must necessarily be similarly confused; if she is fully formed as a character and understands what needs to be done from the outset there is no room for the inner journey any central character within a narrative must be seen to undergo. In adopting what has become a common feature of recent Hollywood films – a strong, central female character – the film immediately creates difficulties for the usual narrative arc of character development. We see the more usual trajectory of character evolution given climactic expression via Jane's statement moments before the assault on her house. In terms of narrative structure, this moment should allow her to come to some new inner awareness before the final action takes place. And the scriptwriters are clear that this is what they were attempting to achieve. Anthony Tambakis, for example, has said: 'What we are building towards in the movie is this arc of a woman who discovers her own sense of self and her own courage, and self-actualizes, and by the end of the film there is a last woman standing, turning the traditional Western archetypes on their head.'[8] The problem, as we have said, is that in the film as we have it Jane already has a fully developed sense of self from the start of the action.

III

One way of viewing this is to suggest this confusion around the central character reflects internal conflict, or uncertainty, amongst the filmmakers regarding the ideological positioning of their film. Indeed, given the difficulties experienced during the film's production, perhaps it would be surprising if there was not some lack of surety of purpose. Because of the troubled production history[9] some of those closely associated with the work expressed almost a sense of surprise that they had managed to deliver a movie with which they were reasonably pleased. Portman, who not only starred in the film but was also, as producer, a driving force behind the whole concept, has been quoted as saying: 'It was a new obstacle not even every day but every hour. It was just one of those movies, and miraculously it turned out as something I'm proud of.'[10] So, it could be argued the uncertainty we have identified at the heart of the central character was the result of this chaotic production period. However, it might also be possible to argue that what is reflected are contradictions, uncertainties and confusions being experienced more widely within American society (and Western society more generally) in the face of a contemporary assault on the values and beliefs of liberal democracy. According to John Schwarzmantel there are a range of possible responses for democracies faced by movements 'using violence' and positioning themselves as hostile to democracy. Through 'dialogue and negotiation' the democracy can 'change its policy to meet the grievances expressed', or the state can resort to increased security and surveillance, or it can attempt 'the use of overwhelming force'.[11]

We can see where the final group of creative personnel behind *Jane Got a Gun* wanted to take things. In their eyes, this is a woman who learns about the necessity of violence (rather than already knowing about this from the beginning). To be blunt, what is being argued here (and this will be expanded on later) is that by extension what is being expressed in this film is the necessity of a nation taking violent action at certain points in its history. The filmmakers seem to be unaware of the way in which within the character arc given to Jane, she does not 'self-actualize' but rather is placed in the position of having to learn from the male hero who knows more than she does and has to take her to this point of realisation. What the filmmakers present to us, it seems without realising it, is not a woman 'doing it for herself' but rather a woman who needs to see that men, and in particular men of a very definite political outlook, are right. What we have is a post-9/11 expression of the traditional Western trope of the need to defend the home as an embodiment of the key social institution of the family. However, the home/family combination is also seen here as the manifestation of civilized values, and therefore as an articulation of the wider concept of the nation. The home and homeland, and beyond this concepts of the nation, and even civilisation itself, are seen as being under threat post 9/11. And, in a sense, as has been suggested in mentioning *Shane* and *The Searchers* above, this is nothing new.

IV

The setting up of the Office of Homeland Security in 2001, along with the enactment of the Homeland Security Act and the publication of the National Strategy for Homeland Security in 2002, brought 'homeland security' not only to the forefront of political debate but also into increased use within popular cultural parlance. The opening to the National Strategy for Homeland Security outlines the basic position: 'Our Nation learned a terrible lesson on September 11. American soil is not immune to evil or cold-blooded enemies capable of mass murder and terror.'[12] The document goes on to explain that the task before the United States government has become that of 'securing the American homeland';[13] defending the home as a metaphorical space of American values has taken on an added dimension post 9/11. However, it is also the case that the right of the individual to bear arms and defend their home should be viewed as a long-standing American expectation. In *Lethal Imagination: Violence and Brutality in American History*, in a chapter entitled 'Armed and Dangerous: Guns in American Homes', Arthur L. Kellermann and Philip J. Cook quote a woman, who armed herself with a .357 magnum after the Los Angeles riots of 1992, as saying: 'I have no one to protect me. If someone comes into my house uninvited, they're dead.'[14] The characterisation given to Jane in *Jane Got a Gun* positions her within a long line of American thought on such matters.

The physical culmination of Jane's journey towards embracing this requirement for the use of extreme force comes after the main attack when she confronts her nemesis, John Bishop (Ewan McGregor), and executes him. As a criminal operating within a genre that carries within its classical generic framework of ideas a central premise of the crucial importance of law and order, Bishop should be taken into custody, tried for his crimes, and sentenced by the courts. Instead, he is summarily executed. Director Gavin O'Connor draws attention to the nature of this act through his choice of shots. The audience is given a low-angle point-of-view shot from Bishop's perspective on the ground looking into the barrel of Jane's handgun: initially, Jane's face is in focus and the gun barrel blurred, then this is changed so the barrel of the gun is brought into focus (Figure 4.2). The execution then climaxes with a cut to an intense white screen coinciding with the sound of a single gunshot.[15] Of course, the Western genre has never shied away from the necessity of meeting violence with violence,

Figure 4.2 Jane, dominant and empowered, as she is about to execute Bishop (Ewan McGregor) in *Jane Got a Gun*.

nor from showing on screen the 'baddie' being killed by a character who (seemingly without irony) employs violence in order to restore law and order. The classic Western, however, might be expected to show this death of the embodiment of evil, or disorder, as arising from a 'fair' fight or, more likely, a fight in which the 'baddie' had attempted to gain an unfair advantage. Here, Bishop is on the ground, unarmed and completely at Jane's mercy.[16] Jane's killing of Bishop is an execution and as such presents a ritualised playing out through the media of the type of deaths US military personnel might necessarily be involved in post-9/11. Osama bin Laden, most famously, is executed by a US special operations team after he is located in Abbottabad in Pakistan: 'I aimed . . . and pulled the trigger twice. Bin Laden's head split open, and he dropped. I put another bullet in his head. Insurance.'[17] The additional element here is that before killing Bishop, Jane needs to employ methods of torture in order to extract information regarding the whereabouts of her daughter. As an embodiment of liberal, female (and on both counts, therefore, weak) America, Jane is shown as being fully prepared to take such extreme measures.[18]

V

Immediately after asserting her determination to defend her home, as mentioned earlier, Jane adds: 'Whatever happens I gotta put my face to it.' The recognition is that 'a man's gotta do what a man's gotta do', with the difference that this man is a woman. The woman, of course, is classically seen in the Western as a home-maker operating within the domestic sphere, and working to create a welcoming, civilised space for the family that exists in stark contrast to the harsh outside world. This would be true of, for example, both Martha Edwards (Dorothy Jordan) and Mrs Jorgensen (Olive Carey) in Ford's effort to create the history of westward expansion in the required mythic image of the 1950s in *The Searchers*. The reality of dirt, dust, mud, insects, and the impossibility of keeping these things out of the home, may have been somewhat different for genuine sod-busters staking a claim and attempting to live in the climactic extremes found in these newly emerging states[19] but in the classic Western's mythic transformation of history there is always a clean table, a matching set of crockery, and freshly-baked produce readily available. Some of the earliest shots in the film show Jane's hands kneading dough. Later, when her former lover, Dan, has arrived at the homestead to try to protect Jane and her husband from the Bishop gang, we have a further series of shots showing Jane in her domestic role washing clothes in the foreground with a bowl of prepared food in the background.

However, although the classic version of woman to be found in Westerns may be tough enough to be stoical in the face of hardship, this Hollywood-created ideal of femininity ultimately needs to be defended by men. For protection, Marian Starrett (Jean Arthur) in *Shane* (George Stevens, 1953), for example, is dependent on not only her husband, Joe Starrett (Van Heflin) but also on the third corner of this film's love triangle, Shane himself (Ladd).[20] Of course, what is being protected here is not only a certain version of 'woman' but also a certain concept of 'the family' and a woman's place within that imagined pillar of societal values. In *Jane Got a Gun* the traditional version of woman has been transformed but in such a way as to allow the former vision to continue to exist. This woman may be able to move beyond the home and out into the world of men, to ride horses and shoot guns, but she is still also the homemaker, mother and wife. And so, the earlier concept of 'woman' certainly has been reshaped, but we are left with the question as to why this may have happened. We will come to that, but first we should note that *Jane Got a Gun* is nothing new in the attention it has given to the representation of women.

Earlier revisionist Westerns, such as *The Ballad of Little Jo* (Maggie Greenwald, 1993), have shown women not only challenging the classic housebound, entrapped (or imprisoned) expression of femininity but also stepping across the strongly entrenched patriarchal boundary between male and female. In *The Ballad of Little Jo*, a film again set in the years of fast-paced westward expansion during the final decades of the nineteenth century, Josephine 'Jo' Monaghan (Suzy Amis) cross-dresses and succeeds in 'passing' as a man. Superficially, Greenwald's film from the 1990s would seem to have similarities to *Jane Got a Gun*. In this later film, Jane not only dresses much like a man but also rides a horse and shoots a gun as we might stereotypically be expected to believe a man would do. But these two films are in fact very different in their political and ideological positioning. In *The Ballad of Little Jo* the focus is on the violence of the attitudes and actions of men towards women. Most telling is the absolute wrath of men – as represented by Percy Corcoran (Ian McKellen) and Frank Badger (Bo Hopkins) – when they become aware of Jo's transgression, that is of her choosing to cross the gender divide and live as a man. Most tellingly, their anger is also clearly seen to be a result of the fact that they feel especially insulted/assaulted by the fact that they have been successfully deceived by Jo's cross-dressing. Jo has succeeded in 'passing' as a man in a similar way to that in which in some films black women have been seen to be able to 'pass' as white. And the outrage of men to the discovery of what has been the unknown presence of a woman in their midst is shown to be similar to the angry response of whites to the unknown presence of a person of colour in the midst of 'their' white society. In both cases, of course, the resulting fury is a direct product of the affronted prejudice, whether misogynistic or racist, of the film's representatives of mainstream society.

Greenwald's film is, then, a genuine feminist film, exposing the hatred at the heart of misogyny and challenging the prejudice embodied in social norms and values. *Jane Got a Gun*, by way of contrast, is a reactionary film presenting itself as feminist but only possessing the most rudimentary surface credentials with which to do so. This film has a central character whose name is in the title of the film and whose story we follow. She is shown to dress as a man and to be able to ride a horse and shoot a gun as a man, but at the same time she is presented as a sexualised Hollywood woman, gazed at by the camera for her feminine beauty. She is also very much a woman of the domestic space, able to perform the traditional female role alongside demonstrating the capability to move within the male realm, but with the crucial proviso that she will defer to male authority within this realm as and when necessary. As such she is celebrated as the perfection of twenty-first-century woman, a redefinition of feminism that is acceptable to redefined twenty-first-century patriarchy.[21] She is also a continuation of the gun-wielding woman found in post-war Westerns, threatening to break out of the box constructed for women by patriarchy but ultimately contained and tamed by genre conventions. With its focus on Jane, the title would suggest the position of women in film has evolved considerably since a Western like *Johnny Guitar* (Nicholas Ray, 1954) in which, despite the centrality of Vienna (Joan Crawford) to the narrative, her name is not found in the title.[22] In fact, *Jane Got a Gun* is a film in which, as Judith Halberstam describes it in *Female Masculinity*, 'what we understand as heroic masculinity has been produced by and across both male and female bodies'.[23] There is no space made available here for a feminisation of the male but instead the whole focus is on the masculinisation of the female. In a post-9/11 world, women (and any other 'feminised' sectors of the community) need to understand what is required within the current global context of 'good' and 'evil'. In *Cold War Femme: Lesbianism, National Identity, and Hollywood Cinema*, Robert J. Corber notes that Vienna in *Johnny Guitar*, 'shifts effortlessly between masculine and feminine gender presentations'[24] and this is what is expected of Jane.

VI

It is Jane's former lover, Dan, who organises the defence of the homestead and shows her what has to be done in a battle between two diametrically opposed forces in order to settle a dispute that offers no room for negotiated peace. She defers to him, not simply because he is a man but because as a man he has the knowledge she does not possess. Crucially, he knows how to take life mercilessly, if and when that is deemed necessary. When one of the Bishop gang, Slow Jeremiah (Sam Quinn), is wounded and at his mercy not only does he eventually execute him but before that he uses torture to interrogate him. Standing over him he forces the heel of his boot into one shoulder wound and then presses the barrel of his handgun into a wound on Jeremiah's other shoulder. Dan is the war veteran who returns with the knowledge of what it takes to defeat a callously brutal enemy. When he talks about his war experiences fighting for the North, or the Union, against the southern slave states, or the Confederacy, in the Civil War it is the Southern forces that have shown the traits he clearly admires. 'You know it took us four years to do what we should have done in a few months because they had will and purpose. If you have got those two things the numbers ain't shit', he says to Jane in an effort to impart more of the special knowledge and understanding he has as a man. In this sense, he is that common type found in Hollywood films of the 'vet' who returns to find that in his absence the world has moved on and that he is unable to re-integrate into society, but who when the crisis emerges is the one who knows how to deal with the situation. He is the one who is prepared to transgress what might be seen as the normal moral code of a democratic society in order ultimately to protect those values. Such 'vets' have frequently been in a positive way equated to vigilantes, righting the wrongs that mainstream society has failed to deal with. What we have are a series of right-wing forms coming out of Hollywood united in their belief that the law as it stands is not strong enough, and that something more is needed in order to deal with the presence of evil in the world.

Within the conceptual framework offered by the film this evil is a simple, inexplicable presence. It is pre-formed and exists as an unexamined inevitable given. In places in *Jane Got a Gun*, the character of John Bishop[25] is performed by McGregor as a comic-book representation of evil but with moments that are given a much fuller sense of menace. When he is garrotting a fur trader who might know the whereabouts of Hammond and his wife, it is the mention by the man of the fact that he has a family that incites Bishop to complete the strangulation. When a member of his gang reveals more information than he would have liked he tells him, in a close-up that employs deep shadow: 'If you cannot hold your tongue, I will cut it out of your head.' We might speculate that this character, like Frost and Jane, has in some sense been formed by his experiences of the Civil War. However, this would be to conjecture beyond anything we are given in the film. His 'associates', as he calls the members of his gang, scarred or tattooed presumably with a record of their kills, are to a man leering, smirking, cartoonish representations of stereotypical notions of evil. They are the not-to-be-understood and the impossible-to-understand expressions of the dark side of humanity. Faced with this brand of evil, relentlessly, remorselessly moving towards you and your family, moving towards your house, what level of response is necessary? Bearing in mind that the right to keep and bear arms is protected under the US Constitution, and given the nature of the genre, there is only one possible reaction and that is, in accordance with the film title and thus in terms that are given special prominence, to 'get a gun'.[26] The gunsmith who serves Jane when she goes into town looking to arm herself notes that she walks out of his shop with 'enough firepower . . . to start another war'.

If we return for a moment to the central female character in *Shane*, Marian Starrett, we see that in addition to being the homemaker/mother/wife she has one other crucial trait attributed to her as a woman: she does not understand the bloody necessity of guns and violence. 'Guns aren't going to be my boy's life', she tells Shane. But he immediately puts her right and by his final phrase makes it clear he is giving her an important lesson: 'A gun is a tool, Marian, no better, no worse than any other tool, an axe, shovel, or anything. A gun is as good, or as bad, as the man using it. Remember that.'[27] In response to this effort to teach her something, and showing she has understood neither the fundamental wisdom of Shane's view for those like her wishing to live in a democracy nor the warning contained in his words, she says, 'We'd all be better off if there wasn't a single gun left in this valley including yours.' There is something critically important occurring at this point in the film. Marian is, within the moral framework of the film, representing two crucial constituencies here. Firstly, she is the film's representative idealised 'woman'. From this perspective, what she has to say is understandable because within the dominant ideology of the period it is the role of women to be delicate, loving and caring, and as a consequence to find it difficult to understand the necessity and importance of those moments when a man has got to do what a man has got to do. Secondly, and more importantly for the ideological tensions within the film at this juncture, she is operating as a representative of left-leaning, liberal society. From this perspective, she is representing that part of society that is soft like a woman, that part of society that advocates peace and lobbies for negotiations rather than military confrontation without any realisation that at some point violence has to be met by violence and that if democracy is to be protected democracy must have within its ranks those who are able to recognise this simple fact (and act on it when necessary). The argument being put forward by the film is that there are times when the norms and values to which you might aspire within a democracy have of necessity to be put to one side in order that the immediate threat, which fails to recognise your norms and values and certainly will not expect to play by them, can be forcefully confronted. Despite the action-girl persona given in various ways to Jane in *Jane Got a Gun* it is important to recognise that as the central female character she is still, with more than 60 years between the two films, playing this element of Marian's role in *Shane*.

After Frost has summarily executed Slow Jeremiah, who is to all intents and purposes a wounded prisoner of war, Jane questions the apparent ease with which he can take a life.[28] And Frost, like Shane, has to point out the realities of the world. 'The only point of a battle, Jane, is to end it in your favour: just kill the other guy otherwise he'll kill you', he says. When Jane comes to the realisation just before the final showdown that, 'Whatever happens I gotta put my face to it', and when she is able to execute the leader of the band that has attacked them while he is defenceless at her feet, this is not simply a filmic representation of a new woman. Much more important is the fact that it is a representation of liberal America coming to understand what needs to be done in the current context of a War on Terror. She has moved from innocence to maturity.[29] This film re-enacts the same scenario seen within the post-war film *Forty Guns* (Sam Fuller, 1957), which again features a powerfully masculine woman, Jessica Drummond (Barbara Stanwyck). There is a violent final shootout in which (in this case) the male hero, in effect, executes the 'baddie' with a series of carefully placed shots in much the same way as Jane kills Bishop. Discussing *Forty Guns*, John Auerbach suggests that such brutality 'raises questions central to virtually all westerns of the period: what are the acceptable or appropriate means to counter dire threats?'[30] During the Cold War with the overseas threat offered by the Soviet Union and the feared domestic threat of communism, Auerbach says, 'the western allowed viewers to displace their growing concerns about geopolitics onto a familiar national register, in effect domesticating their anxiety over foreign affairs'.[31] The correspondence to a post-9/11 world would seem clear.

With regards to gender, what we see in *Jane Got a Gun* are the old masculine spaces of the Western being colonised by new (masculine) fantasies that pose as apparent expressions of a new woman. Neither the space, nor the genre, is feminised. Rather than an empowerment of the feminine, what we have is a taming within violence of the assertive woman, a re-domestication of the overly confident woman. Within a twenty-first-century Hollywood movie that is looking at the (it is suggested) unavoidable nature of the brutality of the defence of home within a new, redefined, fallen-from-innocence era, issues of family and gender are re-positioned within an ideological framework of continuity. In classic Western style the past (in the film, the Civil War, and in the currency of the contemporary present, the post-9/11 world) has to be faced and addressed in order for clarity of purpose to be achieved and the necessity of action in the present to be understood.

Notes

1. Barack Obama, *Public Papers of the Presidents of the United States 2010*, Book 1 – January 1 to June 30, 2010 (Washington: United States Government). Available at <https://www.gpo.gov/fdsys/pkg/PPP-2010-book1/pdf/PPP-2010-book1-Doc-pg597.pdf> (accessed 27 July 2017), p. 597.
2. Highlighting the repetition within Westerns of central issues such as gender (as with defence of the home) across time, John Cawelti explores 'the ambiguity of women playing men's roles' in relation to Joan Crawford's portrayal of Vienna in *Johnny Guitar* (Nicholas Ray, 1954). See John G. Cawelti, *Mystery, Violence, and Popular Culture* (Madison: University of Wisconsin Press, 2004), p. 86.
3. The film opens with Jane telling her daughter a bedtime story about good and bad people. The tale recounts how 'bad' creatures like the lion can be turned to good inside the magical upside-down tree, but how 'good people never turn bad'.
4. Renée Jeffery has highlighted the way in which in the late twentieth century and early twenty-first century there has been 'a renewed willingness to describe the very worst humanitarian atrocities in the most extreme moral terms; that is, to describe both the acts, and in some instances their perpetrators, not simply in terms of their criminality, but to designate them as "evil"'. See Renée Jeffery (ed.), *Confronting Evil in International Relations: Ethical Responses to Problems of Moral Agency* (Basingstoke and New York: Palgrave Macmillan, 2008), p. 3. However, she points out this is not a new phenomenon and that: 'Thinkers from Augustine to Kant and beyond have sought to ascertain the precise sense in which human beings can be held responsible for the evil they cause and, by extension, the extent to which they themselves can be characterized as "evil" individuals' (ibid. p. 4).
5. This is clearly not a scenario restricted to the Western genre, nor one that within this genre is restricted to the current historical context. Adam Lowenstein, for example, has discussed Cronenberg's *A History of Violence* (2005) in similar terms, seeing it as 'a version of the Western narrative where an embattled homesteader defends his family and land from hostile outsiders' produced 'at a time in the United States when variations on this theme were being mobilized to support the fiction of the Iraq War as a defense of the home'. See Adam Lowenstein, 'Transforming horror: David Cronenberg's cinematic gestures after 9/11', in Aviva Briefel and Sam J. Miller (eds), *Horror after 9/11: World of Fear, Cinema of Terror* (Austin: University of Texas Press, 2011), p. 68.

6. Peter Bradshaw, '*Jane Got a Gun* review – laborious and solemn Western with absurd finale', *The Guardian*, 21 April 2016. Available at <https://www.theguardian.com/film/2016/apr/21/jane-got-a-gun-review-laborious-and-solemn-western-with-absurd-finale> (accessed 26 July 2017).
7. John Schwarzmantel deals with the debate around this issue in *Democracy and Political Violence*. Outlining the basic position of the West post-9/11, he says: 'In such a society violence or the threat of violence is continually present, exercised not only by terrorist groups who oppose both the policies and the basic principles of liberal-democracy, but also by agencies of the state who are charged with fighting terrorism and defending the security of the citizens of liberal-democracies.' See John Schwarzmantel, *Democracy and Political Violence* (Edinburgh: Edinburgh University Press, 2011), p. 2.
8. Daniel Dercksen, '*Jane Got a Gun* brings new perspective to the classic American Western', *The Writing Studio*, 3 May 2016. Available at <https://writingstudio.co.za/jane-got-a-gun-brings-new-perspective-to-the-classic-american-western/> (accessed 5 June 2017).
9. It has been well documented how the original director, Lynne Ramsay, left on the day shooting was scheduled to begin, meaning Gavin O'Connor was drafted in at the last minute, and how this resulted in changes to the script with Joel Edgerton and Anthony Tambakis adding to the work of Brian Duffield.
10. Hilary Lewis, 'Natalie Portman on *Jane Got a Gun* off-camera woes: "It gives you the feeling that you can do anything",' *The Hollywood Reporter*, 28 January 2016. Available at <http://www.hollywoodreporter.com/news/jane-got-a-gun-natalie-860212> (accessed 5 June 2017).
11. There is not the space to discuss this further but Schwarzmantel suggests the first of these options can offer 'a way out' whereas 'other responses from the state are less likely to offer a way out of violence'. Schwarzmantel, *Democracy and Political Violence*, 2011, pp. 8–9.
12. Office of Homeland Security, *National Strategy for Homeland Security*, July 2002. Available at <https://www.dhs.gov/sites/default/files/publications/nat-strat-hls-2002.pdf> (accessed 16 June 2017), p. 1.
13. Ibid. p. 1.
14. Arthur L. Kellermann and Philip J. Cook, 'Armed and dangerous: guns in American homes', in Michael A. Bellesiles (ed.), *Lethal Imagination: Violence and Brutality in American History* (New York and London: New York University Press, 1999), p. 425.
15. In the tradition of classic Westerns the blood-splattering reality of execution is avoided, thus affording us the narrative pleasure of the demise of the baddie without any messy details that might cloud our judgement of this moment.
16. One of the references at work here is to Clint Eastwood as Harry Callahan in *Dirty Harry* (1971); but in that film (at a time that is essentially after the main years of American involvement in Vietnam), when Eastwood delivers the much-quoted line 'You've gotta ask yourself a question: "Do I feel lucky?"', there is at least the Russian roulette of a chance given to the criminal.

17. Robert O'Neill, *The Operator: Firing the Shots that Killed Osama bin Laden and My Years as a SEAL Team Warrior* (New York: Simon & Schuster, 2017), p. 310.
18. Although we might also see the noir lighting employed at this stage as pointing toward a dark ambiguity at the heart of Jane's (and America's) actions.
19. See, for example, 'The Ira Watson family of Sargent, Nebraska in 1886' photographed outside their sod-built home, in Marianne Bell, *Frontier Family Life: A Photographic Chronicle of the Old West* (New York: Barnes & Noble, 1998), p. 2.
20. We will return to this film and its connections to *Jane Got a Gun* later.
21. We might note that ultimately (although the script allows her to put her case strongly) it might be said to be her lack of patient fidelity that has destroyed the idyll of the love shared between her and Dan. This places her as the locus of fault, positioning her as woman in relation to man in a continuum stretching back to the Garden of Eden.
22. The posters used for both films show a heavy reliance on the image and name of the female lead in 'carrying' the film. Interestingly, despite the male clothes she is wearing it is the feminine figure of Joan Crawford and the assertiveness of her posture that is emphasised, whereas the low-angle shot of Natalie Portman looking at her bare neck might be said to emphasise her vulnerability and need for protection.
23. Judith Halberstam, *Female Masculinity* (Durham, NC: Duke University Press, 1998), p. 2.
24. Robert J. Corber, *Cold War Femme: Lesbianism, National Identity, and Hollywood Cinema* (Durham, NC: Duke University Press, 2011), p. 103.
25. There seems to have been a John Bishop who was at some stage a member of the Jesse James gang and also in the Confederate guerrilla group, Quantrill's Raiders, during the Civil War. See John N. Edwards, *Noted Guerrillas, or the Warfare of the Border* (St Louis, MO: Bryan, Brand, 1877), p. 333. Available at <https://archive.org/details/notedguerrillaso00edwarich> (accessed 7 June 2017). This latter group was infamous for an attack on the town of Lawrence, Kansas, in 1863 in which around 180 males were massacred. Katie H. Armitage, *Lawrence: Survivors of Quantrill's Raid* (Charleston, SC: Arcadia, 2010), p. 7.
26. Many books address this issue but a good starting point is Adam Winkler's *Gunfight: The Battle Over the Right to Bear Arms in America* (New York and London: W. W. Norton, 2011).
27. Echoing this sentiment, Wayne LaPierre says, 'responsible gun owners know a gun is just a tool that can help protect a family or bring home game for dinner', *Guns, Freedom and Terrorism* (Nashville, TN: WND Books, 2003), p. 89.
28. In an article in *The New Yorker* looking at the deaths of several unarmed Iraqis killed by members of the 101st Airborne Division of the US Army, Raffi Khatchadourian quotes Colonel Michael Dane Steele as saying to his troops, 'If you go out and somebody presents a lethal threat to you, and you shoot him, do not feel bad and think that you should have brought him back,

because I didn't want to talk to him.' Steele told his men to think of themselves as apex predators ('If you mess with me, I will eat you'), but he also insisted that they act lawfully. 'We are not gonna be driving around Iraq raping, burning, pillaging, being undisciplined', he said. 'That's not what I'm talking about. I'm talking about the moment of truth, when you're about to kill the other son of a bitch. I do not want you to choke.' Raffi Khatchadourian, 'The Kill Company: did a colonel's fiery rhetoric set the conditions for a massacre?', *The New Yorker*, 6 and 13 July 2009. Available at <http://www.newyorker.com/magazine/2009/07/06/the-kill-company> (accessed 6 June 2017).
29. Richard Gray discusses fiction since 9/11 as having to grapple with the sense of a Fall from a prelapsarian to a post-lapsarian state. 'There is a recurrent tendency in American writing, and in the observation of American history, to identify crisis as a descent from innocence to experience', he says. Richard Gray, *After the Fall: American Literature Since 9/11* (Malden, MA and Oxford: Wiley-Blackwell, 2011), p. 2. Classically, these dislocations that make writers feel they have entered a new era where all, previously stable, reference points have shifted or disappeared occur around wars, he says, such as the Civil War, the two World Wars, and Vietnam.
30. John Auerbach, 'Cold War films', in Adam Piette and Mark Rawlinson (eds), *The Edinburgh Companion to Twentieth-Century British and American War Literature* (Edinburgh: Edinburgh University Press, 2012), p. 175.
31. Ibid. p. 175.

PART II

The Cinematic Big Screen, Surround Sound, Ride

CHAPTER 5

Updating the Escapism of the Western: *The Lone Ranger* (2013)

I

As Michael Hilger says in *Native Americans in the Movies: Portrayals from Silent Films to the Present*, critical opinion on *The Lone Ranger* (Gore Verbinski, 2013) is divided, with some viewing it as a lightweight spoof and others as 'a more serious satire'.[1] He is right to state, 'both approaches provide valid ways to analyse the movie'.[2] With this in mind, this chapter will examine ways in which *The Lone Ranger* might be seen to articulate a response to the world post-9/11.

One frequent response to the question of what the purpose of narrative film might be is to say it provides audiences with an escape from their daily lives: from financial worries, from the psychological stresses of life and, maybe, from potentially distressing, thoughtful engagement with the chaotic and confusing state of the world. Audiences can be transported into an exciting fantasy world where, although the antagonism between good and evil may be intense and packed with moments that seem to announce the imminent victory of satanic forces, anybody who has paid their money knows this (generally) entitles them in the end to see the defeat of dark forces and the triumph of good. In a large part, this chapter will consider the continuing attempt by Hollywood to create this classic escapist experience for the spectator.

An important attraction of any genre has always been the way it has held this promise of thrilling immersion within a known escapist space, and this is partly what is on offer from *The Lone Ranger* working within the tradition of the Western. However, in common with many contemporary movies this film takes its core genre in a range of directions. Indeed, for many, part of the excitement will be to see just how their genre expectations can be challenged. Others may come to this film having experienced the work done by Verbinski and headline star Johnny Depp in a trilogy of adventure films taking the pirate and swashbuckler subgenres in new directions – *Pirates of the Caribbean: The Curse of the Black Pearl* (2003), *Pirates of the Caribbean: Dead Man's Chest* (2006), and *Pirates of the Caribbean: At World's End* (2007). The scripts for these hugely successful films were written by Terry Rossio and Ted Elliot, and this partnership was responsible for early drafts of *The Lone Ranger*; but in this case another writer, Justin Haythe, was brought in for further re-writes before the script was finalised. Apparently, these later drafts took the film away from earlier heavier involvement with supernatural horror.[3] When it was released, in dramatic contrast to the *Pirates of the Caribbean* series, *The Lone Ranger* was a box office flop after having run up a budget estimated at around $250 million.[4] Our focus, however, is mainly on meanings and understandings that might emerge from the relationship between the film text and audience, rather than on box office success or failure.

II

The production team clearly set out to provide the audience with a thrilling escapist experience. The runaway train sequences at the beginning and end deploy all the tactics of shock, surprise and spectacle open to a Hollywood blockbuster in an age of CGI and surround sound. During these scenes spectators partake of an experience that is designed as the cinematic equivalent of a Disney theme park ride. This is all about providing intensity of bodily experience for the spectator; it is achieved by subjecting the spectator's senses to precipitous combinations of speed and suddenness of movement, and volume and pitch of sound, together with kaleidoscopic changes of shape and colour. This is literally sensational and highly affective, rousing the body to an experience of intensities somewhere beyond, and before, conscious thought. In notes on his translation of Gilles Deleuze and Félix Guattari's *A Thousand Plateaus: Capitalism and Schizophrenia* Brian Massumi talks about 'affect', which is a key idea for understanding the relationship between film form and the spectator that we are looking at here. He describes this as 'a prepersonal intensity corresponding to the passage from one experiential state of the body to another'.[5] In a further attempt to explain this Deleuzian concept, in his essay 'The Autonomy of Affect', Massumi compares affect to 'an emotion' in order to try to explain the difference between the two concepts. 'An emotion', he says, 'is a subjective content, the socio-linguistic fixing of the quality of an experience which is from that point onward defined as personal.'[6] Trying to pin this down more firmly, he describes it as 'intensity owned and recognized'.[7] By contrast, he says, affect is 'unqualified' and 'not ownable or recognizable'.[8]

Massumi claims Benedict de Spinoza helps us understand affect through the way in which he talks about 'the irreducibly bodily and autonomic nature of affect'.[9] Massumi goes on to discuss affect as 'a suspension of action-reaction circuits and linear temporality in a sink of what might be called "passion," to distinguish it from both passivity and activity'.[10] Eric Shouse further clarifies what we are talking about here when he says: 'The power of many forms of media lies not so much in their ideological effects, but in their ability to create affective resonances independent of content or meaning.'[11] The awareness offered here is that we cannot reduce our reaction – neither to the media, nor to the world around us in general – to considered, thought about, reflected upon, analysed responses. What we are considering here is the way in which our body responds to impulses received through the senses without recourse to the mind. This is one aspect of escapism, and as we watch these train sequences in particular in *The Lone Ranger* we are subject to this intensity.

Alongside the thrilling intensity of affect, however, escapism is also about the pleasures of experiencing a different world, identifying with characters from this world, and envisaging the self within this imagined world. In this regard, when watching the more strongly narrative-driven (as opposed to spectacle-driven) sections of *The Lone Ranger* the escapism on offer is of a particularly postmodern sort. This is not escapism into a fully formed, logically thought-through world that in its unity and coherence could be imagined to exist in some parallel space and time. This is escapism into a space of plural possibilities, a terrain of shifting sands positing a range of possible takes on the past and reality, where wrong-footing the spectator is at the very heart of the game being played between production team and audience. The pleasure on offer is, essentially, that of surprise. The world we are given is not one with which we are familiar. Not only are there no rules we can recognise but there are, it appears, quite simply no rules: anything can happen. The surreal, bizarre or merely strange represent the norm because everyday notions of time and space are brought into question. In part here we are talking about the meta-cinematic elements deployed. The central narrative concerning the adventures of Tonto (Johnny Depp) and John Reid (Armie Hammer), alias the Lone Ranger, is framed as being told by an aged Tonto to an impressionable young boy full of Western-genre ideas of 'goodies' battling 'baddies'. The core narrative is then periodically broken into by scenes that return us to this startled child as he finds Tonto's story contradicting his mythic beliefs regarding the Wild West. The classical illusion of reality created by film is thereby repeatedly interrupted, so that we are continually reminded we are watching a film.

Figure 5.1 Tonto (Johnny Depp) gazing at us as spectators watching the film, in *The Lone Ranger* (Gore Verbinski, 2013).

These are also, we might notice, time-shifting moments: when a posse of Texas Rangers that includes Dan Reid (James Badge Dale) and his brother John – the future Lone Ranger – have been ambushed in a canyon and apparently all killed, it is not just the young boy back at the fairground listening to old Tonto's story who cuts into the narrative with a rapid-fire series of questions ('They're dead? All dead? Even, Dan?'), we find we too are suddenly drawn into the narrative frame. At the sound of the young boy's voice saying 'That's not right. It can't be right' the younger Tonto from 1869 (when the original adventures are said to have taken place) looks back over his shoulder from the canyon rim directly towards the camera. He gazes straight at us as spectators watching the film; and as a result his response is directed, not only towards the boy who exists within the film's narrative compass as a visitor to a Wild West diorama in a fairground in San Francisco in 1933 but also towards us wherever we might be in 2011, or beyond (Figure 5.1).

III

Further factors also add to the disorientation experienced by the spectator. Like the boy, when we come to the film we may think we know something about the story of the Lone Ranger – a fictional character in a radio series that was subsequently developed into a series of books, and then into a TV series and several Hollywood films – but we find we actually do not know the 'true' story, that is to say, the one Tonto is now telling us. Which is all very well except that, like the boy in the fairground, we cannot be sure this old man is a reliable narrator; and beyond this we know because we are continually reminded by the meta-cinematic nature of what we are watching that Tonto in any guise, and not least in the guise he is presented to us here, is a fictional character. On a number of levels spectators become uncertain about where to position themselves in relation to the story they are being told. It seems we cannot be sure of anything. This is an experience, perhaps, not unlike walking through a fairground hall of mirrors – reality, that we thought we knew and could be sure of, is reflected back to us in a series of distortions that bring into question the very existence of our original conception.

An early shot provides us with a visual context for San Francisco in 1933, a view across a bay showing the Golden Gate Bridge under construction but not yet finished. Historically, as the film suggests through an on-screen title, it is correct to suggest work on this iconic bridge had started by 1933 but the extent of the construction shown in the film would not be achieved until several years later.[12] Reality/history seems to be referenced and yet what we find is that we are actually moving within an interlocking frame of media constructions. Similarly, it is true to say the first transcontinental railroad link across the United States was completed at Promontory Summit, Utah, in 1869, as suggested by the storyline in the film.[13] However, the railroad personnel are fictional, in particular one of the two key antagonists, Latham Cole (Tom Wilkinson). Further, the main settlement mentioned is that of Colby, Texas, which is not only a completely fictional town but also one that can be nowhere near the line of the actual first transcontinental railroad since Texas is too far south. Complicating things still further the filmmakers insist on shooting much of the film with a Monument Valley backdrop. This fits well with the Western genre since this landscape was famously used by the director, John Ford, in many of his Westerns; but this region on the Utah–Arizona border is far to the south of the rail route and far to the west of Texas. The history on display is, therefore, a potentially confusing mix of fact and fiction; and the geography is, similarly, both spatially and historically inaccurate, and potentially confusing.[14]

References to particular ideas also tend to be dealt with in a similarly haphazard fashion. To take one example, Tonto believes Butch Cavendish (William Fichtner) to be a wendigo, or windigo, a creature taken from Native American beliefs who is seen as an evil spirit, or cannibal monster. This supernatural being has been used in a range of literature and films, perhaps particularly post-2000, but is not usually seen as part of the Comanche culture which is supposedly Tonto's background. Its origins are, instead, attributed to Algonquian folklore:[15] 'In Northern Algonquian traditions, the windigo was the spirit of winter, which could transform a man, woman, or child into a cannibalistic being with a heart of ice.'[16]

IV

Each aspect of the filmmaking so far discussed highlights the postmodern approach that characterizes *The Lone Ranger* as a whole. In this film, fact and fiction collide in such a way as to suggest the impossibility of the existence of realism as a genuine field of cultural possibility. The integration of several key facts of historical record within a surreal fictional world works, not simply in such a way as to deny the existence of history but also in such a way as to actively destroy history as a basis for reasoned discussion. Depp's version of Tonto presents us with a character who has a dead crow on his head throughout every scene he is in. In historical terms this is totally bizarre; certain Native Americans wore feathers in their hair, or in some cases had elaborate feather headdresses, but there are no records of anything like this. Depp has credited a contemporary painting by Kirby Sattler, 'I Am Crow', as giving him the idea for this headwear.

> Sattler had painted a bird flying directly behind the warrior's head. It looked to me like it was sitting on top . . . I thought: Tonto's got a bird on his head. It's his spirit guide in a way. It's dead to others, but it's not dead to him. It's very much alive.[17]

A quote from the artist in the same article places this decision regarding Tonto's costume even more firmly within the eclectic cultural mix of postmodernism.

> The portraits I paint are composites created from a variety of visual references coupled with my imagination . . . While being broadly based in a historical context, my paintings are not intended to be viewed as historically accurate.[18]

This brings the stuffed crow in line with other creative decisions made in relation to *The Lone Ranger*, which is a film within which neither history nor geography exist as coherent, structured possibilities. There is no such thing as 'reality' and as a result it is impossible to arrive at any final, considered position in relation to themes and ideas within the film. In classic postmodern style the film suggests there is no grand narrative to be had which will make sense of all of this. Istvan Csicsery-Ronay has written about the unavoidable, ever-changing nature of the postmodern condition. All is continually and unrelentingly in flux, he suggests, never at rest, never settled, never final, always moving towards, never arriving, so that there is only a continually shifting matrix of positions, a blizzard of possibilities, an unstable plurality of equally valid understandings. In the face of all of this, he says, we now live in a 'culture of coping', a managing-to-get-by state, or what he denotes as 'mutopia'.[19]

V

One of the key ways the filmmakers ensure this sense of everything being in flux is realised is through their use of genre. As with everything else in this film, and in line with the film's postmodern credentials, the genre forms we might attribute to the film are multiple – spoof Western, homage Western, buddy comedy, cannibal horror, surreal fantasy, action adventure. We shift suddenly, often startlingly, from one subgenre to another. As Dan Reid lies dying, after he and his posse of Texas Rangers have been ambushed by Butch Cavendish and his gang, we are suddenly aware that Cavendish is cutting out Dan's heart and preparing to eat it. A classic Western scene of the 'goodies' being ambushed in a canyon is transformed into something out of a cannibal horror movie. The shifts are not always as startling as this but scenes that appear to be of one particular classically authentic Hollywood type are continually being undercut. When John Reid is on a train with a Presbyterian family sitting opposite him, as an audience we know where we are: this is a realistic Hollywood scene with a realistic exchange taking place between the characters. But when John picks up a cuddly toy that a child has dropped and throws it back to her in a game of 'catch' we do not expect the sudden, totally surreal moment of the toy being sucked out of the train window in a backdraft. In genre terms we find ourselves in a moment that in comic tone is like something out of Mel Brooks's *Blazing Saddles* (1974). Later, when Tonto and the Lone Ranger are roasting a rabbit on a spit in the desert at night, rabbits are seen in the foreground watching what is happening. As Tonto tosses a piece of cooked meat to these rabbits they suddenly turn into rabid creatures involved in a monstrous feeding frenzy. This is bizarre and destroys any illusion of reality, existing somewhere beyond two men roasting a rabbit in the desert. (Although, maybe, we could argue it is thematically appropriate for a film about cannibalism as an image for human activity.)

Past Westerns are referenced throughout. Visually the film could be seen as a homage to previous work within the genre. But to what purpose? Is there a suggestion the old values advocated by such films need to be recaptured? If so, this would deny the primacy of postmodernism for the film. Sections of the film such as that provided by the posse entering the canyon and being ambushed are filmed in such a way as to replicate classic Western storytelling and create a massive dislocate with other parts such as the totally surreal fantasy of the final runaway train sequence. As viewers we are left with a series of questions, uncertainties and potential ambiguities.

Again, we might ask whether this is a comedy or a tragedy. Much that happens is played for laughs and involves simple, physical, slapstick comedy; but there are also more complex, verbal repartee and body language exchanges between Depp and Hammer performing as if they are characters in an absurdist drama, or a vaudeville comedy duo. On the flip side, there is also a darker, more tragic seriousness to the film, which is pushed to one side by the extreme craziness of the ending but which is still to be found in poignant moments such as John's recollection of his brother's murder ('All I know is a man killed my brother, and I'll see him hang for it.'), or in the actual murder itself. However much some aficionados of the horror genre may find the references to cannibalism when Dan is killed to be humorous, this remains a horrific incident and is the event that forces John to question the nature of human society more closely.

Beyond this, we might notice that the narrative structure itself is also potentially disorientating. There is uncertainty over who the hero might be seen to be. Is this the Lone Ranger's story, or is this Tonto's story? Even the certainties of storytelling are being taken away from the viewer. On the surface it might seem we are being given the story of the Lone Ranger but, ultimately, this is done in such a way as to place Tonto centre stage. And, as has been suggested, the viewer has no way of gauging how reliable, or unreliable, Tonto might be as a narrator. Furthermore, it is not at all clear how the delivery of Tonto's backstory fits logically into the narrative structure. We are told that when he was a young boy Tonto found Cole and Cavendish dying in the desert and saved them by taking them back to his tribal village. In the film, an elderly tribal chief is telling this story, but within the imagined scenario of the film he only exists inside a narrative told by Tonto to a boy at a fairground in an imagined San Francisco in 1933. And so this seems to be Tonto telling his own backstory through the device of a character within his narrative. Potentially, a moment such as this increases our awareness of the presence of the creators of the film working within a twenty-first-century context. The levels of narration are complex. The filmmakers are telling a story about an old man, Tonto, who is telling a story in the 1930s about events in 1869, and within this at one point another old man, the tribal chief, tells a story about events earlier in the 1800s. We are given a story within a story within a story; and, at one point, a story within a story within a story within a story. The spectator is taken into an unstable, multi-dimensional experience, within which nothing can be depended on to be ultimately 'true' because nothing is fixed, all is in flux, and there are no certainties to be had. Any narrative certainties we may have thought we had have been eroded and we, like the boy we follow into the Wild West Exhibition, are left floundering around for some solid ground on which to stand and take our bearings. In the end, Tonto leaves the boy to wrestle with the idea of how he sees things; whatever sense he makes of it all is in the end up to him. And we are in the same position.

BOY: So, the windigo, nature out of balance, the masked man, it's just a story, right? I mean, I know he's not real. Was he?
TONTO: Up to you, Kemosabi.

This means, of course, that there is no stability, no certainty, outside of the individual's personal perspective on everything. Truth does not exist in any final sense, only a multiplicity of truths dependent upon the individual perspective. The shape of the final story is down to the boy, that is, down to the individual spectator. We might notice how confused the boy has become: time becomes either irrelevant or mixed up for him as he shifts from the present to the past (' . . . he's not real. Was he?').

In discussing literary science fiction, Peter Stockwell talks about the 'frame knowledge required for completion',[20] by which he means the historical knowledge and genre knowledge readers need to bring to bear to complete the 'rounded' fictional world evoked by the author. Here we face a somewhat similar situation. If we are to contextualize the film text we need to bring into play our knowledge of history, geography, Westerns and the nature of theoretical postmodernism. Stockwell discusses works that use a 'chaotic blend'[21] in order to explore their areas of interest, and this would seem to be effectively what happens in *The Lone Ranger*. The difficulty for a reader might come in determining that which Stockwell describes as 'not genuine'[22] – elements of what we are told that do not fit with what actually happened in the period within which the text is supposedly set. We have already discussed certain dislocations of history and geography, and these are a continual feature of the film. For example, the only group of Native Americans identified in the film for the viewer are Comanche. This is Tonto's tribal background and the fictional given ethnicity of the group that attacks the railroad only to be slaughtered by the superior fire-power of the US Army. However, although the First Transcontinental Railroad was attacked by various Native American tribes this is not generally seen to involve the Comanche,[23] whose territory and field of operations were further to the south. This means any discussion of Native Americans in relation to this film exists only, and exclusively, within a complex series of representations within media culture. Or does it?

VI

In all the ways so far discussed this film wants to be a postmodern text. It wants to emphasize the complexity, confusion and plurality of possible understandings of the contemporary experience. It wants to deny the

Enlightenment project that suggests through reason an understanding can be gained of situations facing human society. John Reid is ridiculed as an advocate of reason. When we first see him he is carrying a copy of John Locke's *Second Treatise on Civil Government* (1689), which he describes as his bible. He has a picture of his love interest marking a page on which Locke establishes why men and women stay together in long-term relationships through the application of reason alone and without any recourse to concepts of love, or suchlike![24] Later, Reid 'quotes' Locke in a very precised form in order to summarise his whole social philosophy: 'Wherever men unite into society they must quit the laws of nature and assume the laws of men, so that society as a whole may prosper.'[25] In his beliefs, he is shown by events to be naïve in the extreme. John Reid, that is to say, the Lone Ranger of heroic American myth, is held up to ridicule for his ingenuous beliefs.

The Lone Ranger wants to suggest we live in a world in which all is constantly in flux, so that adopting a final, unequivocal position on anything is impossible. And yet, in contradiction to this, the film cannot draw back from taking a definite position on the presence of evil in the world and how it should be dealt with. Good and evil are presented as constants, as unavoidably present within the human experience of the world. When questioning the nature of his brother's death at the hands of Cavendish, and before he takes up the mantle of being the Lone Ranger, John Reid poses a question to himself and to Tonto: 'He cut out his heart. What kind of man does something like that?' Tonto's immediate response is: 'Not a man, an evil spirit, born in the empty spaces of the desert, with a hunger that cannot be satisfied and the power to throw nature out of balance.' For Tonto, the phenomenon is not explicable in human terms and can only be understood by seeing someone such as Cavendish as being beyond the human. The relevance to a society struggling to conceptualize the world post-9/11 would seem obvious.

This strand of thought within the film, in effect, asserts that 'goodies' and 'baddies', in terms that a young boy from 1933 would understand and that we continue to understand, do exist. The attack on Dan Reid's home while he is away offers us a classic Western scene of the homestead under attack, with those who are within, and good, defending themselves against those who are without, and bad, or Other, existing somewhere beyond the pale for civilisation. The eerie silence that precedes the attack is straight out of *The Searchers* (John Ford, 1956), and Rebecca (Ruth Wilson) defends the home with some of the gunplay skills of Jane (Natalie Portman) in *Jane Got a Gun* (Gavin O'Connor, 2016).[26] In such a world, the Lone Ranger cannot take off his mask at the end of the film because there is no resting place for him. Like Ethan Edwards (John Wayne) at the end of *The Searchers* he cannot settle down; he cannot enter into the space of the home and the family, those twin pillars of American society. Evil will continue to exist in the world. Therefore, there will always be a need for heroes in white hats (and black masks) who are prepared to operate outside of the usual social provisions made for law and order, in order that they may act as, in effect, outlaws for good. They have a necessary role to play in facing down those who dress in black hats because the world is a place of binary oppositions; it is not a place of infinite shades of grey with nothing to choose between them, it is not a place in which things simply happen without any value or sense of relative importance attaching to those things. It is not, in other words, a postmodern space. Instead, it is a place of Right and Wrong, a place where decisions have to be made, where choices have to be made, and where action has to be taken in order to push events in one direction rather than another. As Tonto tells Will, the boy at the fairground, 'Come a time, Kemosabi, the good man must wear mask.'

In his early speech to the people of Colby, reassuring them of the 'good' that would result from the railroad and accompanying 'progress' coming to the West, Latham Cole (Tom Wilkinson) sees outlaws as 'those who prey on the weak'. What this film, working within the well-mined traditions of the Western, makes clear is that there are also outlaws working for good, attempting to counteract the actions of 'baddies' but necessarily needing to work outside of the usual boundaries of civilised society. In effect, we have what we find in so many Westerns post-9/11, the imperative to work within an extra-democratic space in order to deal with the intensity of evil with which democracy is confronted. There is no end to human depravity. People cannot be reformed. Some people are simply evil. Good and evil are at war with each other. There are high moral values that are in an ideal world to be applauded but these things cannot be attained in the real world. Naïve liberals and others who believe in utopian possibilities have to learn. The boundaries of civilised society have to be overstepped in order to protect ordinary people and their society. So-called 'civilised' society is not actually civilised at all.

VII

However, there is one further strand of thought to be found in this film. This line of argument appears to want to go beyond a position that sees evil as simply inexplicable within normal human terms. It wants to see evil as (also) emanating from greed and corruption, and related very clearly to power relationships within society. So, there are layers of possibilities here. The film wants to be cleverly postmodern, seeing all things as relative and suggesting there are no certainties; and yet it cannot turn away from its position as part of the dominant ideology and therefore has to pronounce that there is a position we should adopt which recognises the presence of evil in the world and the necessity of confronting that evil. It announces that ideals such as those advocated by the Enlightenment and adopted by the Founding Fathers are not enough: 'good' has to be prepared to go beyond these ideal positions if it is to successfully combat 'evil'. But, even more interesting than this tension between, on the one hand, postmodernist questioning of both the nature of being and the nature of knowledge, and, on the other hand, the assertion from the perspective of the dominant ideology of clear-cut binary oppositions, is the fact that it seems there is this one further step the film wants to take.

It wishes to recognise the corruption and greed of capitalism itself. The one final certainty the film presents to the viewer is that the world is totally corrupt, and is run by powerful, greedy people with no regard to the common good. It is not just that Latham Cole is corrupt. The railroad chairman's words to the Lone Ranger at the end of the film, with his shareholders from 'the finest families in our country' behind him, prove this. 'Justice' is nowhere to be found and can only be brought about in the most improbable way imaginable within an imagined fairy story narrative that is not of the real world. Before the final fantastical sequence, Reid/ the Lone Ranger says to Tonto, 'You were right, there is no justice. Cole controls everything, the railroad, the cavalry, everything. If men like him represent the law, I'd rather be an outlaw.' The world is under the control of a corrupt, powerful elite.

Before going further, we might note that for this film the world in which evil is inevitably and unavoidably present, the post-lapsarian Christian world, in this case seems to owe nothing to religious philosophy. Religion seems to be consistently rejected in this film, ridiculed almost as much as John Reid. The singing of the hymn 'Shall We Gather at the River' by a migrant congregation on a train near the start of the film carries none of the firm, underpinning certainty of religious belief that accompanies its use in Westerns directed by Ford. The response of one of Cavendish's gang members to a Presbyterian minister saying 'There's no need for violence, my son' is to shoot him in the leg and laugh. The words of the US Cavalry officer as he leads a charge on a Comanche village are clearly designed to satirize the commonly adopted and presumed alliance of God with the powerful and with war: 'Let us bring the pure sceptre of Almighty God to the heathens!' Later, as he orders the unshrouding of a Gatling gun and the decimation of Indian attackers, effectively enacting in miniature the genocide of Native Americans, the same officer cries 'For God and for

Figure 5.2 'For God and for country!': the US Army in *The Lone Ranger*.

country' (Figure 5.2) There is also a moment where Cavendish seems to be about to execute Tonto and this draws from Tonto the line, 'I do not fear what comes next,' to which Cavendish replies, 'Nothing comes next.' This appears to dismiss the whole grand narrative of Christianity (although, of course, the words do come from the film's embodiment of depraved evil).

Early in the film Cole says 'Make no mistake, law and order has come to the Wild West' as he heralds the arrival of the railroad; he follows this with 'The future is bright . . . and it's just around the bend.' But, there is no 'bright future' visible in this film, and there is no 'law and order' other than as a cover for corruption and greed. For the Lone Ranger, there is only unrelenting fire-fighting, countering one expression of greed and corruption only to find another has emerged elsewhere, demanding the attention of an incorruptible hero. The Lone Ranger's brother, Dan Reid, refused to go along with corruption and was killed for his stand, and now the Lone Ranger himself faces the same choice as his brother. At the end of the film, the chairman of the Transcontinental Railroad hands him a reward as 'a small token of our thanks', adding ominously, in an aside to the Lone Ranger that makes it clear this is a bribe rather than anything else, 'There will plenty more where that came from: always nice to have a lawman on the side of progress.' These are the inducements to come inside the System, to enter the fold of society that men like the Lone Ranger, it seems, must refuse.

One of the key moments in the film occurs when Tonto and the Lone Ranger are buried up to their necks in a Comanche village and hear the cavalry coming. Again, it is a moment that, in its tone, reminds us of *Blazing Saddles*. 'Oh, thank God: civilisation!' cries the Lone Ranger. 'We'll just explain the entire situation and we'll get the whole misunderstanding cleared up. The United States Army! Finally, someone who will listen to reason.' The Lone Ranger's appeal to religion ('thank God'), to 'civilisation', to the military and, above all, to 'reason' is shown to be utterly and ridiculously naïve. But his continual evocation of the Enlightenment could be seen as crucial. A considerable amount of ground is covered in Locke's Chapter 7, 'Of Political and Civil Society', in his *Second Treatise on Civil Government* that has been referenced earlier, but in amongst it we find in Section 85 that slaves 'are by the right of nature subjected to the absolute and arbitrary power of their masters' and that the 'chief end' of civil society is 'the preservation of property'.[27] Potentially, the film throws us back to question the very foundational principles of the United States.

VIII

Finally, however, it has to be said that this level of engagement with ideas would not seem to be the likely outcome of watching the film for the majority of viewers. The prominence of spectacle propels us headlong, helter-skelter into the thrill of the ride erasing all else. Viewing the film from this perspective might be most likely to encourage political apathy rather than anything else, perhaps the rejection of the whole possibility of politics on any national, international or global scale. The spectator is diminished and disempowered by such a viewing experience. A shot of adrenaline is provided only as momentary relief from powerlessness and impotence.

From this perspective, this type of filmmaking runs the risk of becoming a purposeless ride to nowhere. Film has always been a fantasy space where anything goes, has always transcended time and space, transporting people in an instant from one side of the world to the other, and taking them back and forth through time as and when the narrative demands. Under postmodernism these possibilities have an amplified intensity but there is nothing that is essentially new.

If, in line with Hollywood's cheerleading role for the United States within global media culture, we accept the dominant ideology as we watch *The Lone Ranger*, then we inhabit a world containing a core binary opposition between 'our' society's definition of 'good' and 'our' society's definition of 'evil'. We focus on the outsider otherness of Cavendish and his gang as deranged, depraved and psychopathic. From this perspective, the film becomes an attempt to return to the supposed 'good guy' values of the American Dream. As one of the two main 'bad' characters in the film, Cole has not only become cynical as a result of his experience of the Civil War, he has also arrived at perverse conclusions. 'I was at Gettysburg: 12,000 casualties before lunch', he says. 'Know what I learned in all that carnage? Nothing is accomplished without sacrifice.' Of all the things you might learn about war from such an experience, Cole has only learned how easily disposable human life needs to be seen to be if you are ever to (in his terms) achieve anything.²⁸ It is clear that what motivates him is power. Describing the latest technology that is able to compress time and space, the railroad, he tells a young child: 'Whoever controls this, controls the future: power that makes emperors and kings look like fools.'

The values Cole espouses need to be defeated and 'white hat' perceptions of values and purpose re-established. And yet, although he takes up the heroic mantle at the conclusion of the film, the Lone Ranger has been shown to be both ineffectual and powerless throughout most of the film. 'There does not have to be a war,' he says to the elderly Comanche chief. But the fact is, even as a legendary American hero, he is unable to stop events taking their course.

In many ways this film offers the viewer the classic, star-driven Hollywood experience. On the surface this is a light comedy Western; and yet it is attempting to deal with seemingly antithetical events such as genocidal massacres, pitiless one-on-one savagery and the argued necessity of extra-legal vigilantism. This could be seen as commonplace, everyday global news of inexplicable violence being packaged within a controlled cinematic experience and thereby tamed. This would allow us to classify the film as Disneyfied, right-wing exploitation of the genre; perhaps as an example of something standing in polar opposition to the radical employment of violence in the Western genre achieved in a film like *The Wild Bunch* (Sam Peckinpah, 1969) in response to American involvement in Vietnam. But, perhaps, there is another way of viewing this.

In denying the film box office success was the audience refusing to move into a re-shaped white-hatted future? Were audiences considering any move back to accepting Lone Ranger-style American values as an absolute impossibility within the contemporary global political context? Or, is this to attribute too much political awareness to audiences? It would not seem film audiences have generally positioned themselves in such a way as to reject the easy consumption and expenditure model of late capitalism, nor to decline the opportunity to view violence as affective thrill. Instead, it may be that the film's attempt to foreground postmodern self-awareness by continually drawing the viewer out of the fantasy world, breaking the illusion and returning them to the here-and-now, was found to be unacceptable since what this aspect of self-reflexive cinema does is to request, almost demand, personal viewer reflection on what is being represented to them.

As is the case with any film, viewers are able to access *The Lone Ranger* at any one of a range of levels, which will involve intensities of pleasure and/or confusion that will lead, finally, to an individually (decided) response to the film. The critically engaged reader is still capable of placing everything that is seen and heard within a film into the contextual dimensions of real life, that is the temporal and spatial parameters of everyday life as experienced by human beings living within a phase of time that moves them from birth to death and within a space that unavoidably demands physical (as opposed to virtual) bodily movement. These dimensions may be obfuscated by digital technology but they cannot be escaped in any real way.

Notes

1. Michael Hilger, *Native Americans in the Movies: Portrayals from Silent Films to the Present* (Lanham, MD: Rowman & Littlefield, 2016), p. 78.
2. Ibid. p. 78.
3. Ed Andreychuk, *The Lone Ranger on Radio, Film and Television* (Jefferson, NC: McFarland, 2018), p. 161.
4. Borys Kit, '*Lone Ranger* budget back up to $250 million', *The Hollywood Reporter*, 22 June 2012. Available at <http://www.hollywoodreporter.com/heat-vision/lone-ranger-budget-johnny-depp-336526> (accessed 1 October 2017).
5. Gilles Deleuze and Félix Guattari, *A Thousand Plateaus: Capitalism and Schizophrenia*, trans. Brian Massumi (London and New York: Continuum, 1980/8), p. xvii.
6. Brian Massumi, 'The autonomy of affect', *Cultural Critique*, 1995, 31: 88.
7. Ibid. p. 88.
8. Ibid. p. 88.
9. Ibid. p. 89.
10. Ibid. p. 89.
11. Eric Shouse, 'Feeling, emotion, affect', *M/C Journal*, 2005, 8(6). Available at <http://journal.media-culture.org.au/0512/03-shouse.php> (accessed 27 July 2018).
12. The Golden Gate Bridge Highway and Transportation District website says it was not until 1935 that the towers were ready to take the main cables. See Golden Gate Bridge Highway and Transportation District, 'Construction timeline Golden Gate Bridge: December 1932 to April 1937'. Available at <http://goldengatebridge.org/research/ConstructionTimeline.php> (accessed 13 July 2018).

    In his book, based on accounts by people working on the construction, Harvey Schwartz says: 'The strands for the cables were spun on-site by the contractor, John A. Roebling's Sons Company, between November, 1935, and May, 1936.' See Harvey Schwartz, *Building the Golden Gate Bridge: A Workers' Oral History* (Seattle: University of Washington Press, 2015), p. 164.
13. Latham Cole announces towards the end of the movie: 'With the natives in retreat, we'll be in Promontory Summit ahead of schedule.'
14. Although we might argue we should not be too concerned since such things never worried Ford. *The Searchers* (1956), for example, despite the Monument

Valley filming for which it is famous was supposedly set in Texas. In a sense, the filmmakers are doing no more than following in a long tradition of re-writing history through the Western.
15. Interestingly, in relation to Depp's interpretation of his character, Shawn Smallman suggests 'windigo' often refers to 'a clown-like being' in Plains Cree belief. See Shawn Smallman, *Dangerous Spirits: The Windigo in Myth and History* (Victoria, BC: Heritage House, 2015), p. 13.
16. Smallman, *Dangerous Spirits*, p. 21.
17. Anthony Breznican, 'Johnny Depp tells EW origins of Tonto makeup from "Lone Ranger"', *Entertainment Weekly*, 22 April 2012. Available at <http://ew.com/article/2012/04/22/johnny-depp-reveals-origins-of-tonto-makeup-from-lone-ranger-exclusive/> (accessed 13 July 2018).
18. Ibid.
19. Istvan Csicsery-Ronay, 'Notes on Mutopia', *Postmodern Culture: Journal of Interdisciplinary Thought on Contemporary Cultures*, 1997, 8(1). Available at <http://www.pomoculture.org/2013/09/21/notes-on-mutopia/> (accessed 13 July 2018).
20. Peter Stockwell, *Cognitive Poetics: An Introduction* (London and New York: Routledge, 2002), p. 102.
21. Ibid. p. 102.
22. Ibid. p. 102.
23. See, for example, John Hoyt Williams's book, *A Great and Shining Road: The Epic Story of the Transcontinental Railroad* (Lincoln: University of Nebraska Press, 19996) (pp. 104, 140, 217), which mentions attacks on railroad workers and the derailment of trains by the Sioux, Cheyenne and Arapaho; or Stephen E. Ambrose's *Nothing Like It In the World: The Men Who Built the Transcontinental Railroad 1863–1869* (New York: Touchstone, 2001), which mentions only these same few tribal groups from further north on the Great Plains.
24. Chapter 7, 'Of political and civil society', Section 80. John Locke, *Second Treatise on Civil Government: An Essay Concerning the True Original, Extent and End of Civil Government* (Wheeling, IL: Harlan Davidson, 1982), pp. 48–9.
25. Locke, *Second Treatise*, p. 53.
26. At this point, Joe (Grover Coulson), as the loyal black farmhand, is playing a classic racially defined role – see, for example, Woody Strode as Pompey in *The Man Who Shot Liberty Valence* (Ford, 1962), or Jester Hairston as Jethro in *The Alamo* (Wayne, 1960). Further emphasising racial integration, Tonto is shown in close-up closing the eyes of the dead African American.
27. Locke, *Second Treatise*, p. 50.
28. In line with Cole's relaxed dismissal of battlefield deaths at Gettysburg, the mass of people do not exist other than at the edges of this film. Rail workers are given objective reality only as a coordinated body able to perform construction tasks as a functional collective organism. They are idealised as part of a

heroic achievement of American nationhood: as they move towards completing the transcontinental railroad, for example, workers are seen silhouetted in low-angle shots with the sun behind them. Cole wishes to provide 'food for the masses', but only in order that they might perform their required functions within his vision of the 'cities' and 'factories' of America. Chinese workers are seen by characters within the film as disposable, a form of 'factory fodder' rather akin to Gettysburg's 'cannon fodder'.

CHAPTER 6

Affect and the Immersive Experience of Bodily Excess: *The Revenant* (2015)

I

One of the attractions of the cinema is the chance to confront yourself with a variety of extreme events within a safe space. Ordeals that would in the real world result in severe injury or even death can be 'undergone' within a virtual space of the stimulated imagination; other people can be viewed suffering assorted agonies while the spectator partakes of the same suffering, either vicariously through identifying with the character, or voyeuristically through their role as the unseen watcher. Normally forbidden, perhaps taboo, areas of human experience can be encountered within a space sanctioned by society to allow such extremes of human experience to be played out. This would seem to be true for cinemagoers of all ages. Linda Williams has described this as one of the factors used by her and her then seven-year-old son when choosing a film to watch. They were looking, she said, for films that promised to be 'sensational' and to give their bodies 'an actual physical jolt'.[1] Their search was for a film that seemed in some way to be 'excessive'. Looking at horror, pornography and melodrama, Williams was interested in the way in which the spectacle of the body featured prominently in these genres, giving 'a quality of uncontrollable convulsion or spasm – of the body "beside itself"'.[2] In both the experience of something being 'gross', or 'excessive', and in its focus on 'body spectacle' *The Revenant* (Alejandro González Iñárritu, 2015) would seem to some extent to be operating in a similar sphere. Williams was focusing in particular on the role of the female body within her chosen genres but even so, there are at least a couple more points at which her analysis becomes pertinent for our discussion. For one thing, she suggested the 'success' of her chosen genres seemed to be 'a self-evident matter of measuring bodily response'.[3] Would this represent the 'self-evident' way to determine the 'success', or otherwise, of *The Revenant*? More importantly, she posited the view that the existence and popularity of particular expressions of horror, pornography and melodrama at the time she was writing was linked to 'rapidly changing notions of gender – of what it means to be a man or a woman' and to the function of the resulting films 'as cultural problem-solving'.[4] The Western has, to some extent, always been about what it means to be a man and often (generally by relegation to the margins) what it means to be a woman. In its strong male focus, is *The Revenant*, to a large degree, about what it means to be a man in an early twenty-first-century American context? Is there some sort of 'cultural problem-solving' taking place? If so, what is the 'problem', and how is it being 'solved'? Indeed, is it being successfully 'solved'?

II

On a trapping expedition in the early 1800s around the Upper Missouri, the central character in *The Revenant*, Hugh Glass (Leonardo DiCaprio), is mauled by a grizzly bear in a bloody attack that occupies almost five minutes of screen-time. This is followed by a scene showing the horrific wounds he sustains being stitched without anaesthetic. The small party of trappers then attempts to carry him on a stretcher until expedition leader, Andrew Henry (Domhnall Gleeson), concludes the rough terrain is making this impossible and Glass needs to be killed. Glass is so badly injured he cannot speak but listening to his spits and grunts of protest, as he has to (and we have to), means Henry cannot bring himself to carry out the 'mercy killing'. Left with him to look after him until he dies and then bury him, trapper John Fitzgerald (Tom Hardy) attempts to asphyxiate Glass by stuffing a rag in his mouth and holding his hand over his nose while Glass is strapped to a stretcher and thereby totally immobilized. When his son tries to protect him, Glass has to watch as he is stabbed to death by Fitzgerald. Left for dead partially buried in a shallow grave, and at first barely able to crawl, Glass attempts to make it to the nearest fort on his own. When he finds on drinking that water simply runs out of a hole in his neck he cauterizes the wound by firing it with gunpowder. When he finds the rotting carcass of a bison he breaks open the bones to eat the marrow. When he manages to trap a fish at the edge of a river he eats it raw. When he finds a Pawnee tribesman eating the raw meat of a buffalo we are shown him doing the same, taking the bloody liver in his hands and gorging himself on it. Later, in a snowstorm, he eviscerates his dead horse, taking out great armfuls of bloody innards, and then sleeps inside the resulting hollowed out carcass in order to keep warm.[5] The brutalization of Glass's body is continually displayed for the audience. The merciless assault on his mind is similarly consistently presented in the experiences we see him undergoing, as are the depths of primitivism required for survival.

On one level, the film becomes a Western offered as a gore fest. And our experience of graphic violence perpetrated against bodies is not confined to what happens to Glass. As an attack begins on a working encampment of trappers where skinned and bloody bodies of animals are piled up, a swish pan edit alerts us to the sudden unexpectedness of a naked man lurching into camp. He is placed at a distance so that we cannot quite be sure what we are seeing, thereby further adding to our confusion. As he falls forward, with an arrow in his back, we cut to see another arrow passing through the neck of a man in medium shot. The impact of these two events, one of which we have to work to make sense of, and the other which we are only too graphically and immediately aware of, is magnified by the contrast in filmmaking approaches. This attack on trappers by Native Americans, who we find out are Arikara, continues in the same vein and includes a man seen in close-up being pierced through the forehead by an arrow before having his head chopped off by an Indian on horseback. These are horror movie tropes that further link us to the film analysis by Williams highlighted above.

We also see, in a series of flashbacks, an attack by soldiers on a Pawnee village where Glass apparently once lived with his wife and son. The images show the village littered with bodies and soldiers torching buildings. On another occasion, later in the film, we are shown another Native American village in similar state after being attacked. Again, there are dead bodies everywhere and only a few, totally traumatized, survivors. We do not know who has been responsible for this attack; it could be white men or maybe a rival Native American tribe. We have seen soldiers attacking the Pawnee village but it is unclear whether these are American troops or, perhaps, British forces. And we hear from Hikuc (Arthur Redcloud), the Pawnee tribesman who helps Glass survive by giving him buffalo meat, that his people have been killed by Sioux. According to John Canfield Ewers, in the period in which the film is set 'intertribal warfare among neighbouring tribes, even those who spoke the dialects of the same basic language, was both common and prolonged'.[6]

Continuing the theme of the abuse of human bodies, it is Hikuc that we see hanging from a tree in an image that recalls the fate of many African Americans (but also others) lynched across the United States, particularly in the later decades of the nineteenth century and the first half of the twentieth century.[7] We are shown Hikuc's lynched body in a series of ever closer shots as Glass walks towards it hanging in a small wooded area (Figure 6.1). Glass then has to hide in this small copse because rival French-Canadian trappers who have committed this atrocity are camped close by. This means he has to spend time with the dead body swaying in full view. Just as importantly, we are placed in the same situation. When Glass is allowed (by the filmmakers) to move forward towards the camp

Figure 6.1 The lynched body of Hikuc (Arthur Redcloud) in *The Revenant* (Alejandro González Iñárritu, 2015).

there is no relief for the audience because we are immediately shown an Arikara woman being raped by a trapper. Shortly afterwards, in another shot that is sufficiently quick and distant for us to have to work to make sense of what we are seeing, the rapist is shown sinking to his knees having been either emasculated (or possibly simply castrated) by his victim.

The bloody abuse of bodies continues throughout the film. Earlier, we have listened to Fitzgerald giving details about the time he was scalped and managed to survive; then, towards the end of the film, Henry is not only killed by Fitzgerald but also scalped, and, in case we have missed this detail, his body is shown slung across a horse with the head bare and the scalping clearly visible. Bodies, human but also animal, are clawed, pierced, slashed, chopped, garrotted, buried, tipped overboard and strewn across the landscape throughout this film. And since what we are being provided with is a total immersive experience in blood and gore it is not just the events and visual images that partake in creating this ordeal for the audience, the tapestry of sound is fully integrated, not into creating realism but into swamping the listener with sounds that intensify the felt, imagined narrative moment. Co-supervising sound editor and designer Martin Hernandez says the director, Alejandro González Iñárritu, was trying to get away from a sound design that was simply 'illustrative' of what could be seen on screen. 'Something coming from a different source material can tell a stronger story, without having to be the exact sound of what you see', says Hernandez.[8] When, within minutes of the opening of the film, a trappers' camp by the river is attacked by Arikara, as outlined above, there are desperate, scared and urgent voices and screams, and there are the slicing sound effects of weapons. These sounds are what might be described as realistic; but there is also a low, distant rumbling and an intrusive, insistent, threatening bass drum, sounds which are all about intensifying the moment of spectatorship.

There are also times when the script works to directly address extreme areas of human experience, or taboos. This is Fitzgerald recounting his experience of being scalped by the Arikara:

> At the start I don't feel nothin'. I just heard the sound o' knives scrapping against my skull . . . Then the blood came. Cold. Started streamin' down my face, in my eyes, and breathin' it in. Chokin' on it. That's when I felt it. Felt all of it.

All of these occasions of brutal assault, bodily excess, and intensified physical spectatorship listed above come before we arrive at the final 'shootout' between Glass and Fitzgerald, in which, in keeping with the rest of the film, blood flows freely. In this encounter, one person is shot through the shoulder, has a finger chopped off by a tomahawk, is knifed in the stomach, has a tomahawk driven into his upper body and is stabbed in the back of the leg; the other is slashed across the face by a knife, stabbed in the thigh, has a chunk of ear bitten off and is stabbed through the hand, pinning it to the ground. And all of this, with the snow around them and their clothes turning red with blood, is before either of them is killed.

III

Responding to the experience of watching *The Revenant*, Carole Cadwalladr opened a newspaper article in this way:

> Ritualised brutality. Vengeful blood lust. Vicious savagery justified by medieval notions of retribution. We all know how dark the world can be these days. A world where men are garrotted and impaled. Where they're speared and disembowelled and have their necks slashed and their genitals sliced off. Where they're killed for no other reason than revenge. This isn't Raqqa, though, it's *The Revenant* . . . [9]

The headline to her article marked out *The Revenant* as 'pain porn'. Despite having been praised as '"immersive" film-making at its finest', she said, this was actually a film in which 'the violence is pointless and the whole thing is meaningless'.[10] Much has been written about early twenty-first-century horror films as 'torture porn'. These films, centring on the series of *Saw* films produced between 2004 and 2010, have been seen as a contemporary subgenre of horror. Aaron Michael Kerner explains, 'Torture porn does not rely on narrative per se, as it is about spectacle, about excessive violence and the body.'[11] In the preface to his book *Torture Porn in the Wake of 9/11: Horror, Exploitation, and the Cinema of Sensation* he describes these films as 'a brand of horror film that emerged in the wake of 9/11 and the War on

Terror' that 'attempts to negotiate the angst-filled years colored by the devastating terrorist attack'.[12] These films 'trade in obscene currency – namely, the American foreign policy that sanctions torture and our sadistic disposition that subsequently fuels the visual culture of torture', says Kerner.[13] In its display of the brutalisation of the body, *The Revenant* would seem to move within this field. This is the 'pain porn' Cadwalladr is reacting against; but, taken within the context of the period, it is not 'meaningless', as she describes it – far from it. It is, actually, packed with relevance to the post-9/11 American experience.

After Glass has been savaged by the bear and they are attempting to stretcher him out of the area over impossible terrain, for example, it is not only the small party of trappers on screen who are faced with a moral dilemma: we, too, are brought face-to-face with the same situation. The script has Fitzgerald asserting that 'The proper thing to do would be to finish him off, quick.' In the field, in enemy territory, could this ever be viewed as the correct course of action? How many US military personnel have been faced with this situation, or similar, in recent years? Are there circumstances that would mean this could be viewed as the humane, civilised response? Michael Sledge says the recovery of the bodies of those who have died in battle can be done at various stages with the most dangerous being 'combat recovery'. 'It is conducted under fire', he says, 'by those bonded to the dead. To them, the soldier's body is still the soldier they knew.'[14] In the introduction to his book *Wounded Rangers: Under Enemy Fire in Afghanistan*, Dominic Hagans discusses the on-going war in that country from a British perspective. 'Not many people understand the devastating nature of the injuries sustained in the Afghan conflict as a result of IEDs and high-velocity bullets', he says. 'I hope this book will give an insight into what soldiers are going through daily and how it affects so many people at home.'[15] In a chapter entitled 'My personal 9/11' Hagans says:

> I looked down, and what happened next seemed to take place in slow motion. I could see that my left leg was hanging off below the knee. My right leg was shattered . . . It was mad, because I should have been in terrible pain, but somehow I wasn't . . . Blood was flowing out of my leg and I felt my heart racing. I was struggling for air, and must have been in shock. I felt my eyes starting to close . . .[16]

In Hagans's book, Phillip 'Barney' Gillespie talks about his experience of being severely wounded in Afghanistan:

> I checked over my body and saw that my right foot had gone and my calf muscle looked like it had been put through a mincer. My shin bone was like a bone hanging out from a piece of meat. It was all very strange . . .[17]

Cadwalladr is perfectly correct in what she observes as happening in *The Revenant*, and she is especially correct to bring 'Raqqa' into her analysis. However, as suggested above, she is incorrect to see it all as 'meaningless'. The body porn and the maleness of the total experience is absolutely appropriate to the contemporary period: a period in which the assault on bodies offered by both war and torture has figured prominently within global events. Urging people to read the book *Winter Soldier: Iraq and Afghanistan: Eyewitness Accounts of the Occupation*, Anthony Swofford warns:

> it will be difficult to believe the blind blood-thirst a unit lives and kills on after suffering casualties; you do not want to know about the constantly loosening Rules of Engagement that eventually debilitate to the point of allowing troops to shoot anyone who makes them feel unsafe. You won't want to believe the 'incentivizing' one marine captain does: be the first to kill with a knife and you'll get some extra days off when the unit rotates home.[18]

IV

Clearly, however, the audience at the cinema is in a crucially different situation to that of troops on the ground in Iraq or Afghanistan. The audience is being offered the opportunity to 'enjoy' brutal experiences and the 'pleasure' of violence within the safety of a virtual space constructed for them by Hollywood. Is there enjoyment to be gained by the spectator from such an experience? Can the graphic detail of violent excess pleasure us? Cadwalladr's response to the film reminds us that, however many awards *The Revenant* may have gained, there is no singular unified audience position on such matters. Just as importantly, Asbjørn Grønstad reminds us that what we experience while watching 'violence' in film are 'a wide variety of artistic modes in which violence is being conceived, conceptualized and configured audiovisually', and that 'one should not confuse the ontology of real violence with that of its cinematic forms'.[19] In other words, a reminder that what we see on screen is a representation of the real thing. But why has the representation that we have here been shaped in the way that it has? How should we understand the shape and form the representation has taken?

Regardless of the insights into the pleasures of cinema that may be offered by psychoanalytical theory's investigation of scopophilia, it is a simple truth, that narratives about the lives of others have always fascinated human beings. David Herman confidently takes us back to basics when he gives a 'working definition' of narratives:

> stories are accounts of what happened to particular people – and of what it was like for them to experience what happened – in particular circumstances and with specific consequences. Narrative, in other words, is a basic human strategy for coming to terms with time, process, and change . . .[20]

However, beyond this basic position, what is implicit in this idea of narrative as a way of 'coming to terms with time, process, and change' is power. Narratives have the power to shape our ways of seeing the world. Who tells what stories to who and in what ways is crucial to the shaping and reshaping of society. Stuart Hall has described the stories a society tells as 'myths that represent in narrative form the resolution of things that cannot be resolved in real life. What they tell us is about the "dream life" of a culture.'[21] Hall was specifically focusing on racism but his general position remains relevant. He spoke of 'popular narratives which constantly, in the imagination of a society, construct the place, the identities, the experience, the histories of the different peoples who live within it'.[22] Did the lives of mountain men, trappers and frontiersmen resemble what we see in *The Revenant*? In your dreams. Or rather, as Hall would have it, in the 'dream life' of our (American/Western) culture. In Grønstad's words given above, what we have is something that is 'being conceived, conceptualized and configured audiovisually', a representation, not real life, not real violence.

Stories of the lives of mountain men, such as Jim Bridger, Kit Carson, John Colter, Hugh Glass and others, have been continually reconfigured and reshaped for successive generations. An early account of Glass's survival story was first published in 1825, just a couple of years after the event, in a journal published in Philadelphia. This was followed by a more elaborate report five years later in *The Southern Literary Messenger*. Further re-workings occurred throughout the nineteenth and twentieth centuries before the novel *The Revenant*, written by Michael Punke, appeared in 2002.[23,24] These legendary characters from the early push westwards have provided Americans with some of the founding myths of their nation, setting standards for endurance in the face of hardship and suffering long endorsed by advocates of nationalism and patriotism. In *The Hero in America: A Chronicle of Hero-Worship*, Dixon Wecter suggested, 'The hero is he whom every American should wish to be. His legend is the mirror of the folk soul.'[25] Discussing the heroes who emerged out of the slightly earlier period of the American Revolutionary War (1775–83), or the American War of Independence, Ray Raphael says,

> writers and orators transformed a bloody and protracted war into glamorous tales conjured from mere shreds of evidence. We still tell these classics today . . . Mere frequency of repetition appears to confirm their authenticity . . . Our confidence is misplaced. In fact, most of the stories were created up to one hundred years after the events they supposedly depict.[26]

The stories of frontiersmen who have become national icons and legendary heroes have similarly been told and re-told in the currency seen by the dominant ideology as required by successive generations. In their Introduction to *Myths, Legends and Folktales of America: An Anthology*, David Leeming and Jake Page suggest legends, although they are based on actual events and persons, 'are carefully tailored, often exaggerated, and serve to express some group aspiration'.[27]

V

In acknowledging Glass's story as one amongst many used in the formation of US national identity, we are beginning to consider the concept of 'American exceptionalism'. In order to understand America and Americans as in some ways 'special' and 'exceptional' when measured against other peoples of the world it is necessary to continually re-work and re-present the foundation myths of national identity to Americans (and to the world). Hilde Eliassen Restad suggests the idea of 'American exceptionalism' is 'a real and significant phenomenon' that has had a profound influence on US foreign policy.[28] 'American exceptionalism entails viewing the United States as *better* than all other nations', says Restad. 'This is different from patriotism . . . If one does not believe that American exceptionalism means *better* rather than *different*, one's Americanness is open to questioning.'[29] While challenging the way the concept has been employed in recent decades, Godfrey Hodgson recognises the crucial importance of the idea. 'Each phase of American history has strengthened the perception among many Americans that the United States is not just one nation among many but a nation marked by the finger of destiny', he says.[30] In *The Rhetoric of American Exceptionalism: Critical Essays*, Jason A. Edwards and David Weiss recognise[31] the importance of 'American heroes' as 'embodiments of American exceptionalism' representing 'everything that the United States is and could be' while also pointing out that 'the images of these heroes are malleable'.[32] William V. Spanos suggests 'the myth of American exceptionalism' took its lead 'from the exemplary self-reliant pioneering or westering spirit of the archetypal backwoodsman or frontiersman'[33] which is where Glass and others of his ilk would seem to come in.

Spanos says the idea of exceptionalism became 'accepted as the essence or truth of the American national identity until it was rendered problematic during the Vietnam War (only to be recuperated in the aftermath of the terrorist attacks on the World Trade Center and the Pentagon on September 11, 2001)'.[34] After the Vietnam War, he suggests there was a 'systematic forgetting' of 'historical actualities' that was achieved 'by way of the combined efforts of the American government, the media, and Hollywood . . . to recuperate the consensus, that is, the American identity'.[35] In his phrase, 'the narcotics of the culture industry' was part of the processing of the Vietnam War by American society that enabled the Gulf War of 1991 to be undertaken. Amnesia over Vietnam was then aided by the events of 9/11 to create a 'fervor' out of which it was possible to announce, 'more or less unilaterally . . . and in defiance of international law', a 'global "war on terrorism"'.[36]

VI

All of this would place *The Revenant* within a clear socio-political context but is unlikely to be part of the mainstream audience's experience of the film. As we have seen, *The Revenant* places extremes of human experience on the screen. It revels in an excess of blood and gore, and a surfeit of suffering. The audience is swamped with an audio-visual excess that induces an immediate bodily response. Such an approach to filmmaking depends on some concept of the 'affective' nature of the medium.

As we said at the beginning of this chapter, part of the appeal of going to the cinema is that events that involve the spectator in confronting fear, and even disgust and extreme anguish, can be indulged within a safe space. In this respect, the relationship between filmmakers and spectators has often been viewed as a game, a knowing liaison in which an audience willingly enters a space in which they not only know they will receive sudden jolts of shock and awe but desire this to happen. At the heart of this experience is 'affect', moments of pure bodily reaction to an intensity of stimulation so sudden that the response occurs even before the brain is able to process events. This is a physical, sensational intensity, taking place as a reaction to what is seen and heard. It is unmediated by consciousness, or by conscious thought. It is registered immediately, and uncontrollably, in our body's response to the intensity of the soundscape and the visual stimulation of the environment created for us. This is a visceral form of spectatorship that fully captures the attention of the spectator to the exclusion of all else.

Following Brian Massumi,[37] Eric Shouse explains that 'affect is not a personal feeling'.[38] Mapping out what he sees as three key regions of our response to the world around us, Shouse says, 'Feelings are *personal* and *biographical*, emotions are *social*, and affects are *prepersonal*.'[39] He says: 'A feeling is a sensation that has been checked against previous experiences and labelled', whereas an affect 'is a non-conscious experience of intensity; it is a moment of unformed and unstructured potential . . . affect cannot be fully realised in language . . . affect is always prior to and/or outside of consciousness'.[40] Attempting to clarify things further, he explains, 'At any moment hundreds, perhaps thousands of stimuli impinge upon the human body and the body responds by infolding them all at once and registering them as an intensity. Affect is this intensity.'[41] He claims, 'the power of many forms of media lies not so much in their ideological effects, but in their ability to create affective resonances independent of content or meaning'.[42] Shouse quotes Virginia Demos as saying, 'Affects are comprised of correlated sets of responses involving the facial muscles, the viscera, the respiratory system, the skeleton, autonomic blood flow changes, and vocalisations that act together to produce an analogue of the particular gradient or intensity of stimulation impinging on the organism.'[43] Demos is listing the body parts involved in any spectator's preconscious response to affective stimulation, but with regard to *The Revenant* these are also the body parts that are displayed in order to create this response. This is very much a film with a focus on blood flows, internal organs and intestines. There is a recurring theme of 'breathing'. The sound of breathing forms a crucial strand on the soundtrack, and the words of Glass's wife given as a voiceover, 'As long as you can still grab a breath, you fight', function as a constant reminder of life as a struggle that demands stoical endurance. Furthermore, because the central character is either on his own on screen or unable to speak because of his injuries, this is a film that is dependent on DiCaprio's facial expressions and vocalisations. For much of the film the audience is overwhelmed by a level of immersive content that allows no room for conscious reflection. In the terms of affect theory given above the audience is infantilised, denied the room to process these intensities into feelings and, therefore, existing within a childlike, preconscious space. Shouse explains that, through their expressions, their breathing, their body language and the involuntary noises they make, infants 'are able to express the intensity of the stimulations that impinge upon them', but they have 'neither the biography, nor the language to feel'.[44]

In these circumstances political issues are left not only unaddressed but also unacknowledged. The focus of the filmmaking is on causing a bodily response from the spectator. As Xavier Aldana Reyes says of 'torture porn', this is 'an essentially corporeal subgenre, for it appeals directly to the bodies of spectators, that is, to their capacity to generate somatic empathy through pain or disgust'.[45] Iñárritu is interested in two things, the existential angst of the individual pushed to the limits of human fortitude and the place of man within the awe-inspiring grandeur of the natural world. Like Werner Herzog, for example, during the filming of *Aguirre, Wrath of God* (1972) and *Fitzcarraldo* (1982), he takes his cast and crew to extreme locations and into extreme conditions in order to add further depth to the exploration of these areas of interest. The focus is, on the one hand, on man's diminutive stature within the breath-taking vastness of the landscape and on the other (in something of a binary contradiction), on the heroic stature of man in the face of the vicissitudes of life. Capturing these themes through cinematography and sound seem to have been critically important for Iñárritu. In one article he says:

> the secret is the light, shooting when God speaks, when everything at that time of day is like seeing Caravaggio in a museum, you are experiencing a beauty in your body and soul and eyes. Painting is that way. The light is everything. The cinema is light and space and time. We shot everything in natural light ... In the right light, you go to another, transcendental level, discovering nature in that moment.[46]

Re-recording mixer Jon Taylor has described what he calls Iñárritu's 'supersensitive ear' for sound: 'it has to be unique, authentic and real ... he only works out of emotions, it's only what moves him that matters'.[47]

VII

There are a few places within the script at which significant political ideas come to the surface but little is made of these ideas. At one point we are confronted with the reality of the likely mind-set of the vast majority of pioneers moving West in America. Andrew Henry is in Fort Kiowa awaiting armed reinforcements. When they arrive, he says, the trappers will be able 'to go back out there and shoot some civilisation into those fuckin' Arikara and get our pelts back'. The words and phrasing are designed to shock but, in this case, rather than the shock of bodily excess we have a form of shock which moves us towards thoughtful reflection. What we might mean by 'civilisation' and who can claim to be 'civilised' is a recurring concern within the Western genre, at least since the post-war period; and the final part of Henry's statement, with its emphasis on recovering the pelts, also suggests the extent to which ideas of 'civilisation' might be bound up with mercantilism/capitalism. David J. Wishart describes the fur trade as 'the primary form of Euro-American activity in the Trans-Missouri West' during the early decades of the nineteenth century.[48] Eric Jay Dolin has suggested this trade 'was a powerful force in shaping the course of American history from the early 1600s through the late 1800s, playing a major role in the settlement and evolution of the colonies, and in the growth of the United States'.[49] The conflict over, what could be seen as nothing more than animal 'pelts' can seem unimportant but at the time this was a massive economic resource that a new civilisation in the region was looking to exploit on an industrial scale.

This is the crucial area the film skirts around. If we could escape the focus on the individual, what we would see in *The Revenant* would be different cultures and belief systems coming into contact and the resulting potential for violent clashes. The conflict here could be seen to be between an indigenous population and an invading white society originating from Europe; great cultural blocs involved in a clash of civilisations. From this perspective, the trappers are invaders employing military strength in order to move into another country. The indigenous population is being swamped; and, ultimately, exterminated by incomers.

On closer analysis, perhaps, finer gradations and divisions become apparent. The French-Canadian trappers simply see Hikuc as an Indian (Native American) and not as a Pawnee displaced from his homeland by the Sioux. Their response to him, in hanging him from a tree with a label round his neck denoting him straightforwardly as a 'savage', fits their own set of cultural prejudices. At the same time, the white trappers are simply economic migrants pushing beyond the boundaries of their communities in order to find work. In response to Henry's question 'Would you rather hold on to the pelts, or your life?' Fitzgerald responds, 'Life. What life you talkin' about. I ain't got no life. I just got livin'. The only way I get to do that is through these pelts.' Both the American and the French-Canadian trappers are the descendants of economic migrants and/or refugees who came to the New World seeking a new life. And the Sioux and other Native American tribes would seem to be constantly transgressing borders. (Or, is it the absence/fluidity of borders that should be seen as the focus within the relationships between native tribes?)

On the other hand, perhaps the focus should be on the inter-marriage and trade between all of these parties. In other words, it is not the violence that should be emphasised but the ability of people from different cultures to interact in a state of comfortable hybridity. It might be argued, for example, that this was the situation for the original French-Canadian woodsmen, the coureurs de bois, before they were replaced from the late 1600s by state-financed voyageurs, working for licensed fur traders. In a pattern consistently repeated during the state-sponsored expansion of European empires around the globe, Ewers explains how after their initial contact with the tribe the French had gone down in the estimation of the Arikara by the early 1800s. He quotes Pierre-Antoine Tabeau as saying, 'It is only a little while since the Ricara deified the French, who, unhappily, have only too well disabused them by their conduct and their talk.'[50] In the film, this would seem to be something of what is at the back of the statement by Elk Dog (Duane Howard) to the leader of the French trappers, Toussaint (Fabrice Adde), when he says: 'You stand there and talk to me about honour.'

Avoiding the political, the film presents a vague mysticism as being the only way of understanding the world. After saying 'Sioux killed my people', Hikuc is clear that all human beings can do is to suffer, stoically and patiently. 'My heart bleeds', he says. 'But revenge is in the Creator's hands.' And throughout the film, Glass is shown as having dreams, or visions, of his

Figure 6.2 Hawk (Forrest Goodluck) viewed alongside an image of the crucified Christ in *The Revenant*.

dead wife; the film concludes with him labouring his way up a mountainside and looking up to see his wife before him. Whether she is encouraging him to carry on or calling him to the 'other side' is not clear.

A dream sequence of Glass with his dead son, Hawk (Forrest Goodluck), is set within the ruins of a Catholic church with extensive wall paintings. As Hawk turns to look towards his father in a low-angle shot he is juxtaposed with an image of Christ on the cross;[51] and as Hawk walks the length of the church, moving towards his father to embrace him, the crucified Christ comes into full view alongside him (Figure 6.2). From a close-up of Glass's face in this embrace with his son, we cut to a long shot revealing him to be hugging a tree that has grown up through the ruins of the church. Earlier we have seen a deer standing at the end of the church where we later see Hawk. These elements create a curious combination of the natural world and religion. Much of the film has been set within a cold, snowbound winter landscape: a beautiful place, and yet a harsh and inhospitable environment for man. In this scene it is again winter, the trees are stark and bare, there is muddy water on the church floor, and these things alongside the broken walls of the church evoke nothing so strongly as the devastation of war.[52] A close-up of a nail through the feet of Christ early in this scene links to the film in reminding us of the excessive violence against the body to be found at the heart of Christian belief.[53] Within minutes of screen time after this dream sequence, Glass finds Hikuc hanging from a tree with his head tilted to the left in an echo of Christ on the cross. As a version of the noble savage who is also the Good Samaritan in his caring for Glass, Hikuc bears a sign that is perhaps the film's final verdict on humanity, 'on est tous des sauvages'.

If we are overwhelmed by the immersive, graphic detail of *The Revenant*, and by the film's dark mysticism, we have a truly bleak film that is impressive in its attempt to address the human condition. If we refuse this passivity and create our own active reading we have a film that, beyond its bleak existentialism, contains specifics that are of the early twenty-first-century moment – battlefield traumas, mental and physical torture, mutilated bodies, cultural clashes, horrific killings and lawless borderland incidents. In her book *Precarious Life: The Powers of Mourning and Violence*, Judith Butler states: 'In the United States, we have been surrounded with violence, having perpetrated it and perpetrating it still, having suffered it, living in fear of it, planning more of it, if not an open future of infinite war.'[54] Maybe Fitzgerald's final words to Glass are more apt, addressed to him as an all-American hero, than we might at first realise: 'You came all this way, just for your revenge. Well, you enjoy it Glass 'cos there ain't nothin' gonna bring your boy back.' Discussing torture porn, Kerner, says the genre 'potentially posits that we have become the very thing that we are fighting. Revelations about abuses at Abu Ghraib and Guantánamo Bay Prison . . . and the rendition programme fuel torture porn narratives.'[55,56]

Notes

1. Linda Williams, 'Film bodies: gender, genre, and excess', *Film Quarterly*, 1991, 44(4): 2–13; p. 2.
2. Ibid. p. 4.
3. Ibid. p. 5.
4. Ibid. p. 12.
5. Karen Brulliard, 'Move over, DiCaprio. This man really did survive the cold inside a dead horse', *Washington Post*, 26 February 2016. Available at <https://www.washingtonpost.com/news/animalia/wp/2016/02/26/move-over-dicaprio-this-man-really-did-survive-the-cold-inside-a-dead-horse/?utm_term=.62697d938411> (accessed 9 December 2017).
6. John Canfield Ewers, *Plains Indian History and Culture: Essays on Continuity and Change* (Norman: University of Oklahoma Press, 1997), p. 4.
7. There is documentation for more than 4,000 'racial terror lynchings in twelve Southern states between the end of Reconstruction in 1877 and 1950'. See Equal Justice Initiative, *Lynching in America: Confronting the Legacy of Racial Terror: Report Summary*, 2nd edn, Equal Justice Initiative, 2015. Available at <https://lynchinginamerica.eji.org/report/> (accessed 27 November 2017). Jeffrey Kirchmeier suggests that 'although details of the large number of lynchings of Native Americans are not well documented, historians know of several recorded instances of the use of extrajudicial mob violence toward Native American victims'. See Jeffrey L. Kirchmeier, *Imprisoned by the Past: Warren McCleskey and the American Death Penalty* (Oxford: Oxford University Press, 2015), p. 124.

8. Woody Woodhall, 'Creating the sounds for *The Revenant*', *ProVideo Coalition*, 2 January 2016. Available at <https://www.providecoalition.com/creating-the-sounds-for-the-revenant/> (accessed 29 November 2017).
9. Carole Cadwalladr, '*The Revenant* is meaningless pain porn', *The Guardian*, 17 January 2016. Available at <https://www.theguardian.com/commentisfree/2016/jan/17/revenant-leonardo-dicaprio-violent-meaningless-glorification-pain> (accessed 28 November 2017).
10. Ibid.
11. See Aaron Michael Kerner, *Torture Porn in the Wake of 9/11: Horror, Exploitation, and the Cinema of Sensation* (New Brunswick, NJ: Rutgers University Press, 2015), p. 14.
12. Ibid. p. ix.
13. Ibid. p. 14.
14. Michael Sledge, *Soldier Dead: How We Recover, Identify, Bury, and Honour Our Military Fallen* (New York: Columbia University Press, 2005), p. 31.
15. Dominic Hagans, *Wounded Rangers: Under Enemy Fire in Afghanistan* (Cirencester: Mereo, 2013).
16. Ibid. pp. 2–3.
17. Ibid. pp. 89–90.
18. Anthony Swofford, 'Foreword', in Iraq Veterans Against the War and Aaron Glantz, *Winter Soldier: Iraq and Afghanistan: Eyewitness Accounts of the Occupation* (Chicago, IL: Haymarket Books, 2008), p. x.
19. Asbjørn Grønstad, *Transfigurations: Violence, Death and Masculinity in American Cinema* (Amsterdam: Amsterdam University Press, 2008), p. 68.
20. David Herman (ed.), *The Cambridge Companion to Narrative* (Cambridge: Cambridge University Press, 2007), p. 3.
21. Stuart Hall, 'Race, culture, and communications: looking backward and forward at cultural studies', in Marcus E. Green (ed.), *Rethinking Gramsci* (London and New York: Routledge, 2011), p. 16.
22. Ibid. p. 16
23. Clay Landry, 'The real story of Hugh Glass – sources', Museum of the Mountain Man, Pinedale, Wyoming. Available at <http://hughglass.org/sources/> (accessed 2 December 2017).
24. A film version of Glass's survival was made in the 1970s, *Man in the Wilderness* (Richard C. Sarafian, 1971), starring Richard Harris as Zachary Bass.
25. Dixon Wecter, *The Hero in America: A Chronicle of Hero-Worship* (New York: Scribner, [1941] 1963), p. 488.
26. Ray Raphael, *Founding Myths: Stories That Hide Our Patriotic Past* (New York and London: The New Press, 2004), p. 4.
27. David Leeming and Jake Page, *Myths, Legends and Folktales of America: An Anthology* (Oxford and New York: Oxford University Press, 1999), p. 5.
28. Hilde Eliassen Restad, *American Exceptionalism: An Idea that Made a Nation and Remade the World* (London and New York: Routledge, 2015), p. x.
29. Ibid. p. 4.

30. Godfrey Hodgson, *The Myth of American Exceptionalism* (New Haven, CT and London: Yale University Press, 2009), p. 27.
31. While discussing Arthur W. Herbig's essay in their collection: 'Discursive characterization as embodiment and critique: the divergent rhetorical trajectories of Pat Tillman as an American hero', in Jason A. Edwards and David Weiss (eds), *The Rhetoric of American Exceptionalism: Critical Essays* (Jefferson, NC: McFarland, 2011), pp. 132–52.
32. Jason A. Edwards and David Weiss (eds), *The Rhetoric of American Exceptionalism: Critical Essays* (Jefferson, NC: McFarland, 2011), p. 6.
33. William V. Spanos, *American Exceptionalism in the Age of Globalization: The Specter of Vietnam* (Albany, NY: State University of New York Press, 2008), p. 66.
34. Ibid. p. 67.
35. Ibid. p. 89.
36. Ibid. p. 90.
37. Brian Massumi, 'Notes on the translation and Acknowledgements', in Gilles Deleuze and Félix Guattari, *A Thousand Plateaus: Capitalism and Schizophrenia* (London and New York: Continuum, [1987] 2004), pp. xvii–xx.
38. Eric Shouse, 'Feeling, emotion, affect', *M/C Journal*, 2005, 8(6). Available at < http://journal.media-culture.org.au/0512/03-shouse.php > (accessed 23 November 2017).
39. Ibid.
40. Ibid.
41. Ibid.
42. Ibid.
43. Virginia E. Demos, 'An affect revolution: Silvan Tompkin's affect theory', in Virginia E. Demos (ed.), *Exploring Affect: The Selected Writings of Silvan S. Tompkins* (New York: Press Syndicate of the University of Cambridge, 1995), p. 19.
44. Shouse, 'Feeling, emotion, affect', 2005.
45. Xavier Aldana Reyes, *Body Gothic: Corporeal Transgression in Contemporary Literature and Horror Film* (Cardiff: University of Wales Press, 2014), p. 125.
46. Anne Thompson, 'Alejandro G. Iñárritu on leading Oscar nominee *The Revenant*: "This was a film that easily could kill you"', *IndieWire*, 14 January 2016. Available at <http://www.indiewire.com/2016/01/alejandro-g-inarritu-on-leading-oscar-nominee-the-revenant-this-was-a-film-that-easily-could-kill-you-175267/> (accessed 7 December 2017).
47. Woodhall, 'Creating the sounds for *The Revenant*', 2016.
48. D. J. Wishart, *The Fur Trade of the American West, 1807–1840: A Geographical Synthesis* (Lincoln: University of Nebraska Press, [1979] 1992), p. 10.
49. Eric Jay Dolin, *Fur, Fortune, and Empire: The Epic History of the Fur Trade in America* (New York and London: W. W. Norton, 2010), pp. xv–xvi.
50. Ewers, *Plains Indian History and Culture*, 1997, p. 28.
51. This may be based on 'The Crucifixion of Christ' (1512) by Hans Baldung Grien (1484/5–1545) in the Gemäldegalerie, Matthäikirchplatz, Berlin.

Refusing a Middle East setting, this work depicts a wooded foreground set against an icy, mountainous backdrop.
52. In particular, the scene is perhaps reminiscent of First World War landscapes on the Western Front.
53. The detail from 'The Inferno' (early fifteenth century), by Giovanni da Modena in the Basilica di San Petronio in Bologna, Italy, which follows this shot of Christ's feet, is from a painting which depicts all manner of bodily tortures based on Dante Alighieri's poem. The violence includes bear-like creatures mauling and eating people.
54. Judith Butler, *Precarious Life: The Powers of Mourning and Violence* (London and New York: Verso, 2004), p. 28.
55. Kerner, *Torture Porn in the Wake of 9/11*, 2015, p. 3.
56. Adam Lowenstein rejects 'torture porn' as a term, in favour of 'spectacle horror'. He discusses this as 'a mode of direct, visceral engagement with viewers'. See Adam Lowenstein, 'Spectacle horror and *Hostel*: why "torture porn" does not exist', *Critical Quarterly*, 2011, 53(1): 42–60. Lowenstein emphasises the importance of seeing on-screen violence in relation to the specific target audience the material is aimed at.

CHAPTER 7

The Anchorless Postmodern Experience within an Ahistorical Filmic Space: *Django Unchained* (2012)

I

Django Unchained (2012) and *Inglourious Basterds* (2009) constitute a linked pair of films within Quentin Tarantino's body of directed work. With these films he addressed two equally horrific episodes from human history. In the earlier war film, *Inglourious Basterds*, Tarantino focused on the Nazi Holocaust during the Second World War; and with the Western, *Django Unchained*, he considered slavery within the United States during the nineteenth century. A connection to Germany was maintained in this second film through the character of Dr King Schultz (Christoph Waltz), a German bounty hunter operating in the Deep South just prior to the American Civil War.[1] Particularly because of this character it becomes difficult for any viewer who knows both films to avoid making connections between the histories of Germany and the United States. Together, the two films constitute what Oliver C. Speck described as a genre unique to Tarantino, 'the historical revenge fantasy'.[2] Speck says:

> There are, of course, countless films that are set in the past and that take liberties with historical accuracy . . . However, only *Django Unchained* and *Inglourious Basterds* allow us to imagine the revenge of the tortured – the Jews, the slaves – on the leader of the oppressive regime – Hitler, the slaveholder.[3]

The parallel is clear: in the same way the monstrous atrocity of the Holocaust looms within Germany's history, so too the hideous human abuse of slavery hangs over America. Both events operate as an unmentionable ghostly presence/absence on the edges of the purview of subsequent generations. Tarantino has said he believes the United States is 'one of the only countries that has not been forced to look its past sins completely in the face'.[4] The German writer W. G. 'Max' Sebald, amongst others, spoke of the post-war 'conspiracy of silence' that operated in Germany:

> Only when we were 17 were we confronted with a documentary film of the opening of the Belsen camp. There it was, and we somehow had to get our minds around it – which of course we didn't . . . In the mid-60s I could not conceive that these events had happened only a few years back.[5]

In considering the German experience, Sebald warned of the dangers for any country in pushing its population towards maintaining a 'silence about the past'.[6,7] On a similar note, Henry Louis Gates Jr, interviewing Tarantino about *Django Unchained*, said he felt people in America had 'become inured to the suffering and pain of slavery'.[8] He believed they had distanced themselves in such a way that they could not 'experience the anxiety, the stress, the terror, the horrible pain, et cetera, that came with the slave experience'.[9]

II

Tarantino has expressed intense interest in the history of the period and place within which this film is set: 'I've always wanted to recreate cinematically that world of the antebellum South, of America under slavery.'[10] For him this would seem to run alongside a passionate belief in the need for the US to face up to the brutal reality of slavery. Commenting on the release of his film in the same period as *Lincoln* (Steven Spielberg, 2012) and *Twelve Years a Slave* (Steve McQueen, 2013) he said: 'Frankly, nothing could have me more excited, from an American storytelling perspective and an American healing perspective.'[11]

However, for Tarantino, this genuine interest and impassioned belief always exists within the context of cinema. What appeals to Tarantino is recreating the antebellum South 'cinematically' and his interest in the coincidence of three films on slavery is within the context of 'American storytelling'. In critically evaluating *Django Unchained* there might be a sense in which it would be wrong to criticise the film for failing to reflect historical reality. This a film which, despite genuine concerns on the part of those involved in its making for the ramifications of slavery for America,[12] does not look to exist in relation to a real space and time but instead within an intense matrix of film references.

What is created is a postmodern textual space, a plethora of images and simulations. What we have presented on the screen is Jean Baudrillard's simulation as 'a real without origin or reality: a hyperreal'.[13] The filmmaker indulges in, and the audience is pleasured within, an endless spiral of filmic play. We are placed within a process of filmic re-play within which we feel ourselves constantly looping into and out of other texts. We are immersed in images that have 'no relation to reality whatsoever'.[14] The film becomes 'its own pure simulacrum'[15] and we find ourselves positioned within a deceptively 'real' unreal 'reality'. In consuming these images, in desiring and seeking out these images, we are placing ourselves inside an alternative reality. Baudrillard's suggestion is that this space within which we plunge ourselves may become more 'real' than 'the real' itself, so that within the experience of hyperreality we are unable to differentiate between reality and simulation. The space into which we are taken and through which we move does not exist in relation in any historical sense but within a continuous present, an exciting, embracing, genre-induced swirl of images.

III

Tarantino's references to films and further elements of culture operate at a variety of levels. Firstly, *Django Unchained* exists in stark contradistinction to Hollywood classics such as *Gone with the Wind* (Victor Fleming, 1939) and *The Birth of a Nation* (D. W. Griffith, 1915). The filmmaker has described himself as 'obsessed' with *The Birth of a Nation* and the making of that film:[16] 'I think it gave rebirth to the Klan, and all the blood that was spilled – until the early sixties, practically.'[17] Tarantino's most obvious visual reference to *The Birth of a Nation* comes in a night-time scene in which a white mob on horseback sets out to attack and kill Schultz and the former slave he has freed, Django Freeman (Jamie Foxx). By focusing on the farce of the vigilantes attempting to ride their horses while unable to see where they are going because of the hoods they are wearing, Tarantino ridicules white supremacists. Just as crucially he also mocks those scenes at the end of *The Birth of a Nation* in which a Ku Klux Klan force on horseback wearing white robes and masks wrest back control of a southern town from former black slaves freed after the Civil War. By extension, he also derides the racist politics embodied in Griffiths's film as a whole. Further, when the white mob flees and Schultz designates them 'cowards' Tarantino effectively labels with that same term the KKK and any similar right-wing organisations that may have continued to exist into the present.

Inevitably, since *Django Unchained* is a Western, Tarantino also sees his film in relation to the work of John Ford. In fact, he sees his film as positioned in opposition to the entire tradition of classical Hollywood Westerns. His distaste for the 'history' to be found in Ford-style Westerns (if we take his words at surface value, at least) could not be clearer. Speaking of Ford, he has said: 'To say the least, I hate him. Forget about faceless Indians he killed like zombies. It really is people like that who kept alive this idea of Anglo-Saxon humanity compared to everybody else's humanity.'[18] In this sentiment and in his research, Tarantino is in line with historical reality. In *The Conquest of Texas: Ethnic Cleansing in the Promised Land, 1820–1875*, Gary Clayton Anderson discusses growing 'vigilantism' in Texas in 1858,[19] that is, in exactly the time and place Tarantino is placing the audience in the opening to his film. 'Put simply,' says Anderson, 'the majority of Anglo-Texans, many of whom played major roles in local government, supported ethnic cleansing in one fashion, or another.'[20]

And yet, even as he rejects the ideology of the American Western tradition, Tarantino pays homage not only to classic character types from the genre, such as the loner and the gunfighter, but also to the stylistic visualisation of the West. It is true that the opening to *Django Unchained* parallels the first scene in Sergio Corbucci's Spaghetti Western, *Django* (1966, Italy/Spain), and this is made explicit by having the same song, composed by Luis Bacalov, on the soundtrack. However, visually the opening is a homage to Westerns directed by Budd Boetticher, such as *The Tall T* (1957), *Ride Lonesome* (1959) and *Comanche Station* (1960), which were shot in the same Alabama Hills in California used here by Tarantino.

IV

The first image of Django is of his back rising into the foreground to display the scars across his back (Figure 7.1). We are immediately confronted with the brutality of the African American experience; but this is

Figure 7.1 Immediate visual representation of the brutality of the African American experience, in *Django Unchained* (Quentin Tarantino, 2012).

also Tarantino referencing the most (in)famous image relating to slavery to emerge during the Civil War, that of a former slave whose disfigured back was photographed after he escaped to Union lines in 1863.[21] By contrast (and Tarantino would hope we are aware of this), the opening to *Gone with the Wind* presents slavery as existing within a rural idyll, 'a land of Cavaliers and Cotton Fields called the Old South'. We are told that 'in this pretty world Gallantry took its last bow', but that it is now 'a Civilization gone with the wind'. This text is placed against a background of contented black farmworkers and a blackface minstrel tune, *Dixie (I Wish I was in Dixie)*, that became an anthem for the South during the Civil War. The notion of a supposed past Golden Age, an Arcadia, that is embodied in this opening could not clash more forcefully than with the scarred backs of the line of slaves and the sound of their clinking leg chains found in the opening to *Django Unchained*.

And yet Tarantino's presentation of black male bodies also offers a very particular, media-mediated representation. The attempt to position *Django Unchained* in direct opposition to the institutional racism of American history and Hollywood film history is clear. However, the image of the maimed bare torsos of black men in chains sets in motion further complex debates. In an article on *Uncle Tom's Cabin, or Life Among the Lowly* (1852), Marianne Noble refers to the concept of 'the sentimental wound', which she describes as 'a bodily experience of anguish caused by identification with the pain of another'.[22] Noble explains that the author of *Uncle Tom's Cabin*, Harriet Beecher Stowe, attempted to bring about an intensity of identification on the part of the reader so that they might empathize with the slave's position but the unintended effect was to create eroticism.

> The effort to provoke in readers an experience of intersubjective connectedness at the level of the body had the unanticipated effect of eroticizing the reading experience, and in so doing, it undermined its own effort to humanize the slaves, who were positioned as erotic objects of sympathy rather than subjects in their own right.[23]

Cassandra Jackson has subjected the Civil War image of the scarred escaped slave, referred to above, to somewhat similar criticism. The disfigured black body, she argues, is brought before the gaze of the viewer and then placed into a narrative by the viewer, therefore becoming subject to the power and control of the viewer.[24] She suggests, 'the wounded black body' functions 'as a means through which an able-bodied white audience could vicariously experience the bodily pain of the mutilated slave, while also being empowered to ameliorate that pain via activism'.[25] Summarising her position on the photograph, she said, 'while it invites the viewer to share in experiencing the body of the subject, it also re-inscribes otherness'.[26]

Could we subject Tarantino's opening images, indeed his whole film, to similar analysis? Is this a 'vicarious' experience for a 'white audience'? Do these images 're-inscribe otherness'? Is there an 'eroticizing' of the black male (and, later, female) body? In analysing Robert Mapplethorpe's photographs of the black male body from the exhibition *Black Males* (Galerie Jurka, Amsterdam, 1980) and within his *Black Book*,[27] Kobena Mercer discusses these images as 'a cultural artefact that says something about certain ways in which white people "look" at black people and how, in this way of looking, black male sexuality is perceived as something different, excessive, Other'.[28] He suggests Mapplethorpe's *Black Book* 'facilitates the imaginary projection of certain racial and sexual fantasies about the black male body'.[29] However much Tarantino may suggest he was interested in presenting through these images the abuse of slavery, the audience is actually being placed within the media/cultural sphere identified by Mercer.[30]

V

Tarantino's film has also been widely discussed in relation to Spaghetti Westerns and blaxploitation (and sexploitation) movies from the 1970s. Dennis Abrams's description of blaxploitation does not suggest this phenomenon was much more than exploitation:

> Roles for black actors may have been available in the blaxploitation era, but the characters were still two-dimensional and cartoonlike. In addition, few opportunities arose for black writers, producers, and directors; almost all of the blaxploitation films were conceived and created by whites.[31]

On the other hand, Jasmine Nichole Cobb and John L. Jackson point out that as much as blaxploitation movies have been criticized they have also been praised for fostering 'racial pride' and for the way they 'emphasize/fantasize the black man's triumph against whiteness and institutional racism'.[32] This is where Tarantino would seem to lay the emphasis. He has described *The Legend of Nigger Charley* (Martin Goldman, 1972, US), for example, as an 'empowering movie'.[33]

The bit-part role in *Django Unchained* of Chicken Charlie (Omar J. Dorsey), a slave-fighter owned by slave-owner Calvin J. Candie (Leonardo DiCaprio), may be a reference to the film *Charley One-Eye* (Don Chaffey, 1973, US/UK) which is perhaps the nearest thing there is to a British Spaghetti Western.[34] This film has a character, The Black Man (Richard Roundtree), who is hung upside down in order to be whipped in much the same way Django is strung up in order to be abused first of all by Billy Crash (Walton Goggins) and then by Stephen (Samuel L. Jackson). The Black Man has lines such as 'I only kills whites', which essentially is the 'job' Django takes up as a bounty hunter.

Other blaxploitation Westerns also place African Americans in central roles. *The Legend of Nigger Charley* features three escaped slaves, Charley (Fred Williamson), Toby (D'Urville Martin) and Joshua (Don Pedro Colley), who flee their plantation after one of them kills the plantation owner. Williamson described his character as 'a guy who starts off as a slave, beats up his slave master, escapes from the plantation, goes West, and becomes a gunfighter'.[35] He felt black audiences had a hunger for 'new and liberating images of themselves'.[36] As the screenwriter for another blaxploitation Western, *Boss Nigger* (Jack Arnold, 1975, US), Williamson wrote a role for himself as a black bounty hunter. The trailer for this film described Williamson, as Boss, and his fellow black bounty hunter, Amos (D'Urville Martin), riding into 'a white man's town' and bringing with them 'black man's law'. The duo's work as bounty hunters is described by Daniel O'Brien – in a phrase that might also describe Schultz's actions in *Django Unchained* – as 'their legally sanctioned, if morally questionable, capitalist enterprise'.[37]

Django Unchained also has clear echoes of *Darktown Strutters* (William Witney, 1975, US). In this film characters portrayed as members of the Ku Klux Klan are used to comic effect, there are black dudes exuding an aura of 'cool', and there is a scene around the dinner table involving house-slaves and a white master who sits at the head of the table and bemoans the fact that he has to 'listen to the darkies complain'. The final comedic 'battle' between the black characters and actors parodying the Klan takes place in front of a white mansion displaying an antebellum neoclassical architectural style.

Darktown Strutters also has female actors, led by Trina Parks as Syreena, performing roles that are reminiscent of the sexploitation movies Tarantino also references. In *The Hot Box* (Joe Viola, 1972, US) female prisoners are punished in a 'hot box', described in trailers as 'a tropical torture chamber'. The treatment of Broomhilda in *Django Unchained* when, after attempting to run away, she is placed inside a metal, coffin-like hot-box is a more realistic portrayal of sadistic brutality but the link is clearly there. Connections to other sexploitation movies are not always so blatant. However, *Black Mama, White Mama* (Eddie Romero, 1973, US/Philippines), like *The Hot Box*, is about people (in these films it is women) attempting to escape imprisonment. In what could be described, like *Django Unchained*, as an interracial buddy movie Lee (Pam Grier) and Karen (Margaret Markov) escape while chained together.[38]

In the Spaghetti Western *Django*, the central character, Django (Franco Nero), is a gunslinger with superhuman fighting prowess. In the final scene, he is cornered in a cemetery by a group of red-hooded, white supremacist vigilantes, but despite having severely injured hands he is able to kill all of them, confirming his status as a figure of folklore or myth.[39] Tarantino sees his hero in a similar vein:

> I guess the reason that made me put pen to paper was to give black American males a Western hero, give them a cool folkloric hero that could actually be empowering and actually pay back blood for blood.[40]

In addition to *Django*, Tarantino references a series of similar Spaghetti (and related) Westerns. In the Zapata Western *Il mercenario/The Mercenary* (Corbucci, 1968, Italy/Spain), for example, Riccioli/Curly (Jack Palance) is shot in similar way to the plantation owner, Candie, in *Django Unchained*. In his use of a fantasy ending Tarantino's film is entirely different to Corbucci's *Il grande silenzio/The Great Silence* (1968, Italy/France), which has the bleakest of finales with the death of the 'hero' and his love interest and the massacre of the townspeople. However, the anti-hero in that film, Loco/Tigrero (Klaus Kinski), is portrayed as a racist: after killing a black man the comment he is given is, 'What times we live in, when a black man is worth as much as a white man.'[41] And thematically, the concept of the 'massacre of the innocents' with which *The Great Silence* concludes and the notion that the law is simply a means of maintaining the status quo between those in power and those who are powerless which runs throughout Corbucci's film are both ideas that are central to *Django Unchained*.

Other Westerns referenced by Tarantino would include *Buck and the Preacher* (Sidney Poitier, 1972, US), *Skin Game* (Paul Bogart, 1971, US) and *The Scalphunters* (Sydney Pollack, 1968, US). In *Buck and the Preacher*, set after the Civil War, Buck (Poitier) leads wagon trains of African Americans west. They are attacked by whites ('night-riders') employed by plantation owners. In the comedy Western *Skin Game*, set during the antebellum period, the central characters, Quincy (James Garner) and Jason (Louis Gossett Jr), form an interracial partnership.[42] There is also a brutal slave hunter who is shown with a group of chained slaves and a plantation owner who has Jason whipped. *The Scalphunters* again features a central black and white pairing. A slave, Joseph Lee (Ossie Davis), agrees to help fur trader Joe Bass (Burt Lancaster) recover hides from a group of Kiowa in the hope of getting to Mexico to escape slavery. The scalphunters of the title are similar not only to the slave hunters in *Django Unchained* but also (ironically) to Schultz and Django as bounty hunters.

Beyond Westerns, Tarantino's film echoes a string of other more mainstream Hollywood movies. Amongst these would be the ultimate interracial buddy movie, *The Defiant Ones* (Stanley Kramer, 1958, US), featuring the central, chained-together, characters of Noah Cullen (Sidney Poitier) and John 'Joker' Jackson (Tony Curtis). There is also the melodrama *Band of Angels* (Raoul Walsh, 1957, US), which follows *Gone with the Wind* in employing a romanticised Deep South plantation context and using Clark Gable as its leading man.[43] Straddling mainstream Hollywood films and cult movies from the 1970s, *Django Unchained* contains obvious references to *Mandingo* (Richard Fleischer, 1975). This film, in which a slave, Ganymede (Ken Norton), is kept by a slave owner as a prize fighter, has been seen as a form of mainstream blaxploitation. The fight between the slaves Ganymede and Topaz (Duane Allen), described as 'a fight to the finish with no holds barred', includes kicking, biting and gouging, and ends with the death of Topaz.

Extending the references to exploitation movies, *Django Unchained* also includes a crucially important mondo documentary, or docudrama, in its chain of allusions. *Addio Zio Tom / Goodbye Uncle Tom* (Gualtiero Jacopetti and Franco Prosperi, 1971, Italy) uses actors to re-stage scenes researched from the history of African American slavery. It begins by looking at the legacy of Martin Luther King Jr in relation to the concept of the 'Uncle Tom', the black man seen as excessively obedient to whites and stoical in response to violence: it ends with a member of the Black Panther Party reading about Nat Turner, who led a violent slave revolt in Virginia in 1831, and fantasising about brutally killing whites.[44] Wilson Jeremiah Moses has suggested the 'black messianic tradition' has not been limited to passive concepts such as 'blessed are the weak' but has also included 'motifs of vengeance and retribution'.[45] Django clearly embodies the role of the messianic deliverer of vengeance; and, while it might be incorrect to align Stephen (Samuel L. Jackson), Candie's house slave-cum-household manager, with Martin Luther King, he is clearly constituted as the ultimate 'Uncle Tom'. Furthermore, *Addio Zio Tom* is based on the premise of Europeans travelling through history to the antebellum Deep South in order to make a documentary. These filmmakers talk of 'Rousseau, Diderot, Voltaire' and, like Tarantino's Schultz, clearly highlight the ideas of the Enlightenment. In addition, the first docudrama scene is set at a dinner table, there is a public castration, runaway slaves are shown being killed by slave hunters, there is a pseudo-scientific discussion of the mental inadequacies of blacks and slaves are shown wearing metal masks and being branded with hot irons.

VI

As mention of the Enlightenment might suggest, *Django Unchained* contains cultural references beyond the cinematic. Typically for Tarantino, these range from the ridiculous to the sublime. Candie runs a plantation called Candyland and, amongst other possibilities, this name would seem to reference the children's board game, *Candy Land*. This is a game of chance with the outcome solely dependent on the shuffling of a pack of cards. There are no strategies players can adopt, nor are there choices or decisions that have to be made. Consequently, the result of the 'game' is totally predetermined. Advertisements for *Candy Land* suggest, 'You don't have to know how to read or count to have loads of fun in Candy Land', but by contrast Tarantino's other cultural references emphasise the importance of education. Strangely perhaps, in view of his occupation as a bounty hunter, Schultz is associated with the European Enlightenment. Discovering the name of Django's lover, Broomhilda, Schultz tells the story of Brünnhilde and Siegfried; or at least a small climactic part of what is an epic saga. Schultz focuses on how Siegfried as the fearless hero rescues Brünnhilde from within a ring of fire. Effectively, Tarantino (and within the film, Schultz) begins to position Django, this non-Aryan, African American, as a warrior capable of matching the status of heroes from white mythology.[46] Django is the black hero who will walk through fire to save the woman he loves. He may also be, if Tarantino is looking towards Richard Wagner's romantic re-telling of Brünnhilde and Siegfried's tale in *Der Ring des Nibelungen* (*The Ring of the Nibelung*), the hero who will sweep away the old gods and usher in a new era founded on human love.

In Candie's library, as Schultz begins talking about the French writer Alexandre Dumas, a further strand of cultural references, perhaps the most important for the whole film, becomes clear. Earlier, the audience witnessed Candie allowing dogs to kill and seemingly eat one of his former prize fighters, D'Artagnan. That name now resonates as we hear Schultz discussing Dumas and recall D'Artagnan was the central character in a series of novels by Dumas. 'I was wondering what Dumas would make of all of this', says Schultz, standing in the Candieland library. And he reveals to Candie that Dumas was black. Moments before, disturbed by flashbacks of D'Artagnan being ripped apart by dogs, Schultz has rushed towards Candie's sister, Lara (Laura Cayoutte), playing Ludwig van Beethoven's 'Für Elise' on the harp. He has demanded she 'stop playing Beethoven'. In forcibly preventing Lara from performing, Schultz reveals how disturbed he is that such an expression of culture should find a place within a house founded on barbarism (Figure 7.2). Since Schultz is

Figure 7.2 Schultz (Christoph Waltz) shows his distress at Beethoven being played in the Candieland mansion, in *Django Unchained*.

German, Tarantino might also be suggesting the hypocrisy of America in seeing itself as morally superior to Germany because of that country's role in the Holocaust. Tarantino is playing out the clash between Enlightenment values and the moral standards of a Deep South slave-owning elite. At the same time, this is also allowing him to confront contemporary right-wing prejudices. The figure of Dumas is critically important to Tarantino (and Schultz) in this respect.

Michel Fabre sees Dumas 'as a dazzling example of French recognition of black literary merit'; adding, 'few French people considered his skin color, but in American terms he was a negro'.[47] Dumas's grandmother was a slave on the French island of Saint-Domingue but his father, Thomas-Alexandre Dumas, also known as Alexandre Dumas, became a general in the French army. This man described himself as a 'sincere lover of liberty and equality, convinced that all free men are equals'.[48] The younger Alexandre Dumas played a small part in a republican uprising in Paris in 1832, and then fled to Switzerland in 1833 when it looked as if he might be arrested for his beliefs.[49] The depth of the references at work at this point would seem undeniable: the younger Dumas as the literary figure and the older Dumas as the principled soldier combining in an image of Enlightenment values embodied within black ethnicity.

VII

Connections and associations to a whole range of classical Hollywood films, blaxploitation and sexploitation movies, operatic and literary sources, and other popular cultural forms are all found within *Django Unchained*.

However, it seems important to be clear that for the majority of spectators most of these layered cultural allusions will not be noticed. Generally, there will be only the generic experience of a pleasuring, postmodern, maelstrom of images. In fact, it is more likely that moments from within Tarantino's own past work will be evoked rather than the films, books and music considered above. Django strung upside down and helpless in an outbuilding and about to be sliced up by Billy Crash (Walton Goggins), for example, will exist in relation to Mr Blonde (Michael Madsen) torturing Marvin Nash (Kirk Baltz) in *Reservoir Dogs*, and other scenes in this vein. And then there are the scenes of shoot-outs and explosions, the distinctive tone of the humour, the use of slow motion and, perhaps above all, the idiosyncratic dialogue. Despite the existence of what has been outlined as an intricately woven fabric of allusions, this particular element of pastiche, of postmodern cobbling together of elements from other works, never really comes into view for the average filmgoer.

This is not to doubt the intensity with which Tarantino has constructed his narrative. It is impossible to argue the cross-referencing at work around Schultz, for example, has not been carried out with careful attention to detail. As an example, consider the scene towards the end of the film in which Django enters the cabin of the slave hunters and slaughters them. Just before he enters we are shown an image from a stereoscope that a female slave hunter is looking at. It shows two people in front of an ancient Greek temple. The most famous building of this sort with columns to the front and sides would be the Parthenon in Athens, but this is actually the Second Temple of Hera in Paestum in southern Italy. The question becomes, why has Tarantino included this image? If you think of Schultz as linked to the European Enlightenment, and you reflect on how young well-to-do men would complete their education by embarking on the Grand Tour, you might recall that this cultural experience often culminated in a visit to Paestum. If you then remember Schultz referring to Dumas and reflect on Dumas as perhaps the ultimate embodiment of Enlightenment belief in 'liberté, égalité, fraternité' you might wonder if Dumas ever embarked on the Grand Tour. And if you find out Dumas wrote several travel books you might discover one of these books refers to him going to Paestum.[50] And if you turn to that book you might come across these lines:

> En rentrant à l'hôtel, un grand jeune homme me croisa ; je crus le reconnaître, et j'allai à lui: en effet, c'était le frère de mademoiselle Schulz, avec lequel j'avais ébauché connaissance il y avait deux mois ... J'exposai à monsieur Schulz les causes de mon retour à Messine. Aussi curieux de pittoresque que qui que ce soit au monde, il m'offrit d'être mon compagnon de voyage.[51]

And you realise just how much integrated depth of cultural reference Tarantino has placed within a seemingly unimportant shot that we glimpse in passing.[52] We would have to conjecture the female slave hunter has become fascinated by a photographic viewing device found amongst the dead Schultz's possessions.[53]

However, despite Tarantino's real investment in research, the experience of the spectator watching *Django Unchained* depends on the creation of a deliberate disjuncture between historical reality and the cinematic event. In contrast to almost all of Tarantino's other movies this film employs moments which attempt to foreground historical reality. The opening, for example, shows slaves being moved as a chain gang from one place to another; and Foxx has spoken of how Tarantino pointed out, in no uncertain terms, that at this stage Django had to be played as a slave with all that might entail in terms of dejection and subservience.[54,55] For the most part though, rather than historical reality this film employs cinematic excess and exists within its own virtual narrative space. The inevitable result is that the audience is able to escape the reality of the slave experience. In a way, this would seem strange given that, as already mentioned, Tarantino has stressed that beyond providing his audience with the excitement of cinema he was also interested in exposing the way America has been able to escape confronting the sins of its past.[56] But in his filmmaking Tarantino is wedded to postmodernism. He cannot escape transporting his audience into an ahistorical space within which all sense of the linear (if highly disputed) narrative of history is lost. His professed interest in history is swamped by his postmodernist cinematic technique. M. Keith Booker's verdict on *Pulp Fiction*, which he says 'openly presents itself as a cinematic spectacle, a collection of references to earlier movies, and as such is a perfect illustration of the phenomenon of pastiche in postmodern film',[57] is absolutely appropriate for *Django Unchained*. For Booker, 'the way *Pulp Fiction*'s allusions to films (and other cultural artefacts) slip and slide around in time suggests not a renewal of the past so much as a refusal to recognize historical sequence or to historicize its various references'.[58] With, first of all, *Inglourious Basterds* (2009) and then *Django Unchained*, Tarantino moved towards historical subjects, but the effect of his filmmaking technique has been to reconfirm the spectator's position within a virtual present. Tarantino and his cast may be able to extract themselves from this position so that in post-screening interviews they are able to re-assert their liberal credentials in relation to race but this may not be so simple for the audience.[59] The audience is left within a seamless media space of 'entertainment'.

Tim Woods discusses *Pulp Fiction* in terms of displaying 'a plurality of styles and voices which circulate within a flattened, de-historicised space'.⁶⁰ In this, he is situating Tarantino's work in relation to theories of postmodernism advanced by Fredric Jameson. Jameson suggested the 'formal features' of postmodernism expressed 'the deeper logic' of the current 'social system', and the keynote of this 'late, consumer or multinational capitalism', he said, was 'the disappearance of a sense of history'.⁶¹ He put forward the proposition that 'our entire contemporary social system' had 'begun to live in a perpetual present'.⁶² For Jameson we lived in a society that had become 'incapable of dealing with time and history'.⁶³ For the audience, the stars of this film, Jamie Foxx, Christoph Waltz and Leonardo DiCaprio, exist more in relation to their other film roles and their media profiles than they do in relation to America's historical past. Similarly, Tarantino's film itself primarily exists within the perpetual presence of his other works. This is the contradiction at the heart of *Django Unchained*: the nature of an internally riven society is clearly apprehended by Tarantino but in the face of this all that can be imaged and presented to the audience is a descent into violence.

> As far as I'm concerned, especially as a quarter Cherokee Indian, America is responsible for two holocausts in its country: the eradication of the indigenous Indians and the slavery that they put Africans, and Jamaicans, and West Indians (under) during the slave trade for 245 years.⁶⁴

The clarity of the vision of the profile of the US only seems to make the decline into fantastical escapism more urgent and desperate in the face of the inability to find solutions to absolute dislocation. Tarantino shows us the criss-crossed scars on Django's back, Broomhilda being whipped and D'Artagnan being ripped apart by dogs, but these experiences are no more than points on the graph of the emotional ride created for us. Tarantino is clear that his business is to make an entertaining movie and that this sits within a different realm to historical reality.

> I wasn't trying to tell a *Schindler's List* movie I was trying to tell an exciting adventure story that you could get caught up in but inside of that I wanted it to take place within the backdrop of slavery.⁶⁵

Ultimately, the immersion in hip/cult, postmodern film culture operates as a 'get-out' clause for a director unable to offer answers. Tarantino's movie begins to knock at the door of 'Otherness'. Its liberal subterfuge is that it is addressing the big, unspoken issue for America, when in fact – even leaving aside its creation of an unreal ahistorical space, within a twenty-first-century context, considering the 'sins of the past' allows us to sidestep the 'sins of the present'. Those detained in Guantanamo Bay have been reported as living in 'cramped conditions, excessive heat, poor sanitation'.[66] The circumstances experienced by individuals within this detention camp carry eerie echoes of slavery:

> The conditions of detention remained harsh – he was at times chained to a wall of his cell and subjected to long periods of loud music. He was continually threatened by soldiers with dogs, sticks, and rifles.[67]

In the deep, deep South, far from the seat of American government, captives shuffle in shackles. They are kept in inhumane conditions because they are seen as being beyond the law, not subject to the democratic rights normally afforded to others.

VIII

Schultz is, perhaps, a peculiar character to have as a carrier of European Enlightenment values. He is a bounty hunter who describes himself as someone involved in 'a flesh for cash business'. The US currently has a foreign policy programme designed to 'take out' suspected terrorists, or suspected associates of terrorists, using exactly Schultz's methods for the execution of Smitty Bacall (Michael Bacall). He is shot in front of his young son by Django and Schultz as he ploughs a field near his homestead. Django, as a trainee operative, is shown Bacall's name on a 'wanted poster' and persuaded by Schultz to kill him from a distance. Faced with Django's moral concerns Schultz tells him, 'Quit your pussyfooting and shoot him', and Django complies. In discussing drone warfare, Ram Manikkalingam has suggested:

> To engage in this kind of killing is not easy. And just as the drone humanizes the enemy – he becomes a living, breathing feeling person – to kill, you must dehumanize him. So drones simultaneously humanize and dehumanize the enemy combatant, noncombatant, bystander, child, father, mother, and grandparent.[68]

Schultz operates with impunity because he has names on 'wanted lists' from the US authorities. Drone strikes have been much documented in recent years, for example:

> On 30 September 2011, a U.S. drone strike killed Anwar Al-Aulaqi, an American citizen who had been placed on government 'kill-list' over a year before, and Samir Khan, another American citizen. Two weeks later, on 14 October, another U.S. drone strike in Yemen killed Anwar Al-Aulaqi's son, 16-year-old Abdulrahman Al-Aulaqi, as he was eating dinner with his teenage cousin at an open air restaurant.[69]

Schultz executes those on his list, confident that they are 'guilty' because their name appears on his 'roll-call' of bad guys.[70]

As Schultz and Django move into Mississippi to rescue Broomhilda they are operating deep within enemy territory. They take the fight behind enemy lines, where they need to live by their wits and are always in danger of being exposed as undercover operatives. In the Anglo-European Western world audiences believe in these sorts of heroes: men who are 'out there' and are prepared to walk through fire to complete their mission. This is 'our' common folkloric myth leading to the worship of men who are able to, as Tarantino described it, 'pay back blood for blood'. Whether the film is directed by Ford or Tarantino, the Western's belief is not in ordinary people but in the 'exceptional' man. As Samuel Perry points out, Tarantino is wedded to the idea of the frontier hero, the self-contained individual who is the bringer of retribution.[71]

David Leonard has described *Django Unchained* as a white-centred narrative that offers white redemption.[72] Apart from Django, none of the other slaves are shown as either willing or able to challenge white supremacy. Tarantino himself has described Django as special: 'the fact is, Django is an exceptional human being. That's why he is able to rise to this occasion.'[73] This idea of the 'exceptional' African American has been a prevalent white American concept stretching back over generations. In a book on US history written before 1900, James Schouler suggested: 'Nothing, however, made American slavery on the whole so tolerable a condition for both enslaver and enslaved as the innate patience, docility, and child-like simplicity of the negro as a race.'[74] His view of African Americans saw them as 'a black servile race, sensuous, stupid, brutish, obedient to the whip, children in imagination'.[75] Writing in the late 1950s, the historian Stanley M. Elkins characterised Frederick Douglass's book *My Bondage and My Freedom* as 'obviously not the work of an ordinary slave'.[76] Disturbingly, Perry has pointed out *Django Unchained* 'chooses to enact very realistic violence on the black characters', whereas 'white characters suffer mostly fantastic harm'.[77,78]

Notes

1. Christoph Waltz played SS Colonel Hans Landa in *Inglourious Basterds*.
2. Oliver C. Speck, 'Introduction: a southern state of exception', in Oliver C. Speck (ed.), *Quentin Tarantino's Django Unchained: The Continuation of Metacinema* (New York and London: Bloomsbury, 2014), p. 1.
3. Ibid. p. 1.
4. Henry Louis Gates Jr, 'Tarantino "unchained": Django trilogy', in Gerald Peary (ed.), *Quentin Tarantino: Interviews, Revised and Updated* (Jackson: University of Mississippi, 2013), p. 194.
5. Maya Jaggi, 'The last word', *The Guardian*, 21 December 2001. Available at <https://www.theguardian.com/education/2001/dec/21/artsandhumanities.highereducation> (accessed 22 March 2018).

6. W. G. Sebald, 'Reflections: a natural history of destruction', *The New Yorker*, 4 November 2002, p. 68.
7. Discussing the devastation of German cities brought about by Allied bombing, causing an estimated 600,000 to 800,000 deaths, Sebald spoke of an 'individual and collective amnesia' regarding these events. See W. G. Sebald, 'Reflections: a natural history of destruction', *The New Yorker*, 4 November 2002, p. 68.

    Interestingly, raising a similarly ignored episode from British history, Sebald said of the bombing: 'As far as I know, the question of whether and how it could be strategically or morally justified was never the subject of open debate in Germany after 1945, no doubt mainly because a nation which had murdered and worked to death millions of people in its camps could hardly call on the victorious powers to explain the military and political logic that dictated the destruction of the German cities.' W. G. Sebald, *On the Natural History of Destruction*, trans. Anthea Bell (New York: Random House, 2003), pp. 13–14. Sebald's interest was in 'the outrage of supposing that history could proceed on its way afterwards almost undisturbed, as if nothing had happened' (ibid. p. 154).
8. Gates, 'Tarantino "unchained": Django trilogy', p. 192.
9. Ibid. p. 192.
10. Ibid. p. 186.
11. Ibid. p. 186.
12. The actors, Jamie Foxx, Leonardo DiCaprio, Kerry Washington and Samuel L. Jackson in particular, along with Tarantino, have consistently said they would not have had anything to do with a film they did not think was making a positive contribution to the debate surrounding issues of race in the US.
13. Jean Baudrillard, *Simulacra and Simulation*, trans. Sheila Faria Glaser (Ann Arbor: University of Michigan Press, [1981] 1994), p. 1.
14. Ibid. p. 6.
15. Ibid. p. 6.
16. Gates, 'Tarantino "unchained": Django trilogy', p. 187.
17. Ibid. p. 187.
18. Ibid. p. 188.
19. Gary Clayton Anderson, *The Conquest of Texas: Ethnic Cleansing in the Promised Land, 1820–1875* (Norman: University of Oklahoma Press, 2005), p. 302.
20. Ibid. p. 324.
21. The image was reproduced in *Harper's Weekly* a couple of months after the slave, named as Gordon, escaped 'from his master in Mississippi'; Harper's Weekly, 'A typical negro', *Harper's Weekly: A Journal of Civilisation*, 4 July 1863, 7(340): 429. Available at <https://archive.org/stream/harpersweeklyv7bonn#page/428/mode/2up/search/gordon> (accessed 26 March 2018).
22. Marianne Noble, 'The ecstasies of sentimental wounding in *Uncle Tom's Cabin*', *Yale Journal of Criticism*, Fall 1997, 10(2): 295.

23. Ibid. p. 296.
24. Cassandra Jackson, 'Visualizing slavery: photography and the disabled subject in the art of Carrie Mae Weems', in Christopher M. Bell (ed.), *Blackness and Disability: Critical Examinations and Cultural Interventions* (Münster: LIT Verlag, 2011), p. 32.
25. Ibid. p. 36.
26. Ibid. p. 37.
27. Robert Mapplethorpe, *Black Book* (New York: St Martin's Press, 1988).
28. Kobena Mercer, *Welcome to the Jungle: New Positions in Black Cultural Studies* (New York and London: Routledge, 1994), p. 173.
29. Ibid. p. 173.
30. Jack Fritscher suggests the film *Mandingo*, in which blacks are presented 'as serious sex objects of white desire', was a powerful influence on Mapplethorpe. See Jack Fritscher, *Mapplethorpe: Assault with a Deadly Camera: A Pop Culture Memoir – An Outlaw Reminiscence* (New York: Hastings House, 1994), p. 208.
31. Dennis Abrams, *Spike Lee: Director* (New York: Chelsea House, 2008), p. 27.
32. Jasmine Nichole Cobb and John L. Jackson, 'They hate me: Spike Lee, documentary filmmaking, and Hollywood's "savage slot"', in Janice D. Hamlet and Robin R. Means Coleman (eds), *Fight the Power: The Spike Lee Reader* (New York: Peter Lang, 2009), p. 257.
33. Gates, 'Tarantino "unchained": Django trilogy', p. 187.
34. The title of this film is taken from the name of a chicken adopted and looked after by a character called The Indian (Roy Thinnes).
35. Jabari Asim, *The N Word: Who Can Say It, Who Shouldn't, and Why* (New York: Mariner Books, 2007), p. 183.
36. Ibid. p. 184.
37. Daniel O'Brien, *Black Masculinity on Film: Native Sons and White Lies* (London: Palgrave Macmillan, 2017), p. 110.
38. This film might be seen to explore the relationship between various liberation movements of the 1970s – women's liberation, black liberation, revolutionary political liberation. 'We're trying to set this island free. Christ, you're black, you understand don't you?', says Karen to Lee.
39. There were paramilitary bands active in the South towards the end of the nineteenth century known as Red Shirts. Their aim was to use intimidation and violence to bring about a resurgence of white power.
40. Krishnan Guru-Murthy, 'Tarantino uncut: when Quentin met Krishnan', *Channel 4 News*, 10 January 2013. Available at <https://www.channel4.com/news/tarantino-uncut-when-quentin-met-krishnan-transcript> (accessed 29 April 2013).
41. Playing the wife of the black man is Vonetta McGee who will become well-known for roles in blaxpoitation films.
42. They are con merchants. Quincy pretends to be a slave owner selling his slave, Jason, but then after he has sold him he helps him to escape.

43. 'The film abounds in stereotyped images of happy, singing slaves, cruel slave owners who flogged their human property as well as kindly, sympathetic slave owners who treated their charges well. This simplistic formula worked against any effort to make the film a serious study or depiction of the slavery problem.' See Larry Langman, and David Ebner (eds), *Hollywood's Image of the South: A Century of Southern Films* (Westport, CT, and London: Greenwood Press, 2001), p. 13.
44. The novel *The Confessions of Nat Turner* (William Styron, 1967) had only recently been published. This was based on *The Confessions of Nat Turner: The Leader of the Late Insurrection in Southampton, Virginia*, written and published in Baltimore by Thomas Ruffin Gray in 1831. Available at <http://docsouth.unc.edu/neh/turner/turner.html> (accessed 20 April 2018).
45. Wilson Jeremiah Moses, *Black Messiahs and Uncle Toms: Social and Literary Manipulations of a Religious Myth* (University Park: Pennsylvania State University Press, 1994), p. 226.
46. Although *Django Unchained* is set in 1858–9 and the premiere of *Das Rheingold*, the first part of Richard Wagner's *Der Ring des Nibelungen* (*The Ring of the Nibelung*), did not take place until 1869, Tarantino seems to follow Wagner in looking to the Norse, rather than the Germanic, version of this myth.
47. Michel Fabre, *From Harlem to Paris: Black American Writers in France, 1840–1980* (Urbana and Chicago: University of Illinois Press, 1993), p. 19.
48. Tom Reiss, *The Black Count: Glory, Revolution, Betrayal and the Real Count of Monte Cristo* (London: Harvill Secker, 2012), p. 159.
49. Although Dumas was not as clear-cut about his politics as, for their purposes, Tarantino (and Schultz) might like him to be. He has been described as 'republican by reason, royalist by instinct', for example. A. Craig Bell, *Alexandre Dumas: A Biography and Study* (London: Cassell, 1950), p. 78.
50. Alexandre Dumas, *Le Capitaine Aréna. Le deuxième volet des Impressions de voyage dans le Royaume de Naples, après Le Speronare et avant Le Corricolo/ Impressions of a Voyage to the Kingdom of Naples, part 2, Captain Arena* (Paris: Michel Lévy Frères, [1835] 1879), p. 275.
51. Ibid. p. 112. 'On returning to the hotel, a tall young man crossed me; I thought I recognized him, and I went to him; in fact, it was Mademoiselle Schulz's brother, with whom I had made my acquaintance two months ago ... I explained to M. Schulz the causes of my return to Messina. As curious as anybody in the world, he offered to be my traveling companion.'
52. Hera was the Greek goddess of marriage and the family, but Dumas refers to the temple in question, not as the Second Temple to Hera but as 'Le temple de Cérès'. In Roman mythology, Ceres was the goddess who protected the rights of the plebeians, or commoners. She was also the mother of the god and the goddess of freedom, Liber and Libera.
53. However, even as we acknowledge the mastery of story detail, we might notice this background context relates not so much to themes and ideas within the

film but to the intensity with which the backstories attaching to characters have been imagined by Tarantino. The interest is, first and foremost, in narrative structure and storytelling.

54. Christopher Hooton, 'Jamie Foxx recalling Quentin Tarantino shouting at him on the *Django Unchained* set doesn't go where you'd think', *Independent*, 30 May 2017. Available at <https://www.independent.co.uk/arts-entertainment/films/news/jamie-foxx-interview-quentin-tarantino-howard-stern-django-unchained-behind-the-scenes-shouting-rant-a7762541.html> (accessed 27 April 2017).
55. Tarantino's main interest though is not in historical accuracy but the trajectory of Django as a character: if he is to become the hero he has to begin his journey from a well-defined low point.
56. Gates, 'Tarantino "unchained": Django trilogy', p. 194.
57. M. Keith Booker, *Postmodern Hollywood: What's New in Film and Why It Makes Us Feel So Strange* (Westport, CT: Praeger, 2007), p. 89.
58. Ibid. p. 90.
59. See, for example, MovieManiacs (2013), 'Django Unchained: meet the press'. Available at <https://www.youtube.com/watch?v=-1QpScB-HJg> (accessed 29 April 2018).
60. Tim Woods, *Beginning Postmodernism* (Manchester and New York: Manchester University Press, 1999), p. 211.
61. Fredric Jameson, 'Postmodernism and consumer society', in Hal Foster (ed.), *Postmodern Culture* (London: Pluto Press, 1985), p. 125.
62. Ibid. p. 125
63. Ibid. p. 117.
64. See Welt, 'Django Unchained - Die komplette Pressekonferenz zur Deutschlandpremiere,' *Welt*, 8 January 2013. Available at <https://www.youtube.com/watch?v=hPsBl8pBEd0> (accessed 5 May 2018).
65. Ibid.
66. Helen Duffy, *The 'War on Terror' and the Framework of International Law* (Cambridge: Cambridge University Press, 2005), p. 382.
67. Martha Rayner, 'You love the law too much', in Jonathan Hafetz (ed.), *Obama's Guantánamo: Stories from an Enduring Prison* (New York: New York University Press, 2016), pp. 90–1.
68. Ram Manikkalingam, 'Foreword', in Bradley Jay Strawser (ed.), *Opposing Perspectives on the Drone Debate* (New York: Palgrave Macmillan, 2014), p. x.
69. Ezio Di Nucci and Filippo Santoni de Sio (eds), *Drones and Responsibility: Legal, Philosophical and Socio-Technical Perspectives on Remotely Controlled Weapons* (London and New York: Routledge, 2016), p. 57.
70. Attempting to define who should be on the 'kill-list', the Obama administration 'designed a "disposition matrix" that defines the parameters for which individuals should be targeted'. See Mikkel Vedby Rasmussen, *The Military's Business: Designing Military Power for the Future* (Cambridge: Cambridge University Press, 2015), p. 139.

71. Samuel P. Perry, 'Chained to it: the recurrence of the frontier hero in the films of Quentin Tarantino', in Oliver C. Speck (ed.), *Quentin Tarantino's Django Unchained: The Continuation of Metacinema* (New York and London: Bloomsbury, 2014), pp. 205–26.
72. David J. Leonard, 'Django blues: whiteness and Hollywood's continued failures', in Oliver C. Speck (ed.), *Quentin Tarantino's Django Unchained: The Continuation of Metacinema* (New York and London: Bloomsbury, 2014), pp. 269–86.
73. Gates, 'Tarantino "unchained": Django trilogy', p. 186.
74. James Schouler, *History of the United States of America, Under the Constitution: 1801–1817; Jefferson Republicans* (New York: Dodd, Mead, 1894), p. 264.
75. Ibid. p. 267.
76. Stanley M. Elkins, *Slavery: A Problem in American Institutional and Intellectual Life*, 3rd edn, (Chicago and London: University of Chicago Press, 1976), p. 5.
77. Perry, 'Chained to it', 2014, p. 220.
78. In sharp distinction to many of the points made here, Kate Temoney has suggested Tarantino actually creates a 'bearable space' for human rights discourse to take place. See Kate E. Temoney, 'The "D" is silent, but human rights are not: *Django Unchained* as human rights discourse', in Oliver C. Speck (ed.), *Quentin Tarantino's Django Unchained: The Continuation of Metacinema* (New York and London: Bloomsbury, 2014), pp. 123–40.

PART III

The Cinema of Contemplative Reflection

CHAPTER 8

Employing Religious Concepts to Address the Political Situation Post-9/11: *The Three Burials of Melquiades Estrada* (2005)

I

This chapter considers *The Three Burials of Melquiades Estrada* (Tommy Lee Jones, 2005, France/USA) in relation to its use of the key Christian concepts of forgiveness of sins and redemption. The central focus of *Three Burials* is seen as being its recourse to Christian ideas, not only in relation to timeless spiritual questions regarding the relationship of human beings to an all-powerful deity but also in relation to the contemporary historical/political moment. The presence of evil in the world, the struggle between good and evil, the concept of sin, the character who travels towards redemption, these are staple elements not only of Westerns but of Hollywood films in general. In *Three Burials*, director Tommy Lee Jones and scriptwriter Guillermo Arriaga are interested in ideas that might be seen as central to New Testament Christianity.

The central incident, around which everything revolves, is the killing of an illegal immigrant from Mexico, Melquiades Estrada (Julio Cesar Cedillo), by a US Border Patrol officer. After the killing, a ranch foreman, Pete Perkins (Jones), who has employed Melquiades and become his friend, takes the officer, Mike Norton (Barry Pepper), hostage. Pete gets Mike to exhume Melquiades's body and then takes Mike with him as he crosses the Rio Grande to take the body home to Mexico. Following the usual approach of neo-Westerns, *Three Burials* deploys the classic iconography of the genre – cowboys on horses moving through a rugged frontier landscape – within a present-day context, in this case that of pick-up trucks, helicopters, Border Patrol officers, and illegal immigrants on the US–Mexico border. In narrative terms, again pursuing a classic approach, the hero sets out to seek redress for a wronged friend, while aiming, in the process, to correct a current defect in the administration of law and order. The filmmakers employ *the* American film genre par excellence[1] to address political realities within the contemporary world. In overall terms, this film addresses: the personal – the distress of two men, Pete and Mike, attempting to come to terms with a death; the philosophical – the value of ideas such as mercy and repentance in the modern world; and the political – economic migration and views of the 'Other' within contemporary world affairs.

The New Testament focuses on Christ's offer of salvation for sinners. His 'message' is seen as being not so much for the 'righteous' but for those who have sinned. The only condition attaching to being 'saved' is that sinners should truly repent. This is a frequently repeated New Testament idea. For example, Luke 5: 32: 'I have not come to call the righteous but sinners to repentance' (KJV); or, Luke 15: 7: 'joy shall be in heaven over one sinner that repenteth, more than over ninety and nine just persons, which need no repentance' (KJV). What we see in *Three Burials* is a sinner brought not simply to the point of being sorry for his previous actions but to the depths of a painfully felt repentance. Beyond this, we are shown that this type of transformation cannot take place without an equally suffering-filled application of the concept of Christian 'mercy'. However, the main point to be taken from the film is not solely to do with the relevance of Christian values to personal relationships and individual spiritual development. These things are seen as having direct application to the wider political context. The suggestion is that if America is to come through the crisis of the opening years of the twenty-first century the country has to 'go back to basics'. As a country founded on Christian precepts and democratic principles it has to scrutinise itself to see how it currently measures up to these underpinning values. On the evidence of this film, for Jones and Arriaga, these foundations represent the strength of the United States and it is these values that need to be displayed both within the country and when coming into contact as a nation with other countries, cultures and belief systems.

For more than half of the film Pete has Mike, the man who has killed his best friend and against who, in the spirit of the genre, he should be seeking revenge, totally at his mercy. And yet we can only conclude by the end of the film that what Pete has achieved through showing mercy is Mike's salvation. From being an utterly 'lost soul' – condemned by his partner, Lou Ann Norton (January Jones), as a 'son of a bitch' who is 'beyond redemption' – Mike has been taken on a journey that has transformed him. Although that journey starts at the very point that marks the culmination of his previous 'sinful' life, that is, at the time he shoots and then realises he has killed Melquiades, he is only able to plumb the depths of his anguish during the course of his trek through the wilderness with Pete.

II

During the opening sections of the film we are introduced to Mike as someone who is angry, violent, cold, distant and detached. At home with his wife he has a permanent scowl on his face and shows no signs of affection or warmth. When, with other Border Patrol officers, he confronts migrants attempting to enter the US from Mexico, we see him revel in the confrontation. He chases two would-be migrants, catches one – a man – and kicks him brutally, and then punches the second – a woman – before shouting to her to 'Stay down, bitch'. In his 'love-making' with his wife he displays the same stark disregard for others. He is consistently shown, not only as having no sympathy for other people, but also as having no ability to empathise. Jones presents us with the ultimate – perhaps, inevitable – outcome for such an individual working within law enforcement when he has Mike shoot Melquiades from a distance with a rifle. As he tentatively walks towards the dying man Mike calls 'Hey, man, you okay?', and from this point begins his movement towards becoming another person. We see Mike literally going through the process of being 'born again'.

Jones and Arriaga are careful to show the original Mike as an inevitable product of the society in which he lives. He is not an aberration. It is not that everyone will turn out to be like Mike but he is one of the unavoidable consequences of the boring, mundane, valueless existences led by so many. Brent Strang is more specific, suggesting, 'his attitudes and behavior are the performative effects of the intensification of border security in the post-9/11 United States'.[2]

Within a few minutes of the opening we see Mike and Lou Ann negotiating to buy a mobile home. The scene begins with the US flag flying over a mobile home park before the camera moves down to reveal the state of the nation. Initially the salesman is on the phone talking to somebody else and paying little real attention to the young couple. When he does begin to talk to them all he has to offer is his sales patter. There is no empathy between any of the characters and an advertising hoarding announcing 'Liberty Means Freedom from High Interest Rates' proclaims just how degraded American values have become.

Mike and Lou Ann's lives are defined by a bored, functional interest in popular culture. Before having sex in the kitchen, Mike has a fishing channel on the TV in the living room. While she is 'taking part' in sex in the kitchen Lou Ann is watching a soap drama on a second TV. This character defines her life largely through shopping. She asks, for example, to be taken by Mike to a 'mall' on Saturday, as if this is the most exciting thing possible. Mike feels he has a solution to the fact that she is bored at home on her own when he tells Lou Ann he is going to buy her a 'Nintendo'. Shortly afterwards, in a restaurant talking to a waitress, Lou Ann seems to display a touching longing for the beauty of her hometown of Cincinnati, until, that is, she delivers the second part of her sentence. 'Cincinnati is really pretty in the springtime,' she says, 'there's lots of malls.' Sitting in the restaurant Lou Ann flicks through a celebrity magazine and looks apathetically out of the window while the 'Stars and Stripes' is positioned prominently behind her.[3] In his pick-up truck Mike flicks through a porn magazine. Later, just before he shoots Melquiades, he settles down in the countryside to masturbate. These are lives that are mundane at every level; and this sense of humdrum existences and shallow interests is seen as extending into the world beyond the characters introduced to us. When Lou Ann is in a motel room with Melquiades she turns on the TV only to find it has been left on an 'adult channel' by the previous occupant(s).

Beyond Mike and Lou Ann, everybody we see in this small town performs their life in a detached, indifferent way. The pathologist who carries out the post-mortem examination of Melquiades's body is nonchalantly dismissive of the whole process and mainly concerned about the fact that he has 'gotta be in El Paso tomorrow'. Rachel (Melissa Leo), the waitress in the restaurant, indulges in sex with various men in the town in a largely dispassionate manner, in much the same way as she is shown mopping the floor without ever being engaged with the task. For her, the sex is a momentary distraction from the boredom of her existence. When we see the burial of Melquiades we are shown a purely functional operation carried out by a digger driver. As the heavy metal bucket of the digger is used to push down the soil of Melquiades's grave this entirely impersonal operation is watched by a deputy police officer who is clearly in the cemetery to oversee a process rather than to mourn a death.

Pete, however, is seen as being different. The first shot we are given of him shows him violently vomiting. It is only when we cut to the dead body of Melquiades that we realise why this has happened. Because we cut from the previous scene straight to Pete being sick without an establishing shot setting up the context of the mortuary within which this is occurring, and because this is our introduction to this character, the impact of what we see is magnified. Pete is not cold and detached. He empathises and he feels. He sits alone in his room mourning for Melquiades for two days. Later, when Melquiades has been buried without Pete being informed we are shown his distress in a close-up on his face. He does not respond with anger to the slight of not being told the burial was taking place but with uncertain confusion: 'It seemed like you'd at least . . . (*pause in delivery*) . . . notify me.' Later, when Pete has Mike as his hostage and orders him to disinter Melquiades and on uncovering the body Mike vomits this links him to Pete's original action in the film and shows he has embarked on his process of transformation.

III

There are, in point of fact, two strongly contrasting types of detachment at work within *Three Burials*. One is the apathetic disinterest in the world and other people we have already considered and the other is its polar opposite. When, after having shot Melquiades, we see Mike sitting on the back steps of his mobile home we find him within a detached space of contemplation. Although, in his emotional distance from Lou Ann as she comes to join him on the steps, this appears similar to his previous state, the space he is now occupying actually amounts to one of engagement with the lives of others rather than estranged dislocation from the lives of others. Specifically, he is reflecting on the taking of a life that has just, as it were, almost inadvertently happened to him; and what we see on his face is torment and concern rather than the self-centred arrogance and bravado of his earlier incarnation. Two short scenes placed one after the other show a crucial link between Pete and Mike, even before their journey into Mexico together to take Melquiades's body home begins. In one, Pete sits on the ground next to Melquiades's grave drinking a beer, and in the next, Mike sits in his truck haunted by the horror of Melquiades's death as his wife walks off towards the bland, everyday ordinariness of a shopping mall. In both cases, these men are detached from the world around them and contemplatively alone with their thoughts of Melquiades.

In terms of the internal logic of the film the two forms of detachment identified here are also crucial for the spectator. In viewing a film we can passively allow the images and the sounds to wash over us, or we can actively engage with the material; these are very different positions in relation to the material placed before us, and yet, both can be considered as forms of detachment. In his role as director, Jones uses intertitles, so that sections of the film are denoted by something like chapter headings on a plain black screen. These titles are: 'The First Burial of Melquiades Estrada', 'The Second Burial of Melquiades Estrada', 'The Journey', and 'The Third Burial of Melquiades Estrada'. This use of intertitles is a device frequently associated with the concept of distanciation: an effort to disengage the audience from immersion within the narrative so that they might reflect more carefully on what they are seeing. In fact, one of the things that happens in the film is that the filmmakers in effect ask us to consider the whole idea, or experience, of mediating the world through screens.

As we have already seen, both Mike and Lou Ann are shown looking at TV screens in an unthinking, disengaged manner. Furthermore, in a shot that contributes nothing towards moving the story forward and, therefore, is driven by no narrative necessity, Melquiades is shown looking into a shop window displaying an array of the latest flat screen plasma televisions. Symbolically, these are screens as consumer products, but they are also (and this is linked to the idea of consumption) screens seen as representing detachment from the real world. As we view Melquiades across the street looking in the window of this electrical shop the camera positions us so that we are viewing him through the window of his pickup truck. In other words, our attention is drawn even more strongly to the framing that is taking place; that is, to the set-ups being chosen by the filmmakers, and to the idea of viewing through screens. We are looking at a screen within which we are looking through a further framing device at a character looking through a window at images on TV screens. This distancing of the viewer, so that we are made more conscious of our voyeuristic looking in on others, is used again by Jones when we see Mike on the back steps of his mobile home. In this case, we look through Lou Ann's (predominantly pink) washing that is hanging out to dry. Like Rachel and Lou Ann, who in their boredom are frequently looking through windows at others, we become observers watching the lives of other people. We are placed in a position of detached observation and, because detachment carries with it the binary possibilities we have been discussing, this can do one of two things; it can motivate considered reflection, or it can simply be left to express the estranged way in which human beings within contemporary existence experience the world.

IV

The only section of the film given a title that does not refer to a burial is that marked out as 'The Journey'. In this way, a concept that is invariably important within narratives is drawn to the viewer's attention. And, in this connection, it is important to notice that it is not only Mike who is undertaking a journey. Pete, too, is on a journey, firstly, to fulfil a promise he made that if Melquiades were to die in Texas he would take his body to his home town to be buried, but beyond this there is a sense in which Pete is searching to regain something which has been lost with Melquiades's death. The death of a friend leaves an emptiness which has to be addressed in some way, and a need to recalibrate, or rebalance, one's life. As with Mike, whose journey of transformation actually begins with the death of Melquiades, so too with Pete. He sits for days in his cabin after Melquiades's death, and when somebody comes to visit him the depths of his grief are registered in the performance by Jones and by a choice of shot that confronts us with his anguish, head on and in close-up. Pete turns to society and the law for redress, asking for his friend's death to be investigated, but when nothing comes of this he has to take his journey through grief in a new, deeper and more challenging direction in an effort to re-find an acceptable order, shape and structure for the world.

Journeys through intense grief and a loss of faith have been undertaken before in the Western. In *The Outlaw Josey Wales* (Clint Eastwood, 1976), for example, a wooden cross symbolically gives way beneath Josey Wales (Eastwood) as he buries his family and attempts to place the signifier of his faith at the head of his young son's grave.[4] From that point on Eastwood's film is about Josey's journey back to a position where he can, again, believe in the possibility of a better world. However, *Three Burials*, in its focus on the dual aspect of the journey – not only in having two people travelling together, but also in emphasising the conceptual importance of the binary unit of forgiveness of sins and redemption, with the first allowing for the possibility of the second – would seem to be interestingly different.

Whether they are conscious of it or not, what Jones and Arriaga reject in *Three Burials* is any overriding concept of evil. There is no sense of this being a struggle between good and evil, nor that evil is the central, unavoidably ever-present force in the world determining the tensions that exist. In fact, despite initially being led in the direction of believing him to be a character moulded in the 'bad guy' Hollywood tradition, what we are shown very clearly is that Mike is a pretty ordinary person who has moved along a certain path up until the point at which he has been confronted with the full horror of the trajectory he has embarked upon. To begin with he is presented as cold, distant, verging on psychotic; but Melquiades's death presents Mike, and the viewer, with the frightening awfulness of what it means to shoot somebody. The dying man is shown in close-up on the ground coughing up blood, which we can hear gurgling in his throat. His eyes blink and he groans slightly. A shot across his body shows Mike running towards him while he makes small head and upper body movements that indicate he is still alive. For the first time in the film Mike shows signs of empathy with another person. We can hear it in his nervous, tentative delivery of the line, 'Hey, man, you ok?' He carries his rifle hanging from his left hand like some sort of limp, useless encumbrance. He even attempts a pathetic use of

Figure 8.1 For the first time in the film Mike (Barry Pepper) shows signs of empathy with another person: *The Three Burials of Melquiades Estrada* (Tommy Lee Jones, 2005).

Spanish: 'You, bueno?' (Figure 8.1). When he kicks Melquiades's foot, it is something we can imagine the old Mike doing but the half-hearted way in which he now performs the action reveals the impact this event has already had. We see him panicking in close-up. In the body language of bringing his hand to his head and turning through 360 degrees as he looks around what we have, for the first time, is a fully emotionally engaged response to the world around him.

Alongside this realistic representation of Mike as an ordinary person, who cannot be dismissed in the usual simplistic, media-invoked terms of the deranged individual who has been born evil and embodies evil, we are shown the low-level corruption within the system that means the immediate response to an event such as this is to cover it up as quickly as possible. Again, it is the ordinariness of all of this that is emphasised. What happens, as almost everybody attempts to ignore the fact that a man has been killed, is not the result of malicious calculation but the seemingly inevitable result of the bland, mundane nature of the world these people inhabit. Captain Gomez (Mel Rodriguez), who is in charge of the Border Patrol officers, simply wants an easy life. As he tells Mike within the first few minutes of the film, when Mike has been too violent with the Mexican migrants attempting to cross the border: 'I don't like trouble, boy. I don't like it at all.' Strang points out Gomez is not concerned about Norton's overt racism but just that he might as a result get into trouble. What this signifies, says Strang, is Gomez's 'complicity in a more systemic racism endemic to neoliberal multiculturalism'.[5] The local sheriff, Belmont (Dwight Yoakam), sees Melquiades as a 'wetback', that is, an illegal immigrant, and, therefore, within the moral framework Belmont's experience of life has given him and within this 'systemic racism', somebody without rights. He tells Pete, 'You're not his family, I don't have to notify you about a goddam thing. He was a wetback.'[6] Those in authority in *Three Burials* are shown to be keen to (literally) bury this incident as quickly as possible, not because they are malevolent but because this is the instinctive reaction within the parochial world in which they exist. As a result of his erectile dysfunction Belmont may be the butt of a series of (what are presented as) comic moments but he is also shown as a far from bad person. We notice, for instance, the way in which he turns to Pete to tell him they have already buried Melquiades. What he has to say may quickly turn into the forceful tones of the line given above about Pete not being family, but it starts in a tone of gentle conciliation. Later, when Pete has taken Mike hostage, Belmont has a chance to shoot Pete, but he cannot bring himself to fire. In this he is linked to Pete who later has a chance to shoot Mike as he makes a bid to escape but cannot take the shot.

V

When he has taken Mike hostage the first thing Pete does, as mentioned earlier, is to order Mike to dig up Melquiades's body. Pete then takes Mike to Melquiades's small home where he orders Mike to take the body into the very bare and basic house and to place the body on the bed. Pete's words make it clear he is determinedly placing Melquiades's life into a very human, very real context for Mike. 'Melquiades lived here', he says. 'That was his bed. Kept his clothes right over there. That was his plate. And that was his cup.' Mike, who has been unable to empathise with others, and particularly not with the foreign 'Other'[7] as represented by Melquiades, is forced to experience another person's life. He is compelled to place himself within the poverty of the space occupied by a Mexican immigrant, but also to consider the extent to which one person's life is much like anybody else's – eating, drinking, sleeping, getting up, getting dressed, etc. Mike is required, highly symbolically, to drink from Melquiades's cup and then to put on the dead man's everyday working clothes (Figure 8.2). Within the film this is one character experiencing another person's life, but it is also the viewer being presented with the very restricted existences of Mexican workers in the USA over successive generations. The film is working within the philosophical realm but also within the sphere of contemporary politics.

Three Burials encourages viewers to question the way in which the Mexican 'Other' is (and, by extension, all 'Others' are) viewed within the US and represented within the media. This has become a growing issue since this film was made in 2005, perhaps.in particular in recent years

Figure 8.2 Mike is required, highly symbolically, to drink from Melquiades's cup: *The Three Burials of Melquiades Estrada*.

with Donald Trump highlighting in his presidential campaign the importance he was placing on strengthening the border with Mexico.[8] But the topic has a long history in which both the levels of immigration, legal and illegal, and attitudes towards this have been driven largely by economic fluctuations. Often, migrants from Mexico, both official and unofficial, have been welcomed in southern states by businesses in need of workers. Speaking about the Texas–Mexico border in relation to his film, Jones claimed: 'there is one country there, one culture in that river valley, and it doesn't have a lot to do with Mexico City or Washington D.C. – the Rio Grande valley has its own culture. It is a superficially imposed barrier. A sort of enforced schizophrenia.'[9] The way in which Pete is shown as being 'at home' on both sides of the border demonstrates the point Jones is making and highlights a general difficulty with national borders which is sharpened during periods of substantial migration.[10]

9/11 has been viewed as a factor in determining immigration policies in America in recent years.[11] Certainly, there have been increasingly negative reactions towards immigrants. Gloria Anzaldúa, who has written much on Mexico–Texas border issues, clearly saw 9/11 as something of a turning point: 'On September 11 as I listened to the rhetoric of retaliation and war, I realized it masked feelings of bewilderment, sorrow, and fear – the U.S. borders of "safety" had been violated and many people could no longer see our country the same way.'[12] Summarising the population data, Leal and Rodriguez say: 'According to the US Census, the foreign born in 2010 constituted 12.9% of the overall population, or 40 million people', and this reflected 'continual growth since the 1970 low point of 9.6 million individuals and 4.7%', although 'the foreign-born percentage was higher in the late nineteenth and early twentieth centuries'.[13] It has been estimated in total there are 11 million illegal immigrants in the US, with two-thirds of them having lived in the country for more than ten years, and about a half of the 11 million believed to be Mexican.[14] Debates about how this issue should be handled, whether President Barack Obama was too lenient or not, and whether the border with Mexico should be further strengthened, continue to be hotly contested. It is within this atmosphere and what he describes as 'the accelerating discursive shift that sees immigrants as dehumanized criminals' that John Riofrio has framed *Three Burials* as part of 'the search for a national identity' post-9/11.[15]

Peter Andreas says that since 9/11 there has been a keen and widespread focus on national borders:

> In both political debates and political policy, borders are very much back in style. Rather than simply being dismantled in the face of intensifying pressures of economic integration, border controls are being retooled and redesigned as part of a new and expanding "war on terrorism."[16]

Hilary Cunningham says the post-9/11 world has been seen by many in terms of 'separation and division' rather than the 'hybridities' that had seemed possible under the globalisation of the previous decade.[17] There is 'a growing sense, *or the proliferation of a sense*, that we now live in a newly bordered reality, *or a reality that needs to be bordered in new ways*' (her italics), she says.[18] However, she counsels against thinking that border security between Mexico and the US was becoming more relaxed in the 1990s, showing how as borders were tightened in this period migrants took to using increasingly dangerous routes with the inevitable consequence of hugely increased death tolls.[19]

VI

Intriguingly, the border in question has also been characterised as 'increasingly militarized and violent'.[20] The authors of a paper looking at the increased military-style build-up on the frontier with Mexican claim that: 'In recent years, border enforcement strategy has centered on the development of a militarized logic and a strategic plan for enforcement that emphasizes pain, suffering, and trauma as deterrents to undocumented migration.[21]

What is occurring along the Mexican border is a form of war with American personnel – using trucks and helicopters in *Three Burials* (and, beyond the film, increasing levels of technological surveillance) – hunting down small bands of the infiltrating enemy. In Melquiades's death we are presented with the frightening awfulness of what it means, both to kill somebody in battle and to watch somebody die on the battlefield. And the landscape within which all of this takes place is reminiscent of all those places American troops have found themselves deployed in recent years. This is dusty, rocky, desert terrain.

Melquiades asks that, if he should die 'over here', Pete should take his body home for burial. 'Over here' is the classic phrase of the soldier fearing he may die in a war he is fighting on foreign soil. Pete remembers him as saying: 'Promise me one thing, Pete, if I die over here carry me back to my family and bury me in my hometown.' The recovery of bodies from the battlefield and the securing of a 'decent' burial for fallen comrades is considered by soldiers to be an almost a sacred duty. Interestingly, Mike is placed in a somewhat similar position to Melquiades. Talking about the life of a Border Patrol officer but through the language used placing himself in the position of military service personnel, Mike says: 'We're always a long way from home.' *The Guardian* reports that 'By 2010 the border patrol had more than 20,000 agents', and in order to hire people quickly the agency 'drew heavily on veterans from the wars in Iraq and Afghanistan' to the point where vets made up almost 30% of agents. This brought 'a military ethos to the policing job' and occurred alongside 'the emergence of a homeland security industry in which military suppliers repurposed weapons, surveillance technologies and vehicles for use inside the US'.[22]

Amongst a range other literary texts (not least various books from the Bible) *Three Burials* references William Faulkner's novel *As I Lay Dying* (1930), in which after her death, Addie Bundren's family, following her wishes, journey with her body to her hometown in order to bury her. Discussing this book, John Limon makes the point that it is permeated with death and as such is linked to the experience of the First World War.[23] 'Perhaps nowhere in actual First World War literature is polluted trench life, a miasma of mud and guts and decomposing bodies, rendered better than in *As I Lay Dying*', he says.[24] We might suggest that perhaps nowhere is the reality of American troops-on-the-ground involvement post-9/11 rendered better than in *Three Burials*. Most of the time the experience is one of dull boredom, monotony and inactivity. The moment of action and death comes unexpectedly, almost by chance, but it affects the whole of the rest of your life. Nothing can prepare you for seeing the life of another person ebbing away (as a result of your actions). Death lives with you, it accompanies you: the smell of death, the recurring images of death; until finally (if you are lucky) it can be put to rest.

Limon describes *As I Lay Dying* as 'a surfeit of mud and blood and guts, a satiety of everything that the coffin is supposed to hide or withstand'.[25]

If we substitute 'sand and dust' for 'mud' (see, for example, Pete entering the restaurant in a dust storm twenty minutes into the film) we have a fairly good description of *Three Burials*, in which we are forced to witness the steady, unrelenting decomposition of Melquiades's body.[26] Susan Scott Parrish points out that the 'muddiness' of Faulkner's novel is also the mud of the 'Mississippi watershed'.[27] And, in a similar way, the terrain of *Three Burials* remains redolent of the landscape of the US–Mexico border while also conjuring images associated with US ventures overseas.[28]

VII

Three Burials is a wonderful film. It challenges the viewer in so many ways. In the final analysis, however, it fails to address the underpinning economics that have caused all of this to exist. There is one mention made by Melquiades of 'the boss' of the ranch where he and Pete work, who lives in Houston. 'Fuckin' mama's boy', says Melquiades. 'He says he's a rancher, just because they bought him this ranch, but I ain't seen him here bustin' his ass.' In addition, we do see the poverty of Melquiades's home. But there is no real investigation of the economic reasons underlying the fact that, as Cunningham puts it:

> For much of the world's mobile population, the experience of transnational interconnection entails rivers and oceans to be crossed (often in unsafe and overcrowded vessels), electrified fences guarded by border patrols, stretches of desolate desert, or the interrogation cell in the basement of a port of entry.[29]

Discussing Anzaldúa's writings around 'cultural otherness' Matthew Carter talks of 'the fallacy of geo-political attempts to establish a border along national or racial lines, a binary to "distinguish *us* from *them*"'.[30] However, although such attempts may in some sense be a 'fallacy', borders and all that they enforce in terms of economic disparities are very much an international political reality, and a reality that is felt every day in the lives of the poor on both sides of these, in many senses but not in an economic sense, arbitrary lines of demarcation. As Slavoj Žižek has it in talking about Europe: 'This is the truth of globalisation: the construction of new walls safeguarding prosperous Europe from the immigrant flood.'[31]

In being ordered to put on Melquiades's clothes and drink from his cup, Mike is an everyman figure. Audiences are being urged by the film to set aside prejudices and empathise with 'wetbacks'. Mexicans are literally 'neighbours' to a country that advocates Christianity with its core commandment of 'love they neighbour' as a bedrock to its democratic values. Towards the end of this Western, Pete fires his gun but only in such a way as to drive Mike towards enacting the real 'final shootout' which is between the person he once was and the person he is in the process of becoming. But, for the viewer, as this happens the 'War on Terror' remains an unavoidable presence. Mike kneels in the manner of a man about to be executed by terrorists,[32] but what he receives is neither the vengeance of the Western genre, nor the brutal justice of a vengeful Old Testament god. Instead, he experiences the 'mercy' of a loving god that is able to bring about redemption. What is suggested is that there is another way beyond revenge and its unrelenting cycle of the meting out of death. This Christian approach leads through pain and suffering, confession and contrition, to forgiveness and redemption. As Pete in his role as a mythic figure (in stark contradistinction to his role as the confused very ordinary individual) rides off into an unknown future, Mike calls out to him, 'You gonna be alright?' There is no answer to this, as there is no answer to such a question for any of us, but it does echo Mike's words to the dying Melquiades – 'Hey, man, you okay?' – and it leaves Mike as a man who is now able to at least attempt to reach out towards friendship across the gulf that divides one person from another. Joseph S. Walker is correct to characterise this film as a text that reflects 'the confusion, ambiguity, and anxiety that have marked the age of the War on Terror'.[33] This national state of being is essentially what the filmmakers are attempting to address, and the ending contains the essence of their considered response.

After the waters of Mike's anguish have broken in a torrent of regret – 'I'm sorry! I swear to God, I'm sorry. I swear to God. I swear to God. I did not mean to kill him. It was a mistake. I didn't want it to happen. It hurts me, and I regret it, every single day.' – he sleeps a long and peaceful sleep, like a baby as they say. But for Pete, who like Shane[34] will soon wend his way off into the landscape, there is no rest. He is shown standing on a hillside, looking into a blazing fire, alone with his thoughts again, in a detached, contemplative space. As Mike kicked Melquiades's foot when he was dying, so now Pete kicks Mike's foot to wake him to a new day and a new life. Melquiades could not be roused but Mike is back from the dead.

As Carter has counselled, we should be careful not to treat the Western genre as 'either historically vacant or ideologically monolithic', simplistically replicating 'the mythic binarism and triumphalism of Anglo-American frontier narratives'.[35] He very correctly suggests this would be to 'underestimate the enormous complexity with which the myth is dealt with in the genre'.[36] *Three Burials* is a film that steps outside of and beyond the normally permissible (carefully bounded) liberalism of Hollywood in order to look at America's position in the world post-9/11. Its setting on the borderlands of the United States and its movement beyond the designated territorial space of the United States is apt. It moves beyond the usual mainstream bounds of political discussion in America. *Three Burials* pushes towards extreme liberalism: the film does not have a hero who meets fire with fire but one who is able to show mercy. However, to restate the position of this chapter, in the final analysis it does not address the fact that borders should be understood as:

> a fundamental part of what might be called the machinery of mobility and enclosure in a global landscape and they function not in isolation, but in coordination with larger systems that secure capital and wealth in our global village.[37]

The significant absence in the film, that which is barely mentioned, are these larger structures apportioning wealth and poverty. In its focus on Christian values *Three Burials* ultimately fails to address the central fact that the border which is being defended is the one that exists between rich and poor, between the 'haves' and the 'have nots'. And because it never addresses the economic basis to prejudice the film fails to engage with anything beyond a vague sense of common humanity. What we have is the retreat from harsh economic reality into the false consciousness of religious and liberal platitudes dealing with the 'human soul' and the 'human condition'. We are requested to recognise our common humanity as if this will address issues attaching to borders between people, that is to say, between different space-configurations of wealth and poverty. Arriaga said of the film: 'It can be understood for what's going on in the world. We are suspicious of each other right now. But we have much more things in common.'[38] In a liberal society sentiments such as these are to be applauded but such attitudes can never offer a starting point for successfully addressing the central issue because they fail to engage with the real economic basis of people's lives.

Notes

1. Jean-Louis Rieupeyrout, *Le Western: ou, Le cinéma américain par excellence* (Paris: Éditions du Cerf, 1953).
2. Brent Strang, 'Disinterring the Western in *Three Burials of Melquiades Estrada* and *No Country for Old Men*', in MaryEllen Higgins, Rita Keresztesi and Dayna Oscherwitz (eds), *The Western in the Global South* (New York and London: Routledge, 2015), p. 237.

3. There is also a Lions Club banner behind Lou Ann. This organisation aims to 'foster a spirit of understanding among the peoples of the world'. But also to provide 'a forum for the open discussion of all matters of public interest; provided, however, that partisan politics and sectarian religion shall not be debated'. See Lions Clubs International, 'Purpose and ethics'. Available at <http://www.lionsclubs.org/EN/who-we-are/mission-and-history/purpose-and-ethics.php> (accessed 6 November 2017). It is difficult to understand how you can have 'open discussion' while ruling out politics and religion.
4. John White, *Westerns* (London and New York: Routledge, 2011), p. 74.
5. Strang, 'Disinterring the Western', 2015, p. 237.
6. The term 'wetback' (an illegal Mexican immigrant who has crossed the Rio Grande, therefore 'wetback') is a highly controversial term that is now generally seen as an unacceptable racial slur. See, for example, Gregory Korte, 'Mexican slur has long history in politics', *USA Today*, 29 March 2013. Available at <https://www.usatoday.com/story/news/politics/2013/03/29/mexican-immigration-slur-history/2036329/> (accessed 7 November 2017) and Frank Ortega, 'What's wrong with "Wetback"?: what a congressman's slur reveals', *Racism Review*, 11 April 2013. Available at <http://www.racismreview.com/blog/2013/04/11/whats-wrong-with-wetback-what-a-congressmans-slur-reveals/> (accessed 6 November 2013).
7. '... political geographers have used the concept of the "other" to examine how powerful countries dominate less powerful countries, regions or localities in an effort to legitimize their exploitation'. Alison Mountz, 'The other,' in Carolyn Gallaher, Carl Dahlman, Mary Gilmartin, Alison Mountz and Peter Shirlow, *Key Concepts in Political Geography* (London and Los Angeles: Sage, 2009), p. 333.
8. 'The promise to build a wall along the US–Mexican border was a feature of Mr Trump's presidential campaign, during which he accused Mexican immigrants of "bringing drugs" and "bringing crime". The President claims the wall is necessary to protect against illegal immigration.' Emily Shugerman, 'Donald Trump says Mexico will pay for border wall after meeting with President Peña Nieto,' *Independent*, 7 July 2017. Available at <http://www.independent.co.uk/news/world-0/us-politics/donald-trump-mexico-pay-border-wall-meeting-president-pena-nieto-immigration-a7829266.html> (accessed 7 November 2017).
9. Stephen Applebaum, 'Tommy Lee Jones: *The Three Burials of Melquiades Estrada*', *BBC*, 24 September 2014. Available at < http://www.bbc.co.uk/films/2006/03/30/tommy_lee_jones_melquiades_2006_interview.shtml> (accessed 7 November 2017).
10. A key element of this is Pete's comfortable fluency in Spanish, emphasised throughout the film.

11. '... the 9/11 terrorists entered the country on temporary visas and had authorization (if fraudulently obtained) to be in the U.S. Yet in the 11 years since the attack, we've devoted enormous resources to securing the southern border and deporting non-criminal immigrants. The leading countries of origin for people removed from the U.S. in 2011 were Mexico, Guatemala, Honduras, and El Salvador.' Ted Hesson, 'Five ways immigration system changed after 9/11', *ABC News*, 11 September 2012. Available at <http://abcnews.go.com/ABC_Univision/News/ways-immigration-system-changed-911/story?id=17231590> (accessed 8 November 2017).
12. Gloria Anzaldúa, '(Un)natural bridges, (Un)safe spaces', in AnaLouise Keating (ed.), *The Gloria Anzaldúa Reader* (Durham, NC, and London: Duke University Press, 2009), p. 247.
13. David L. Leal and Nestor P. Rodriguez (eds), *Migration in an Era of Restriction and Recession: Sending and Receiving Nations in a Changing Global Environment* (New York: Springer, 2016), pp. 2–3.
14. Jens Krogstad, Jefferey S. Passel and D'Vera Cohn, 'Five facts about illegal immigration in the U.S', Pew Research Center, 27 April 2017. Available at <http://www.pewresearch.org/fact-tank/2017/04/27/5-facts-about-illegal-immigration-in-the-u-s/> (accessed 7 November 2017).
15. John D. 'Rio' Riofrio, *Continental Shifts: Migration, Representation, and the Struggle for Justice in Latin(o) America* (Austin: University of Texas Press, 2015), p. 139.
16. Peter Andreas, 'A tale of two borders: the U.S.-Canada and U.S.-Mexico lines after 9-11', in Peter Andreas and Thomas J. Biersteker (eds), *The Rebordering of North America: Integration and Exclusion in a New Security Context* (London and New York: Routledge, 2003), pp. 1–2.
17. Hilary Cunningham, 'Nations rebound?: crossing borders in a gated globe', *Identities: Global Studies in Culture and Power*, 2004, 11: 331.
18. Ibid. p. 332.
19. Ibid. p. 338. Brent G. McCune and Dennis L. Soden, amongst others, support Cunningham's basic position: 'In the 1990s, there was the militarization of the U.S.-Mexico border through "Operation Gatekeeper" and "Operation Hold-the-Line." And now, through post-9/11 legislation, there is a hardening of the southwest border.' See McCune and Soden, 'Regulating the push and pull of migration in the post-9/11 era on the southern border', in Matthew J. Morgan (ed.), *The Impact of 9/11 and the New Legal Landscape: The Day That Changed Everything?* (New York: Palgrave Macmillan, 2009), p. 197.
20. Jeremy Slack, Daniel E. Martinez, Alison Elizabeth Lee and Scott Whiteford, 'The geography of border militarization: violence, death and health in Mexico and the United States', *Journal of Latin American Geography*, 2016, 15(1): 8.
21. Ibid. p. 8.

22. Reece Jones, 'Death in the sands: the horror of the US-Mexico border', *The Guardian*, 4 October 2016. Available at <https://www.theguardian.com/us-news/2016/oct/04/us-mexico-border-patrol-trump-beautiful-wall> (accessed 8 November 2017).
23. John Limon, *Writing after War: American War Fiction from Realism to Postmodernism* (Oxford: Oxford University Press, 1993), pp. 123–4.
24. Ibid. p. 124.
25. Ibid. p. 122.
26. There is a whole issue here attaching to the macabre humour of *Three Burials* that we do not have the space to address. Suffice to say that, as Cleanth Brooks noted, the same issue exists in relation to Faulkner's *As I Lay Dying*. He said Faulkner had created 'a complexity of tone that has proved difficult for some readers to cope with'. See Cleanth Brooks, *William Faulkner: The Yoknapatawpha Country* (Baton Rouge: Louisiana State University Press, [1963] 1991), p. 141.
27. Susan Scott Parrish, '*As I Lay Dying* and the modern aesthetics of ecological crisis', in John T. Matthews, *The New Cambridge Companion to William Faulkner* (Cambridge: Cambridge University Press, 2015), p. 77. Parrish looks particularly to the catastrophic Mississippi flood of 1927.
28. In situating the film in Texas the filmmakers are placing the action within a wealthy, oil-producing region. The Permian Basin has around half of the state's 800-plus oil and gas production sites. Jennifer Hiller, 'A 21st-century oil boom in the Lone State', *San Antonio Express-News*, 25 February 2013. Available at <http://www.mysanantonio.com/business/article/A-21st-century-oil-boom-in-the-Lone-Star-State-4303192.php> (accessed 14 November 2017).
29. Cunningham, 'Nations rebound?: crossing borders in a gated globe', 2004, p. 345.
30. Matthew Carter, '"I'm just a cowboy": transnational identities of the borderlands in Tommy Lee Jones' *The Three Burials of Melquiades Estrada*', *European Journal of American Studies*, 2012, 7(1): 11.
31. Slavoj Žižek, *Welcome to the Desert of the Real: Five Essays on September 11 and Related Dates* (London and New York: Verso, 2002), p. 149.
32. In 2002 (i.e. before this film was made), for example, Daniel Pearl, a journalist working for the *Wall Street Journal*, was beheaded after being captured by terrorists in Pakistan. See Wall Street Journal, 'Reporter Daniel Pearl is dead, killed by his captors in Pakistan', *Wall Street Journal*, 24 February 2002. Available at <https://www.wsj.com/articles/SB1014311357552611480> (accessed 14 November 2017).
33. Joseph S. Walker, 'Coen, Coen on the range: Rooster Cogburn(s) and domestic space', in Scott F. Stoddart (ed.), *The New Western: Critical Essays on the Genre Since 9/11* (Jefferson, NC: McFarland, 2016), p. 66. Although Walker often seems to want to interpret events in the film in a too literal manner.
34. *Shane* (George Stevens, 1953).
35. Carter, '"I'm just a cowboy"', 2012, p. 16.

36. Ibid. p. 16.
37. Cunningham, 'Nations rebound?: crossing borders in a gated globe', 2004, p. 346.
38. Christian Moerk, 'An actor, a writer and the silent border between them', *New York Times*, 11 December 2005. Available at <http://www.nytimes.com/2005/12/11/movies/an-actor-a-writer-and-the-silent-border-between-them.html> (accessed 15 November 2017).

CHAPTER 9

Living in a World of Fear and Inexplicable Evil: *The Assassination of Jesse James by the Coward Robert Ford* (2007)[1]

I

The Assassination of Jesse James by the Coward Robert Ford, directed by Andrew Dominik, presents the viewer with a central theme that has been a mainstay of Western culture for centuries, the confrontation between good and evil. Much of this conflict is played out through the film's representation of Jesse James, who is shown as a man who possesses both a 'good' side and a 'bad' side; and in the course of presenting this struggle, the film delivers a potent mix of powerfully suggestive images confronting us with a world in which the presence of evil seems explicable only via recourse to concepts of religion and mysticism. The film becomes an illogical mess of ideas, full of confused and contradictory ideological positions.

It could be argued that this confusion represents a deliberate strategy used by the filmmakers to express the states of mind of both the character of Jesse James and his eventual assassin, Robert Ford. However, after offering a critical reading of the film's engagements with the notions of good and evil and the nature of celebrity, this chapter will argue that the film's contradictory ideological positions actually say more about the muddled state of the dominant ideologies of modern Western nations and their media than they do about the mindsets of the historical characters that are being represented.

II

In keeping with the peculiar line of religious thought taken by the writer, Ron Hansen, who was responsible for the original novel from which the script was developed, the assassination of Jesse James (Brad Pitt) is presented as in some way paralleling the death of Jesus Christ. It is implied that Jesse is Christ-like in his ability to see into the hearts of others (and even to foresee his own impending death). The narrative shows him to be betrayed, like Christ, by somebody from within his own coterie; and Dominik's construction of the death scene suggests he goes willingly, lamb-like, to his slaughter. According to Nancy Tischler, Hansen's usual approach to his work is to view the stories he is writing through the lens of his Catholicism: 'Taking a moment in history, dealing with actual people, fleshing this out with historical research and speculation, and envisioning it through the perspective of his Catholic faith, he builds a series of fascinating stories.'[2]

Speaking about the connection between his writing and his religious belief, Hansen himself has said:

> For me, writing, art, is a way of registering what my prayer is like. I was once asked how writing and prayer differed and I couldn't identify how they were different because when I pray, when I write, it feels the same way and I think God speaks to me sometimes through my writing and sometimes through my prayer and sometimes in other ways.[3]

In the same interview he went on to discuss the way in which people with religious faith were able to see the world with a richness that was beyond other people:

> I think people with strong religious faith see in colour and other people see in black and white. We are just aware of a bigger range of things going on and we see the relationships between things. We see God's personality revealed in so many different ways; and other people are very sequestered and limited, I think, if they don't have a religious faith. They're not stepping outside themselves, they're always within themselves, or, just with their friends and family, but not reaching beyond to that other level, not seeing the supernatural and its evidence in nature and other places.[4]

Looking at *The Assassination of Jesse James by the Coward Robert Ford* from this perspective, Robert Ford (Casey Affleck) is immediately thrown into the context of being a version of Judas Iscariot. Unlike Ford, who shot Jesse James in the back of the head, Judas did not kill Christ directly, but he was, like Ford, the disciple who most clearly betrayed him. Robert Seesengood and Jennifer Koosed introduce a further dimension to this line of interpretation when they suggest Jesse can also be viewed in relation to David, the King of Judah from the Old Testament. 'Hansen's reconstruction of Jesse James is thoroughly informed by the lives of Jesus and David', they claim.[5] They point out that 'both Jesse and David are bandits' who 'hide out in the wilderness and gather around them a group of disaffected locals'. Going further, they suggest 'Jesus has much the same profile' in that 'he too hid out in the wilderness and assembled around him a group of disaffected locals'. Furthermore, the apparent rejection in the film by Jesse of any Christ-like status is, they suggest, ambiguous.

> Hansen has James reject the divinization of Ford's ardor with a succinct rebuke – 'I ain't Jesus.' But it is a rejection that is also an identification – otherwise, why even mention Jesus in this context?[6]

When we near the point of the murder, or 'assassination', we are told by the narrator that 'The day before he died was Palm Sunday'; and, while Jesse attends church with the rest of the family we see Robert Ford alone in the house musing on the wounds of Jesse, 'the scars where Jesse was twice shot'. Furthermore, just before Jesse is 'assassinated' the audience is given a view of him standing in a window of his home with his face distorted by the imperfections in the glass so that within the composition of the shot our attention is drawn to the cross of the wood within the window frame (Figure 9.1). The script then mentions Jesse's age at the time of his death as being thirty-four, something that has already been stated at the start of the film. The Christian connotations attaching to each of these aspects of the script are clear; and this drawing out of parallels to Christ's death, alongside a lauding celebration of Jesse the man, is found throughout the build-up to the climactic scene. The day of Jesse's death is announced through an intertitle proclaiming 'APRIL 3RD, 1882' in white lettering on a black background, as if this was some special date worthy of remembrance. We are shown clouds scudding from right to left across the sky, Robert Ford using a hand-pump to draw water and a point-of-view shot recreating the moment when, as Ford splashes water

Figure 9.1 Jesse (Brad Pitt) boxed and framed in relation to 'the cross' in *The Assassination of Jesse James by the Coward Robert Ford* (Andrew Dominik, 2007).

over his face by bringing his two hands up to cover his eyes, he is plunged into darkness. The cinematography and the editing ensures each of these moments is layered with implied significance as the filmmakers both follow and embellish the mythology attaching to the historical figure of Jesse James. In addition, the concept of 'assassination' clearly carries further connotations in American society which could be argued to work towards bracketing Jesse James with a series of further iconic figures such as Martin Luther King Jr, Presidents Abraham Lincoln and John F. Kennedy, and presidential candidate Robert 'Bobby' Kennedy.

III

Diametrically opposed to this way of seeing Jesse as Christ are those elements of the film that associate Jesse with darkness and evil. Much of the film is shot using subdued lighting, creating classic film noir images that are dark and full of shadow. Visual and scripted associations between Jesse and the forces of evil are found throughout the first half of the film, up until the point at which we begin to approach Jesse's death when his image shifts from predominantly 'prince of darkness' to predominantly 'divine being'. From this point on Jesse is increasingly placed within bright interior spaces and brilliantly sunlit exterior locations, but prior to this both the lighting used around him and the way in which he is described is very different.

At the start of the film he is seen firmly in opposition to concepts of law and order, regretting 'neither his robberies nor the seventeen murders he laid claim to', we are told by the narrator (Hugh Ross). When he prepares himself for the attack on a train at Blue Cut, Missouri, we see him dressed in black, standing in the darkness and pulling a black kerchief (actually described as being *blue* in Hansen's novel)[7] over his face and nose so that only his eyes are showing (Figure 9.2). The series of shots which follow move in ever closer on the small part of Jesse's face we can see in the darkness before continuing past him to present the audience with a screen of complete blackness while the sound of the approaching train rings like a metallic echo in a pitch-black chamber. We are journeying into a demonic other world, and the atmosphere of fear and uncertainty is further accentuated by the camera shots that follow, accompanied as they are by threatening music. The light from the lamp at the front of the oncoming train falls across slender trees and creates shadowy lines that run the full vertical length of the frame. While his men rush around firing their guns, attempting to ensure the occupants of the train are suitably terrified, Jesse emerges like some otherworldly being out of the steam given off by the engine that has been brought to a halt.

Figure 9.2 Jesse dressed in black and standing in darkness in *The Assassination of Jesse James by the Coward Robert Ford*.

Later that night, sitting talking to Robert Ford about the robbery, in response to Ford's musing about what an amazing day he has had robbing a train and now 'chatting with none other than Jesse James', Pitt has to deliver the line 'Yeah, it's a wonderful world', and what he does is interesting. He speaks the line not as if he is in character as James but as a reprise of the voice of Detective David Mills, the role he played in *Seven* (David Fincher, 1995), a film which as movies of moral darkness go ranks with the most frighteningly and unremittingly grim. The depth of the ironic tone achieved in the delivery is magnified through the reference. In keeping with the recurring presentation of this implied dark side of the world and of man, at various moments through this scene Pitt turns his head slightly to one side so that in the noir lighting half his face is cast into deep shadow. The use of a half shadowed face to symbolically signal the presence of Jesse's 'dark' side occurs at other points in the film and it is also applied to other characters. In the sequence currently being discussed a similar effect is projected onto the face of Affleck's Robert Ford before the scene ends by fading to black.

When he moves house in Kansas, Jesse is further linked to darkness. We see him as a shadowy figure, moving belongings into his new home 'at night', the narrator tells us, 'so that the neighborhood couldn't get a good look at them'. Continuing the theme of Jesse's association with darkness, when he arrives at Ed Miller's (Garret Dillahunt) shack Jesse's mere presence clearly terrifies this man. As he appears on horseback over a distant rise, moving across a frosty landscape, the editing shows him appearing to be able to 'jump' through time as he traverses the distance between the horizon and the shack. When Miller opens the door to let Jesse in, Miller's face is given in close-up through the glass that is set in the door, giving a ghostly aspect to his image and prefiguring his fate. As he steps back to allow Jesse in, the back of Jesse's black hat moves across the screen in extreme close-up, obliterating Miller's face and further confirming his fate. And as Jesse moves into the room a reverse shot shows Jesse's face in complete shadow, further confirming his association with the darker aspects of human nature. A little later in the scene, after Miller and Jesse have talked, Jesse puts on his black hat revealing his black glove in the process; and, as he moves the hat up towards his head within a head and shoulders shot, the hat momentarily wipes his face from the screen. Then, as the 'new' – after the wipe – Jesse looks out at the grey sky, an out-of-focus bird flies up and out of the shot, and cutting to a low-angle shot looking up at Jesse as he invites Miller to dinner in town we see his face again half in shadow. Finally, the scene ends with a shot of Miller, which fades out to a black screen. Visual confirmation of Miller's death is actually delayed until a later flashback but the audience already understands that his fate is sealed thanks to the close thematic alignment between *mise en scène*, cinematography, editing and performance that is displayed within the sequence set in his shack. Interestingly, the content of Miller's death scene again serves to underscore the idea that Jesse possesses good and evil sides. In the darkness of night Jesse is shown callously shooting Miller in the back; but, in a sudden contrast of action and manner, Jesse immediately shows a capacity for tenderness as he comforts his horse, which has been startled by his gunfire.

When Jesse pays a surprise visit to another gang member, Dick Liddil (Paul Schneider), it is the middle of the night. Liddil comes cautiously downstairs to find Jesse already sitting at a table in his house. Jesse's face is lit from below and to one side so that, again, he is given the trademark, face-half-in-shadow look. As Liddil is asked by Jesse if he is 'ready to go for a ride' a shot of Liddil dissolves into a ghostly image and we are left to wonder if, as with Ed Miller, this prefigures his fate. Again, when Jesse chooses to have a one-to-one chat with Charley Ford (Sam Rockwell), it is the middle of the night and, again, he surprises the person concerned. To the sound of Charley's snoring the audience is shown the silhouette of Jesse standing in the doorway to the bedroom; and, although his body is nothing more than a black silhouette the outline of his gun, the instrument of death, can be seen on his right hip. Jesse is thus recurrently associated with the idea of his being a supernatural bringer of fear and potential death. In this particular night-time chat, Jesse explains to Charley how he has had a discussion with himself in which his 'good side won out', implying of course that the debate that went on was between his good and bad sides. He goes on to tell Charley about the night he killed Ed Miller, but as he does so Jesse refers to himself in the third person, saying, 'Ed and Jesse, they argued on the road . . . '. What does this particular use of language signify? Is it that Jesse views his bodily actions at a detached distance, as if from some sort of godlike perspective? Is this use of illeism a projection of an out-of-body experience? Or is it that Jesse wants to distance himself from the dark half of himself with which he now feels uncomfortable? At this point we are taken into the flashback showing Miller's death through a transition that sees a shadowy image of Jesse dissolve into a shot of a cloudless, starlit sky at night, so that the two – Jesse and the night sky – are in some way associated with each other. And this is reinforced when, as he prepares to kill him, Jesse's first lines to Miller in the flashback probe at some mysterious or mystical relationship between human beings and the cosmos:

> JESSE: You ever count the stars. I can't ever get the same number. They keep changing on me.
> ED: I don't even know what a star is exactly.
> JESSE: Your body knows. It's your mind that forgot.

Concluding the story of the murder for Charley, Jesse retains the third person address: 'When push came to shove, Jesse shot and killed him.'

If we recall the opening of the movie we can see the way in which right from the start Jesse is ascribed supernatural powers. The narrator's voiceover tells us: 'Rooms seemed hotter when he was in them, rains fell straighter, clocks slowed, sounds were amplified.' What do these things suggest? That the experience of life is especially intense around Jesse? That he is in some sense a presence that is able to alter the natural world? Certainly the opening shots of the film provide images that mark Jesse as a special person in some way, suggesting a self-contained character who is different from others, distant, detached and thoughtful. At other points in the film he is seen as a being who others believe to be telepathically aware of what they have been doing. The sheriff, who is attempting to capture him, for example, says: 'I can't guess how he does it but he's always knowledgeable about what's going on.'

IV

Linked to these interpretations of Jesse as an extramundane being associated with Christ on the one hand and Satan on the other is the idea of the celebrity status of the historical Jesse James who was idolized, in particular across the southern states, during the latter years of his life as well as after his death. In the film this 'fan-base' comes to be embodied in Robert Ford, who tells Jesse he has a copy of 'The Train Robbers, or a Story of the James Boys' by R. W. Stevens beside his bed.[8,9] Indeed, the later years of Jesse James's life did coincide with the emergence of mass media celebrity culture across the United States nurtured by newspapers, comic books and the relatively new technology of photography. In the United States news photography including snapped images of battlefield dead[10] originated with the American Civil War; and, by the time of James's death in 1882 newspapers were competing for readership within a boom industry. Indeed, 'the number of daily newspapers in the United States rose from 574 in 1870 to 2600 in 1909, their circulation increasing from 2.6 million to 24.2 million.'[11] Newspapers outside of Missouri attacked that state for not bringing the James brothers and other outlaws to justice. Newspapers within Missouri divided along political lines, either defending the gang as wronged Civil War vets, or calling for something to be done about them. And, as the newspaper debates continued and stories about the gang and Jesse James in particular increased, interest in the activities of the gang grew. William Settle[12] explains that, in addition to the many newspaper reports written in the period, in 1880 'at least three authors wrote "histories" of the band in full-length book form',[13] and from 1881 the *Five Cent Wide Awake Library* began to publish stories about the gang in the dime novel genre.[14]

To return to the film, we could add one further dimension to the character of Jesse as presented in this particular version of the legend that has been built, developed and reshaped by generation upon generation. In a scene with Jesse and Charley on a frozen lake, we find Jesse portrayed neither as a satanic bringer-of-death, nor really as a Christ-like figure, but in a more mortal guise. It may be that he is like Christ in that he longs for an end to his life and is not attached to the body ('You ever consider suicide?' he asks Charley, before firing several shots at his dark outline reflected in the ice beneath his feet) but he is also very human. Still, even as a human being he is an outsider in that he is different to an ordinary guy like Charley. 'You won't mind dyin' once you've peeked over the other side', he says, more to himself than to Charley, and implying he has indeed already looked over to 'the other side'. Within this representation, he is aware of both the existentialist absurdity of the world around us all and the risible nature of the world around the composite myth/legend/celebrity that is 'Jesse James'. His response to Charley's assertion that his brother, Robert Ford, thinks highly of Jesse is 'All America thinks highly of me'.

V

So, what exactly is happening with this particular representation from 2007 of the violent robber and murderer of the historical record, Jesse James? What we are confronted with is (as with all former representations of the legend) something that tells us as much about the period in which we are living as it does about any historical reality from the late nineteenth century. On the one hand, the film is an exploration of the creation of a legend examining the role of the media in manufacturing celebrities and in constructing fans as consumers of celebrity. When Jesse 'rises from the dead' as the table on which his body has been laid out is lifted before the camera of an actor playing the role of a photographer from the period we are also, in effect, asked to consider the role of the camera in media storytelling. Tom Gunning[15] has suggested the key property of the cinematic image is its 'absent presence', and this is a phrase that is totally appropriate for an exploration of both legendary status and stardom, since both stars and legends are most precisely defined as 'absent presences'. And so, the film considers the gap between the 'star' construct and the real human being, and the relationship between fans and the imagined entities of celebrities. On the other hand, the suggestion that the life and death of Jesse James could have some sort of parallel to the life and death of Christ is clearly utterly ridiculous; as is the suggestion of Jesse James as having some sort of supernatural powers, whether satanic or divine.

Because *The Assassination of Jesse James by the Coward Robert Ford* is a product that is perfectly in keeping with the media found within twenty-first-century Western society we find ourselves confronted by a confused (and, for the viewer, confusing) text. The film cannot escape being part of the media it is, in part, purporting to be examining. That media is dominantly conservative in outlook and politically right wing, as quick to construct paragons of virtue to be admired as it is to create figures of evil deemed responsible for the desperate state of the world. More crucially, because it is generally unwilling to accept the role social conditions play in the formation of individual character, it is a media that is seldom prepared to consider the role that a society itself may play in causing acts of 'evil'. Both the presentation of this particular story of Jesse James within this particular film, and the representation of the modern world delivered to the public by the wider media, are founded on a culture of fear that is at the heart of the society inhabited by the film's audience. Frank Furedi has suggested:

> Western societies are increasingly dominated by a culture of fear. The defining feature of this culture is the belief that humanity is confronted by powerful destructive forces that threaten our everyday existence.[16]

Moreover, Furedi says, 'there is a tendency in society to seize on the exceptional, extreme and abhorrent acts as confirmation of the kind of diseased world that we inhabit'.[17]

Clearly thinking along similar lines, Martin Kuška notes that:

> on the one hand, a person must face the ever stronger tides of media-accentuated sources of fear, while on the other hand, the individual continues to actively search for, demand and purchase threatening information (news, movies, literature).[18]

VI

The central character we have here – the version of Jesse James with which we are being presented – enters the constructed film world of *The Assassination of Jesse James by the Coward Robert Ford* with his personality already fully formed. He is a legend in his own short lifetime, a bank robber and murderer with a fearsome reputation. There is no exploration of his past, and therefore no sense of how he came to be the cold, calculating killer who so clearly terrifies Ed Miller. The crucial implication of such a representation of Jesse James is that people should be seen as being born as they are rather than as being created out of the circumstances of their experience of life. From the evidence presented to the audience, Jesse is a product of nature, not of the failure of nurture; he simply is an evil person, a psychopath, who is capable of deranged brutality at one moment and gentle tenderness with his children the next. Jason Horsley suggests that 'although we never really come to know him, Pitt's performance suggests that Jesse is an enigma even to himself'.[19] He is presented as a mystery to everyone, including the audience, existing for the most part beyond the boundaries of the normal, everyday world. Importantly, the conclusion we are forced towards as a result of the particular construction of the film world with which we are confronted is that evil simply is unfathomable, inexplicable, and therefore not subject to understanding. When Jesse briefly cries after having arrived, dressed from head to foot in black, at a small farmstead and violently beaten a young teenage boy for information the audience can see no real explanation as to why. Only if they know something of the biography of the historical figure of Jesse James might viewers link this to a reported similar experience of his own as a teenager at the hands of Unionist troops during the Civil War. As John N. Edwards has reported:

> Jesse was at home with his step-father, Dr. Reuben Samuels, of Clay County. He knew nothing of the strife save the echoes of it that now and then reached his mother's isolated farm. One day a company of militia visited this farm, hung Dr. Samuels to a tree until he was left for dead, and seized upon Jesse, a mere boy

plowing in the field. With a rope about his neck, the soldiers abused him harshly, pricked him with sabres, and finally threatened him with certain death if it was ever reported to them again that he had given aid or information to Guerrillas.[20]

Jesse was sixteen when he joined the Southern guerrilla bands and became intimately involved in a 'war' that became an unremitting cycle of atrocities. According to T. J. Stiles, Jesse's brother, Frank, said, "'If you ever want to pick a company to do desperate work . . . select young men from 17 to 21 years old . . .'".[21] Stiles sets the scene for chapters in his book entitled 'Terror' and 'Horror' by saying:

> They had no lines, no objectives, no strategy, no command structure. Theirs was a purely tactical war, a war to inflict pain, to punish, to kill and destroy. Every barn and brook was a battlefield; every civilian, either an ally or a target. By stepping into that brooding, deathlike camp, Jesse James entered a race to find and kill as many enemies as he could.[22]

Discussing child soldiers in general, Michael Wessells suggests that:

> When children are engaged as soldiers, spend their formative years immersed in systems of violence, and construct their values and identity guided by military groups, they become vehicles for violence rather than citizens who can build peace.[23]

Much recent research has been devoted to the psychological effects of war on child combatants, particularly relating to the experiences of children in African wars, and we should be careful not to make sweeping statements relating to post-traumatic stress and associated psychological outcomes. However, just a little reading around the brutal acts committed by the guerrilla groups with which Jesse was associated in the Civil War will make clear the need for taking this aspect of his 'nurture' into account. As an example of the brutalities that became commonplace, discussing the group of guerrillas operating under the command of William Clarke Quantrill, J. Dennis Robinson gives a report of a single incident in 1863:

> Quantrill and 450 raiders, including Frank James, brutally attacked the town of Lawrence, Kansas. In four hellish hours on August 21 they burned the place to the ground. Following Quantrill's orders to kill every male old enough to hold a gun, the bushwhackers murdered 200 men and boys.[24]

Of course, the filmmakers have made a deliberate choice to focus on the final months of Jesse's life and the emerging relationship in that period with Robert Ford, the person who is to kill him, and they are not obliged to go over every event in the outlaw's life even if that were possible. And so the film might claim to be examining the psychology of James in his final days in a more in-depth fashion than previous films have attempted, and, in looking at the relationship between Jesse and Robert Ford, it might claim to focus on a previously under-explored aspect of the story. Yet, it is not a definitive exploration of even this small portion of James's life and interesting alternative perspectives could have formed the cornerstone of the narrative. The almost cameo-like role in the story that Frank James (Sam Shepard) plays offers a clear example of another key relationship that might have been used as a focal point. Similarly, a view from the perspective of Jesse's wife, Zee James (Mary-Louise Parker), would offer fascinating narrative possibilities. The simple fact is that filmmaking choices, especially ones so fundamental to the structure of the narrative, have consequences. And it must therefore be acknowledged that to ignore causes for the evolution of a character and to present a personality without reference to the formation of that personality creates a particularly pointed experience for the audience.

VII

In the end the film is merely one more version of a story constantly re-played and re-interpreted in the United States over a period of well over 100 years. Like all of the other written, drawn, filmed and staged versions, this one exists in relation to a particular society that has produced it at a particular moment in its history. And so, to again re-phrase our central question, why does this particular version of the Jesse James legend with its already fully formed central character emerge early in the new millennium? The suggestion here is that amongst the things a version in the early 2000s might be said to reflect would be a fascination, not simply of contemporary American society but also of early twenty-first-century UK society, with a certain limited concept of the psychology of 'evil'. In some ways connected to this, there is also a sense of being enthralled by the nature of celebrity and fame. There is no doubt that all of this plays out against a backdrop of a society that is fascinated by celebrities, defined by Karen Sternheimer as 'anyone who is watched, noticed, and known by a critical mass of strangers'.[25] Going further, there might be said to be a desperate psychological need amongst audiences to search for answers to the increasingly chaotic nature of modern life. Faced with a world in which we are continually being asked to consider the location of the 'axis of evil', a return to religious certainty becomes increasingly alluring, even to the extent of imposing Christian imagery in the most unlikely and illogical of places.

The relationship between the public and their idols (and monstrous others), both in the late nineteenth century and today, is at the heart of this film. In the period in which this film is set the emerging mass media of newspapers, magazines and 'dime novels' created a 'star' out of Jesse James. According to Gregory Morris, 'Jesse James began paying attention to his press clippings in the 1870s, and effectively manipulated the editorial pages of the Kansas City papers. And that is how Robert Ford first learned about him and later became obsessed by him.'[26] In the Western world post-2000 we too live in a society fascinated by the cult of the individual who manages to stand out from the crowd, who gains fame or infamy, who expresses our aspirations and fears, who seems to explain to us the nature of contemporary human existence. To some extent, this has always been the case, but in some societies in other periods the corollary to this – the sense that evil is explicable, that community and society are at least as important as the individual – balances the sense of fear generated by the lurking, inexplicable nature of evil and such an unhealthy focus on the individual. In 'Communicating the terrorist risk: Harnessing a culture of fear?' Gabe Mythen and Sandra Walklate argue: 'Instead of appealing to collective desires for the good life, the language of politics increasingly taps into individualized insecurities and fears.'[27] According to John Horn, Andrew Dominik wanted *The Assassination of Jesse James by the Coward Robert Ford* to be 'a dark, contemplative examination of fame and infamy'.[28] And certainly it is 'dark' and it is about 'fame and infamy', but there is no 'contemplative examination' here, there is only the presentation of 'fame and infamy' as simple facts of contemporary experience. As with all films dealing with historical incident, the interests presented relate at least as much to the present as to the past in which the narrative is set. Mythen and Walklate suggest: 'A burgeoning "culture of fear" has taken root in western cultures, promoted by state institutions and exacerbated by those working within the media and security industries.'[29]

This is a film that attempts to establish itself as a serious contribution to the Western genre, setting out to position itself in relation to movies such as *McCabe and Mrs. Miller* (Robert Altman, 1971) and *Days of Heaven* (Terrence Malick, 1978), for example. As such, it is a rich and interesting film that repays analysis in relation to approaches to film such as those offered by genre analysis, star studies and auteur theory, but to do so too easily places the reader in a naïve position of complicity with an ideological base that works to reinforce some of the most dangerous aspects of the currently dominant Western view of the world. The psychosis of late modernity is a state in which, on the one hand, we idolize certain people beyond all reason, setting them on pedestals to be worshipped as gods, and, on the other hand, we trust nobody and fear everybody. Making an explicit link (while acknowledging the creation of fear as an ever-present aspect of media history) David Altheide suggests, 'the role of the mass media in promoting fear has become more pronounced since the United States "discovered" international terrorism on September 11, 2001'.[30] He also points out that this is political since 'the discourse of fear promotes the politics of fear'.[31]

The contemporary state of being is perfectly captured in *The Assassination of Jesse James by the Coward Robert Ford*. The content of the film, aided by the style in which it is filmed, creates an atmosphere of anxiety and foreboding. In reality, the historical Jesse James was just one more victim of war, a brutalized child soldier, but the film works to mark him out as special, a being who is in some way other-worldly. Any acceptance by modern day audiences of the version of the Jesse James legend found in *The Assassination of Jesse James by the Coward Robert Ford* is loaded with irony. The film's simplistic outlook, much like that of most modern Western media, serves only to obscure the all too apparent real nature of the modern world in which new victims of war are created every day.

Notes

1. Some of the ideas found here first appeared in an early form in John White, *Westerns* (London and New York: Routledge, 2011), pp. 159–63.
2. Nancy Tischler, *Encyclopedia of Contemporary Christian Fiction: From C.S. Lewis to Left Behind* (Santa Barbara, CA: ABC-CLIO, 2009), p. 148.
3. 'Ron Hansen: Get to know Ron Hansen – Biola University Chapel', Biola University (2014). Available at <https://www.youtube.com/watch?v=695gYyqVyIg> (accessed 11 November 11 2015).
4. Ibid.
5. Robert Paul Seesengood and Jennifer L. Koosed, *Jesse's Lineage: The Legendary Lives of David, Jesus, and Jesse James* (New York and London: Bloomsbury, 2013), p. 10.
6. Seesengood and Koosed, *Jesse's Lineage*, p. 135.
7. Ron Hansen, *The Assassination of Jesse James by the Coward Robert Ford* (New York: Knopf Doubleday, 1983), p. 17.
8. Presumably this is the writer William Settle refers to as D. W. Stevens. Settle claims almost all of the dime novels put out by the publisher Frank Tousey on the subject of the James brothers were written by this person, 'who is identified by authorities on the dime novel as John R. Musick'. See William Settle, *Jesse James Was His Name: or, Fact and Fiction Concerning the Careers of the Notorious James Brothers of Missouri* (Lincoln: University of Nebraska Press, 1977), p. 188.

9. There are a series of ways in which Robert Ford is seen as a child and, additionally, as existing in something of a father–son relationship with Jesse.
10. See, for example, Alexander Gardner's *Dead Confederate Soldier on the Battlefield at Antietam*, September 1862, Metropolitan Museum of Art, New York. Available at <http://www.metmuseum.org/toah/works-of-art/1970.537.4> (accessed 11 November 2015). Also, Timothy H. O'Sullivan's *Field Where General Reynolds Fell, Battlefield of Gettysburg*, 1863, Metropolitan Museum of Art, New York. Available at <http://www.metmuseum.org/toah/works-of-art/2005.100.502.1> (accessed 11 November 2015).
11. Philip Jenkins, *A History of the United States*, 3rd edn (Basingstoke and New York: Palgrave Macmillan, 2007), pp. 171–2.
12. Settle, *Jesse James Was His Name*, 1977, p. 109.
13. The works referred to are J. A. Dacus's *Life and Adventures of Frank and Jesse James and the Younger Brothers, the Noted Western Outlaws*; James William Buel's two-volume work, *The Border Outlaws* and *The Border Bandits*; and R. T. Bradley's *Outlaws of the Border, or The Lives of Frank and Jesse James*. (R. T. Bradley, *Outlaws of the Border, or The Lives of Frank and Jesse James, Their Exploits, Adventures and Escapes, Down to the Present Time* (Chicago, IL: J. S. Goodman, 1880); James William Buel, *The Border Outlaws: An Authentic and Thrilling History of the Most Noted Bandits of Ancient or Modern Times, The Younger Brothers, Jesse and Frank James, and Their Comrades in Crime* (St Louis, MO: Historical Publishing Company, 1881); James William Buel, *The Border Bandits: An Authentic and Thrilling History of the Noted Outlaws, Jesse and Frank James, and Their Bands of Highwaymen* (St Louis, MO: Historical Publishing Company, 1881); J. A. Dacus, *Life and Adventures of Frank and Jesse James and the Younger Brothers, the Noted Western Outlaws* (New York and St Louis, MO: N. D. Thompson, 1882).) These works joined that of Southern apologist and newspaperman John N. Edwards, *Noted Guerrillas, or The Warfare of the Border* ((St Louis, MO: Bryan, Brand, 1877). This last work is available at the Internet Archive, at <https://archive.org/details/notedguerrillaso00edwarich> (accessed 7 November 2015).
14. Eventually these works would come to be published on an industrial scale, contributing massively to the development of the legend. 'Ralph F. Cummings, former editor of the *Dime Novel Round-Up* . . . reports that stories about the James brothers were published in the following series: *Boys of New York, Golden Weekly, Young Men of America, Wide Awake Library, New York Detective Library, Boys of New York Pocket Library, Morrison's Sensational Series, American Weekly, Jesse James Stories, James Boys Weekly Adventure Series, New York Ledger, Bandit Stories*, and other papers.' Settle, *Jesse James Was His Name*, 1977, p. 187.
15. Tom Gunning, 'Those drawn with a very fine camel's hair brush: the origins of film genres', Iris, 1995, 20: 60.
16. Frank Furedi, *Culture of Fear: Risk-Taking and the Morality of Low Expectation* (London and New York: Continuum, 2002), p. vii.

17. Ibid. p. 109.
18. Martin Kuška, 'New sources of fear in a late modern society: the globalization of risk', in Radek Trnka, Karel Balcar and Martin Kuška (eds), *Re-Constructing Emotional Spaces: From Experience to Regulation* (Prague: Prague College of Psychosocial Studies Press, 2011), p. 113.
19. Jason Horsley, *The Secret Life of Movies: Schizophrenic and Shamanic Journeys in America* (Jefferson, NC: McFarland, 2009), p. 184.
20. John N. Edwards, *Noted Guerrillas, or The Warfare of the Border* (St Louis, MO: Bryan, Brand, 1877), p. 167. Available at <https://archive.org/details/notedguerrillaso00edwarich> (accessed 7 November 2015).
21. T. J. Stiles, *Jesse James: Last Rebel of the Civil War* (London: Vintage, 2007), p. 101.
22. Ibid. p. 101.
23. Michael G. Wessells, *Child Soldiers: From Violence to Protection* (Cambridge, MA: Harvard University Press, 2006), p. 3.
24. J. Dennis Robinson, *Jesse James: Legendary Rebel and Outlaw* (Minneapolis, MN: Compass Point Books, 2007), p. 34.
25. Karen Sternheimer, *Celebrity Culture and the American Dream: Stardom and Social Mobility* (New York: Routledge, 2011), p. 2.
26. Gregory L. Morris, *Talking Up a Storm: Voices of the New West* (Lincoln: University of Nebraska Press, 1995), p. 145.
27. Gabe Mythen and Sandra Walklate, 'Communicating the terrorist risk: harnessing a culture of fear?', *Crime Media Culture*, 2006, 2(2): 124.
28. John Horn, 'With both barrels', *Los Angeles Times*, 2 May 2007. Available at <http://articles.latimes.com/2007/may/02/entertainment/et-pitt2> (accessed 1 June 2014).
29. Mythen and Walklate, 'Communicating the terrorist risk', 2006, p. 126.
30. David L. Altheide, 'Fear, terrorism, and popular culture', in Jeff Birkenstein, Anna Froula and Karen Randell (eds), *Reframing 9/11: Film, Popular Culture and the 'War on Terror'* (New York and London: Continuum, 2010), p. 12.
31. Ibid. p. 19.

CHAPTER 10

Conclusion

> The threat is from the future. It is what might come next. Its eventual location and ultimate extent are undefined. Its nature is open-ended. It is not just that it is not: it is not in a way that is never over. We can never be done with it. Even if a clear and present danger materializes in the present, it is still not over. There is always the nagging potential of the next after being even worse, and of a still worse again after that. The uncertainty of the potential next is never consumed in any given event.
>
> Brian Massumi, *The Future Birth of the Affective Fact*[1]

I

This book has focused primarily on eight contemporary Westerns. It has been suggested each of these films has distinctive thematic and stylistic elements that have been shaped as a result of their production during the period post-9/11. This is to say no more than each film reflects the ideological contestations of the time and place of its inception. Countless studies have shown films to reflect the anxieties of the periods in which they have been made and in many cases to employ the same keynote responses to contemporary concerns from period to period, positioning heroes in relation to the problems of the age, for example, and/or re-emphasising the main strands of a collective national myth for the audience. It has been suggested, for instance, that one way to account for the success of Westerns immediately after the Second World War is to see the genre as 'providing reassuring, imaginary resolutions to real-world anxieties and contradictions'.[2] The additional interest here has been in the fact that, since media texts contribute towards shaping ideological perceptions, these Westerns will also be helping to shape audience attitudes towards the world around them. The overall experiential force of each film will work towards pinning the audience in a particular ideological position.

Every age faces the same question in a different guise: what is the answer to the crisis in which we find ourselves? And every age mobilises the culture at its disposal to think its way through possible solutions. Susan Kollin sees the Western as being 'an important cultural form' in the post-9/11 era, 'deployed in some instances as a discursive weapon in the U.S. war on terror, while in other cases used to reassess the triumphalist and exceptionalist beliefs that became prevalent'.[3] Routinely, as part of the mainstream media, Hollywood films will battle to conserve what are seen as sacrosanct elements of the current social fabric. Frequently they will attempt to bolster their society's core beliefs and values. Less often they might look to modify attitudes and behaviours in order to create a re-invigorated society able to withstand threatening external forces. Occasionally they might view an external challenge to the global capital of which they are a part as an opportunity for deeper reflection on society's commonly accepted principles and ideals.

As an introductory structural framework for the central chapters in this book a single keynote idea was identified for approaching each focus film. So, the films were seen to be:

- reinforcing the myth of America
- endorsing the use of extreme force in dealing with enemies
- highlighting the importance of defending the homeland
- providing audiences with exhilarating escapist entertainment
- delivering an immersive experience of visceral body abuse
- engulfing audiences within an ahistorical postmodern space
- foregrounding religious concepts of forgiveness and redemption
- contributing towards a contemporary Western culture of fear.

Such a list of conceptual approaches could be applied to a range of films beyond Westerns, and indeed to a range of media texts beyond films. To take the final idea in the list: the notion of living within a culture of fear, or the concept of the media as constructing the world as a place of threat, has become widespread. In looking at the news media, for example, David Altheide radically reverses more conventional usage of the word 'terrorism' in suggesting:

> Fear in a democratic society requires the mass media. If these media are perpetuating claims about the 'other' – the likely targets of future state action – then this fear-generating endeavour becomes an act of mass media terrorism on the 'public body,' if not individuals who subsequently suffer from state actions.[4]

The one-line core positions suggested as starting points for the examination of our eight individual films remain important indicators of differences between the films, but might also, taken as a whole, operate to highlight key aspects of contemporary American (Western) culture.

As each of the eight films was considered in detail, overlaps between the concerns to be found in each became apparent. Time after time in these films, for example, a relatively weak force finds itself confronted by what seems to be an overwhelmingly powerful foe; and time after time those under threat need to demonstrate the depths of their resourcefulness in overcoming their enemy. And yet what was also discovered was that beyond these similarities each film was also the site of its own complex ideological entanglements.

II

Although, in general, these films have claimed to offer the spectator various forms of liberating experience – the kick-ass female in *Jane Got A Gun* (Gavin O'Connor, 2016), or the spectacle of *The Lone Ranger* (Gore Verbinski, 2013), for example – they have in reality, it has been suggested, worked to restrict and control audience response in line with the dominant ideology. In the final analysis, although there may be all sorts of ideological struggles at work and ideological ruptures to be found within the films under discussion, most if not all of these films have promoted an ideology centring on a generally agreed national myth of America. Frequently, liberal attitudes – such as the empowerment of women or racial equality – are foregrounded with conscious intent and as a direct challenge to more conservative ideologies relating to these fields of social exchange. Quentin Tarantino and the rest of the cast and crew involved in creating *Django Unchained* (2012), for example, are clearly intensely serious and politically driven in their advocacy of racial equality. And yet, as we might expect within a mainstream film, *Django Unchained* does not question the fundamental ideological basis of Western democracy, nor does it challenge specific ideas underpinning the myth of the nation as embodied in Bush's presidential speeches quoted in the Introduction here. Ultimately, this particular film encloses both the viewer and the filmmakers within a postmodernist box of relativities from within which there is no hope of intervention in the real world because such engagement is not possible given an understanding of the world shaped by postmodernism.

At the same time, within this general situation of there being limited surface ideological contestation and little challenge to the concept of America as an exceptional place with a necessary destiny to fulfil,[5] since the conscious intent of the filmmakers is one thing and the ideology embodied in a text something altogether different, there are clear incongruities and difficulties to be found in each film. *Open Range* (Kevin Costner,

2003), for example, has a central character who is able to kill with absolute cold-blooded efficiency and yet is supposedly gentle and kind-hearted. The contradictions at play within the advocacy of a mainstream concept of an 'America' that is family-orientated but also able to commando into a compound and 'take out' Osama bin Laden cannot be entirely successfully subsumed within the cultural product. *The Three Burials of Melquiades Estrada* (Tommy Lee Jones, 2005) shines an intense spotlight on American attitudes towards (economic) migrants but seemingly believes it is simply a matter of liberal recognition of the humanity of the 'other' that is required, rather than some address to the inequalities of global capital.

It remains true that, despite whatever attempts there may be to pin an audience to an acceptance of limited ideological challenge, individual readers are able to produce their own readings of each of these films. Each member of the audience has, as Chomsky would have it, the ability to 'make the effort'[6] and question these films more deeply. The aim of this book is, very definitely, not to argue in favour of the unchallengeable existence of a blanket ideology. It is the case, however, that dominant audience positions in relation to each of these films are being offered to readers; and these dominant positions are derived not primarily from the ideological perspectives of those involved in creating the films but from wider dominant perspectives within society. As an ideological arena of struggle contestation is taking place within each of these films but it also remains the case that a preferred reading exists for each film.[7] In consideration of gender, obviously the dominant narrative within Westerns would classically be characterised as masculine: this is clearly challenged within a range of contemporary Westerns, such as *Jane Got a Gun* and *The Keeping Room* (Daniel Barber, 2014). In terms of race, besides *Django Unchained* the classical position would also be challenged by Westerns such as *The Revenant* (Alejandro González Iñárritu, 2015) and *The Three Burials of Melquiades Estrada*. And, in the case of both gender and race, these films would be seen as following in the wake of a series of Westerns stretching back into the 1950s that have taken on what might be seen as the dominant conservative agenda of Westerns. There is, however, no smooth progression in the discussion of issues of either gender or race that can be traced through some progressive trajectory of development. The ways in which such matters are dealt with in film reflect the socio-historical, socio-economic and socio-political context of the period in which they are made. As with revisionist Westerns in general over a longer period, the more recently described post-Western, is only 'positive' in its advocacy of certain perspectives on key structures of society such as gender and race, within the context of liberal ideology. The inclusion of liberal notions within the ideational framework of the Western constitutes a move towards a political position of liberalism, or a liberal expression of social values. It is also often a conscious attempt by those who are responsible for producing the film to shift the wider political agenda within their society in this direction. That is to say, it is not an effort to undermine the basis of Western society but an attempt at hegemonic realignment. In order to study film in relation to contemporary socio-political, socio-historical and socio-economic contexts, it is necessary to move beyond what directors and writers may have to say about the product they were involved in bringing to the screen. The film directed by Quentin Tarantino, *Django Unchained*, may indeed be 'about' those things he professes it to be about, primarily the unspoken-about, holocaust-like period of slavery in American history, but it has also come into existence during a period in American history when under acts of 'extraordinary rendition' the United States government has been responsible for 'shipping' prisoners in chains and manacles to Guantanamo Bay. It also, as with *The Three Burials*, erases the economic other than as an implied underpinning, not-to-be-debated functionality.

III

Stanley Corkin suggested the role of mainstream Westerns in the Cold War period was 'to help audiences adjust to new concepts of national definition'.[8] In parallel with this, we could propose contemporary Westerns during the period of the declared 'War on Terror' have been an attempt to do the same sort of thing. But this would be a mistake. Certainly 'national definition' is what is at stake but what we have witnessed has been an ideological process taking place rather than some procedure for 'helping' audiences. Michael Klein is surely right to point out that it is 'the start of the Civil Rights era'[9] in America that signals the emergence of narratives to challenge the 'myth of a harmonious slave society'[10] that had previously been seen in Hollywood films epitomised by *Gone with the Wind* (Victor Fleming 1939). Further, Klein is also correct to highlight the fact that 'during the years of the Vietnam War *and the protests against it*'[11] there was only one Hollywood film set in Vietnam – *The Green Berets* (John Wayne, 1968). In other words, there is some relationship between the level of ideological struggle and protest 'on the streets'[12] and expressions of ideology within film. Klein also observes that in the Western 'indirect criticism' of the Vietnam War appeared at the time, giving the examples of *Soldier Blue* (Ralph Nelson, 1970) and *Little Big Man* (Arthur Penn, 1970).[13] These are films he describes as offering 'a critique of white U.S. civilisation as essentially colonialist, barbarous, hypocritical, and life-denying'.[14]

This book is, therefore, in many ways an old-fashioned one,[15] arguing for the importance of history as something that although it may be deeply contested can be known through close investigation and understood in terms of its political manifestations, and maintaining that there is a crucial linkage between historical events and films that needs to be critically evaluated if the study of film is to have any meaning. As the historian Timothy Snyder warns, with special resonance for film in his use of the word 'spectacle':

> To abandon facts is to abandon freedom. If nothing is true, then no one can criticize power, because there is no basis on upon which to do so. If nothing is true, then all is spectacle.[16]

This does not mean we are unaware of Ernesto Laclau and Chantal Mouffe's counsel that 'there is not an *in-itself* of history but rather a multiple refraction of it, depending on the traditions from which it is interrogated';[17] rather, it is an acknowledgement of the fact that it is a necessity of being-in-the-world to take up a political position.

The interest here is in Westerns as a cultural barometer of media tendencies, as a means of exploring the ways in which films are working to position their audiences and shape audience responses. Often in these films we find audiences are placed within a dark world of confusion and uncertainty. Frequently the horror of the world, the monstrousness of the world or the sudden unpredictability of the world threatens to overwhelm characters. Repeatedly these films create an atmosphere of fear making the world seem a dangerous place. Usually they work to deny access to any form of genuine historical context, replacing it by a myth of the past that is endorsed by the wider media and confirmed over time by an even wider culture of storytelling. Of course, this is in some ways simply part and parcel of narrative structure but that does not mean that in these cases it is not being employed specifically to address the concerns of the age. It is interesting to reflect on the number of times in these films it is the war 'vet' who is shown to be the one who has the 'knowledge' required to deal with the threat that is being experienced. It is fascinating to consider the range of moments in these films in which the enemy has to be interrogated (tortured), or executed without mercy. Although there are plenty of examples of close quarters combat, it is also thought-provoking to consider the number of times an enemy is 'taken out' at long range by somebody using a particularly powerful piece of technology from the period.

The central argument to be found here is that, in the face of the threat posed to American self-confidence by the spiralling consequences of the 'War on Terror' and the escalating involvement of both the military and the secret services in overseas affairs, the genre has been employed as a space for re-establishing/bolstering a confident, assertive Americanism. At the same time it is recognised that to some extent these films have also functioned as an arena within which to question at least some aspects of contemporary American foreign policy. Overall, the genre has been used by a range of filmmakers since 2001 in a variety of ways but always in a manner that, if it is to be fully understood, needs to be seen in relation to American overseas policy. To take another example, *Hostiles* (Scott Cooper, 2017) is billed as a 'journey towards respect, reconciliation and forgiveness'[18] between former enemies, US Army officer Joseph Blocker (Christian Bale) and Cheyenne warrior Yellow Hawk (Wes Studi). However, what we see in the film is something altogether different. We discover that although there are 'good' Native Americans (such as Yellow Hawk), who may once have been enemies but with whom we can now work, there are also other 'bad' Native Americans who remain our implacable foes and who need to be hunted down and killed before they hunt you down and kill you. Behind black warpaint that erases any sense of common humanity these 'baddies', these 'outsiders', these cultural 'Other' descend on an idyllic little house on the prairie in the opening scene, destroying it utterly and mercilessly (Figure 10.1).[19]

To some extent there may have been a re-employment of the Western by Hollywood as a genre that 'works' for examining the post-9/11 period (as it worked for considering the Cold War period); what is happening here is neither unique to the Western genre nor unique in the sense of

Figure 10.1 Warpaint erasing any sense of shared humanity in *Hostiles* (Scott Cooper, 2017).

not previously occurring. The Western is the genre par excellence for the expression (and the exploration) of the binary opposition of good and evil, civilisation and barbarism, although the same relationship of film to ideology and to history is to be found within other genres, and within this and other genres during other periods of history. Cultural products are produced out of, and (therefore) address, current social concerns. Both the features of individual films and trends across groups of films need primarily to be seen within socio-political contexts.

Each of the films considered here may be seen to endorse the 'War on Terror', and in places to attempt a critique of this dominant aspect of American foreign policy. Each of them should be recognised as attempting to create specific controlled audience responses. These attempts to direct spectators may be resisted and, even, rejected; but, the larger question (implied by the references here to wider media contexts) might be: what are the possibilities for audience resistance in the face of a Hollywood product sitting securely within the repeated blizzards of media immersion offered to mainstream audiences?

At its heart this book considers the extent to which audience members are asked to sympathise, empathise and identify with the presented position of a central character, the extent to which they are pushed towards critical evaluation and the complexion of any critical evaluation they might be urged take up. The aim has been to consider the nature of the filmic interface as it encourages the viewer towards, sometimes contemplative consideration, but more generally unthinking acceptance. Despite at times considerable financial losses and critical failure Hollywood has continued to fund these addresses to the dominant concerns of the age. Interestingly, economic decisions are, perhaps, shown to be taken within the urgency of a contemporary socio-cultural context; that is to say, within a context of continual hegemonic negotiation and renegotiation.

Recent Westerns have responded to the political climate as Westerns always have done. To this extent, this book is nothing more than a statement of the obvious, in that any genre in any medium must necessarily have responded in some way to the changed circumstances of America post-9/11. Trauma impacts. A beleaguered culture (naturally) renegotiates its hegemony, restates its values, and attempts to energize its population to resist outside forces that wish to destroy that culture. In the end it is very straightforward: these films are 'War on Terror' Westerns. How do we know that? Simply because they are about:

- the violent, uncivilised brutality of the enemy with which you are faced
- the fear of surprise attack, whether in hostile territory, or at home

- refusing to give way when tested to the utmost extremes of your endurance
- being tortured and being prepared to torture
- sacrificing yourself for others, particularly loved ones
- meeting death, or the possibility of death, with equanimity
- being willing to suffer horrendous injuries that will leave you maimed for life in order to achieve your chosen ends
- being prepared to unmercifully bring the greatest firepower possible to bear on your enemies
- retaining a sense of civilised values such that they are seen to give validity to even your most violent actions.

In these films, in undertaking a mission into enemy territory against a terrifying foe what you have to demonstrate is tenacity and dogged determination, or in waiting for the enemy to descend upon you what you need to display is resourcefulness and a determination to do whatever it takes. Despite barely contained concerns, about corruption amongst society's elected officials and about 'our' side being as brutal and uncivilised as the enemy, these films are ultimately largely in line with the sentiments of the presidential speeches quoted in the opening pages to this book.

The major arena of struggle all of these films side-step is economics. At root, *The Lone Ranger* is not about the 'birth' of a mythical hero of the people but about the irresistible spread of capital across a continent, but the cinematic ride has been of such swish-back rapidity that this is barely noticed. The everyday depth of anti-migrant sentiment in *The Three Burials* is not to be understood, fundamentally, in terms of race but in terms of economics. At base, Glass's story in *The Revenant* is not about against-the-odds personal survival but only exists in an understandable fashion within the context of imperialist ventures in pursuit of lucrative resources. The real story of Jesse James is not that of a romantic outlaw but of dirt poor families living a life of grinding poverty within a society with very clearly defined class divisions. In the same way, the War on Terror is not a war of ideas: wars never are. Wars are economic in their origin, pursuit and resolution.

Notes

1. Brian Massumi, 'The future birth of the affective fact: the political ontology of threat', in Melissa Gregg and Gregory J. Seigworth (eds), *The Affect Theory Reader* (Durham, NC, and London: Duke University Press, 2010), p. 53.

2. Andrew Patrick Nelson (ed.), *Contemporary Westerns: Film and Television Since 1990* (Lanham, MD: Scarecrow Press, 2013), p. xiv.
3. Susan Kollin, *Captivating Westerns: The Middle East in the American West* (Lincoln and London: University of Nebraska Press, 2015), p. 146.
4. David L. Altheide, *Creating Fear: News and the Construction of Crisis* (New York: Aldine de Gruyter, 2002), p. 12.
5. *The Homesman* (Tommy Lee Jones, 2014) would be the key film to consider in this regard. This film does not appear to be 'about' the War on Terror. It is a bleak exploration of the human condition – the intense loneliness of the isolation of the individual to which the only logical response is suicide. However, because it destroys the American Dream and the notion of Manifest Destiny, according to the producer, it could not have been made without overseas finance. See Andrew Pulver, 'Tommy Lee Jones on *The Homesman*: "It's a consideration of American imperialism"', *The Guardian*, 18 May 2014. Available at <https://www.theguardian.com/film/2014/may/18/tommy-lee-jones-the-homesman-cannes-film-festival-hilary-swank> (accessed 15 August 2018).
6. Mark Achbar (ed.), *Manufacturing Consent: Noam Chomsky and the Media.* (Montreal and New York: Black Rose Books, 1994), p. 20.
7. This we should recall is not that reading 'preferred' by those producing the film, nor by the director as auteur, but that which is determined by the presence within society of dominant ways of seeing/ways of understanding the world. Stuart Hall said preferred readings 'both have the institutional/political/ideological order imprinted in them and have themselves become institutionalized'. See Stuart Hall, 'Encoding/decoding', in Stuart Hall, Dorothy Hobson, Andrew Lowe and Paul Willis (eds), *Culture, Media, Language: Working Papers in Cultural Studies, 1972–79* (New York and London: Routledge, [1980] 2005), p. 124.
8. Stanley Corkin, *Cowboys as Cold Warriors: The Western and U.S. History* (Philadelphia, PA: Temple University Press, 2004), p. 3.
9. Michael Klein, 'Historical memory, film, and the Vietnam era', in Linda Dittmar and Gene Michaud (eds), *From Hanoi to Hollywood: The Vietnam War in American Film* (New Brunswick, NJ, and London: Rutgers University Press, 1990), p. 20.
10. Ibid. p. 19.
11. Ibid. p. 20. My italics.
12. Timothy Snyder, Richard C. Levin Professor of History at Yale University, has suggested: 'Protest can be organized through social media, but nothing is real that does not end on the streets.' See Timothy Snyder, *On Tyranny: Twenty Lessons From the Twentieth Century* (London: Bodley Head, 2017), p. 84.
13. Klein, 'Historical memory, film, and the Vietnam era', 1990, p. 20.
14. Ibid. p. 21.
15. Flagging up Stuart Hall for one thing!

16. Snyder, *On Tyranny*, 2017, p. 65.
17. Ernesto Laclau and Chantal Mouffe, 'Post-Marxism without apologies', *New Left Review*, 1987, 1(166): 99.
18. *Hostiles*, DVD package, directed by Scott Cooper. USA: Entertainment Studios, 2017.
19. It should be added that this film also offers a prolonged examination of American brutality in war. At one point, a soldier says to an officer: 'I don't know how you done it all these years, Captain. Seeing all the things you've seen. Doing all the things you've done. Makes you feel inhuman after a while.'

Bibliography

Abrams, Dennis, *Spike Lee: Director* (New York: Chelsea House, 2008).
Achbar, Mark (ed.), *Manufacturing Consent: Noam Chomsky and the Media* (Montreal and New York: Black Rose Books, 1994).
Akins, Jerry, *Hangin' Times in Fort Smith: A History of Executions in Judge Parker's Court* (Little Rock, AR: Butler Center Books, 2012).
Altheide, David L., *Creating Fear: News and the Construction of Crisis* (New York: Aldine de Gruyter, 2002).
Altheide, David L., 'Fear, terrorism, and popular culture', in Jeff Birkenstein, Anna Froula and Karen Randell (eds), *Reframing 9/11: Film, Popular Culture and the 'War on Terror'* (New York and London: Continuum, 2010), pp. 11–22.
Ambrose, Stephen E., *Nothing Like It In the World: The Men Who Built the Transcontinental Railroad 1863–1869* (New York: Touchstone, 2001).
Anderson, Gary Clayton, *The Conquest of Texas: Ethnic Cleansing in the Promised Land, 1820–1875* (Norman: University of Oklahoma Press, 2005).
Andreas, Peter, 'A tale of two borders: the U.S.-Canada and U.S.-Mexico lines after 9-11', in Peter Andreas and Thomas J. Biersteker (eds), *The Rebordering of North America: Integration and Exclusion in a New Security Context* (London and New York: Routledge, 2003).
Andreychuk, Ed, *The Lone Ranger on Radio, Film and Television* (Jefferson, NC: McFarland, 2018).
Anzaldúa, Gloria, '(Un)natural bridges, (un)safe spaces', in AnaLouise Keating (ed.), *The Gloria Anzaldúa Reader* (Durham, NC, and London: Duke University Press, 2009).
Applebaum, Stephen, 'Tommy Lee Jones: *The Three Burials of Melquiades Estrada*', *BBC*, 24 September 2014, <http://www.bbc.co.uk/films/2006/03/30/tommy_lee_jones_melquiades_2006_interview.shtml> (accessed 7 November 2017).
Aquila, Richard, *The Sagebrush Trail: Western Movies and Twentieth-Century America* (Tucson: University of Arizona Press, 2015).
Armitage, Katie H., *Lawrence: Survivors of Quantrill's Raid* (Charleston, SC: Arcadia, 2010).
Asim, Jabari, *The N Word: Who Can Say It, Who Shouldn't, and Why* (New York: Mariner Books, 2007).
Auerbach, John, 'Cold War films', in Adam Piette and Mark Rawlinson (eds), *The Edinburgh Companion to Twentieth-Century British and American War Literature* (Edinburgh: Edinburgh University Press, 2012).

Bakir, Vian, *Torture, Intelligence and Sousveillance in the War on Terror: Agenda-Building Struggles* (London and New York: Routledge, 2016).

Bandy, Mary Lea and Kevin Stoehr, *Ride, Boldly Ride: The Evolution of the American Western* (Berkeley and Los Angeles: University of California Press, 2012).

Baudrillard, Jean, *Simulacra and Simulation*, trans. Sheila Faria Glaser (Ann Arbor: University of Michigan Press, 1981/1994).

Bell, A. Craig, *Alexandre Dumas: A Biography and Study* (London: Cassell, 1950).

Bell, Marianne, *Frontier Family Life: A Photographic Chronicle of the Old West* (New York: Barnes & Noble, 1998).

Booker, M. Keith, *Postmodern Hollywood: What's New in Film and Why It Makes Us Feel So Strange* (Westport, CT: Praeger, 2007).

Bradley, R. T., *Outlaws of the Border, or The Lives of Frank and Jesse James, Their Exploits, Adventures and Escapes, Down to the Present Time* (Chicago, IL: J. S. Goodman, 1880).

Bradshaw, Peter, '*Jane Got a Gun* review – laborious and solemn Western with absurd finale', *The Guardian*, 21 April 2016, <https://www.theguardian.com/film/2016/apr/21/jane-got-a-gun-review-laborious-and-solemn-western-with-absurd-finale> (accessed 26 July 2017).

Breznican, Anthony, 'Johnny Depp tells EW origins of Tonto makeup from "Lone Ranger"', *Entertainment Weekly*, 22 April 2012, <http://ew.com/article/2012/04/22/johnny-depp-reveals-origins-of-tonto-makeup-from-lone-ranger-exclusive/> (accessed 13 July 2018).

Briley, Ron, 'John Wayne and *Big Jim McLain* (1952): The Duke's Cold War legacy,' *Film & History: An Interdisciplinary Journal of Film and Television Studies*, 2001, 31(1): 28–33.

Brodhead, Michael J., *Isaac C. Parker: Federal Justice on the Frontier* (Norman: University of Oklahoma Press, 2003).

Brody, Richard, 'Hits and misses: *True Grit* vs. *The Social Network*', *The New Yorker*, <https://www.newyorker.com/culture/richard-brody/hits-and-misses-true-grit-vs-the-social-network> (accessed 8 January 2018).

Brooks, Cleanth, *William Faulkner: The Yoknapatawpha Country* (Baton Rouge: Louisiana State University Press, [1963] 1991).

Brulliard, Karen, 'Move over, DiCaprio. This man really did survive the cold inside a dead horse', *Washington Post*, 26 February 2016, <https://www.washingtonpost.com/news/animalia/wp/2016/02/26/move-over-dicaprio-this-man-really-did-survive-the-cold-inside-a-dead-horse/?utm_term=.62697d938411> (accessed 9 December 2017).

Buel, James William, *The Border Bandits: An Authentic and Thrilling History of the Noted Outlaws, Jesse and Frank James, and Their Bands of Highwaymen* (St Louis, MO: Historical Publishing Company, 1881).

Buel, James William, *The Border Outlaws: An Authentic and Thrilling History of the Most Noted Bandits of Ancient or Modern Times, The Younger Brothers, Jesse and Frank James, and Their Comrades in Crime* (St Louis, MO: Historical Publishing Company, 1881).

Bumgarner, Jeffrey B., *Federal Agents: The Growth of Federal Law Enforcement in America* (Westport, CT: Praeger, 2006).
Bush, George W., 'Victory speech, 2000', 13 December 2000, *American Rhetoric: Online Speech Bank*, <https://www.americanrhetoric.com/speeches/gwbush-2000victoryspeech.htm> (accessed 11 May 2018).
Bush, George W., 'Address to joint session of Congress following 9/11 attacks', 20 September 2001, *American Rhetoric: Online Speech Bank*, <http://www.americanrhetoric.com/speeches/gwbush911jointsessionspeech.htm> (accessed 11 May 2018).
Bush, George W., 'Address to the nation – ultimatum to Saddam Hussein', 17 March 2003, *American Rhetoric: Online Speech Bank*, <http://www.americanrhetoric.com/speeches/wariniraq/gwbushiraq31703.htm> (accessed 15 August 2018).
Butler, Judith, *Precarious Life: The Powers of Mourning and Violence* (London and New York: Verso, 2004).
Cadwalladr, Carole, '*The Revenant* is meaningless pain porn', *The Guardian*, 17 January 2016, <https://www.theguardian.com/commentisfree/2016/jan/17/revenant-leonardo-dicaprio-violent-meaningless-glorification-pain> (accessed 28 November 2017).
Caldwell, Thomas, 'Film review – *True Grit* (2010)', *Cinema Autopsy*, 2011, <https://blog.cinemaautopsy.com/2011/01/24/film-review-true-grit-2010/> (accessed 8 January 2018).
Carter, Matthew, '"I'm just a cowboy": transnational identities of the borderlands in Tommy Lee Jones' *The Three Burials of Melquiades Estrada*', *European Journal of American Studies*, 2012, 7(1): 1–18.
Carter, Matthew, *Myth of the Western: New Perspectives on Hollywood's Frontier Narrative* (Edinburgh: Edinburgh University Press, 2014).
Carter, Matthew, '"I've been looking for you": reconfiguring race, gender, and the family through the female agency of *The Keeping Room*', *Papers on Language and Literature*, Winter 2018, 54(1): 25–45.
Cawelti, John G., *Mystery, Violence, and Popular Culture* (Madison: University of Wisconsin Press, 2004).
Cinema Review, 'OPEN RANGE, production notes – about the production', *Cinema Review*, <http://cinemareview.com/production.asp?prodid=2177> (accessed 22 June 2018).
Cobb, Jasmine Nichole and John L. Jackson, 'They hate me: Spike Lee, documentary filmmaking, and Hollywood's "savage slot"', in Janice D. Hamlet and Robin R. Means Coleman (eds), *Fight the Power: The Spike Lee Reader* (New York: Peter Lang, 2009), pp. 251–72.
Coen, Ethan, '2016 election thank you notes', *New York Times*, 11 November 2016, <https://www.nytimes.com/2016/11/13/opinion/sunday/2016-election-thank-you-notes.html?_r=1&register=facebook> (accessed 30 January 2018).
Cogburn, Brett, 'The real Rooster Cogburn: remembering my great-grandfather's role in the creation of a classic western character', *True West: History*

of the American Frontier, 19 March 2011, <https://truewestmagazine.com/the-real-rooster-cogburn/> (accessed 3 January 2018).

Cogburn, Brett, *Rooster: The Life and Times of the Real Rooster Cogburn, The Man Who Inspired True Grit* (New York: Kensington Books, 2012).

Corber, Robert J., *Cold War Femme: Lesbianism, National Identity, and Hollywood Cinema* (Durham, NC: Duke University Press, 2011).

Corkin, Stanley, *Cowboys as Cold Warriors: The Western and U.S. History* (Philadelphia, PA: Temple University Press, 2004).

Cousins, Mark, 'America seeks comfort in Westerns', 16 October 2003, *Evening Standard*, <https://www.standard.co.uk/go/london/film/america-seeks-comfort-in-westerns-6956608.html> (accessed 4 January 2018).

Csicsery-Ronay, Istvan, 'Notes on Mutopia', *Postmodern Culture: Journal of Interdisciplinary Thought on Contemporary Cultures*, 1997, 8(1).

Cunningham, Hilary, 'Nations rebound?: Crossing borders in a gated globe', *Identities: Global Studies in Culture and Power*, 2004, 11: 329–50.

Dacus, J. A., *Life and Adventures of Frank and Jesse James and the Younger Brothers, the Noted Western Outlaws* (New York and St Louis, MO: N. D. Thompson, 1882).

Dean, Eric T., '"We will all be lost and destroyed": post-traumatic stress disorder and the Civil War', *Civil War History*, 1991, 37(2): 138–53.

Deleuze, Gilles and Félix Guattari, *A Thousand Plateaus: Capitalism and Schizophrenia*, trans. Brian Massumi (London and New York: Continuum, [1980] 1988).

Demos, Virginia E., 'An affect revolution: Silvan Tompkin's affect theory', in Virginia E. Demos (ed.), *Exploring Affect: The Selected Writings of Silvan S. Tompkins* (New York: Press Syndicate of the University of Cambridge, 1995), pp. 17–26.

Denton, Robert E. (ed.), *The George W. Bush Presidency: A Rhetorical Perspective* (Lanham, MD: Lexington Books, 2012).

Dercksen, Daniel, '*Jane Got A Gun* brings new perspective to the classic American Western', *The Writing Studio*, 3 May 2016, <https://writingstudio.co.za/jane-got-a-gun-brings-new-perspective-to-the-classic-american-western/> (accessed 5 June 2017).

Di Nucci, Ezio and Filippo Santoni de Sio (eds), *Drones and Responsibility: Legal, Philosophical and Socio-Technical Perspectives on Remotely Controlled Weapons* (London and New York: Routledge, 2016).

Dolin, Eric Jay, *Fur, Fortune, and Empire: The Epic History of the Fur Trade in America* (New York and London: W. W. Norton, 2010).

Duffy, Helen, *The 'War on Terror' and the Framework of International Law* (Cambridge: Cambridge University Press, 2005).

Dumas, Alexandre, *Le Capitaine Aréna. Le deuxième volet des Impressions de voyage dans le Royaume de Naples, après Le Speronare et avant Le Corricolo/Impressions of a Voyage to the Kingdom of Naples, part 2, Captain Arena* (Paris: Michel Lévy Frères, [1835] 1879).

Eberwein, Robert (ed.), *The War Film* (New Brunswick, NJ: Rutgers University Press, 2005).

Edwards, Jason A. and David Weiss (eds), *The Rhetoric of American Exceptionalism: Critical Essays* (Jefferson, NC: McFarland, 2011).
Edwards, John N., *Noted Guerrillas, or the Warfare of the Border* (St Louis, MO: Bryan, Brand, 1877) <https://archive.org/details/notedguerrillaso00edwarich> (accessed 7 June 2017).
Elkins, Stanley M., *Slavery: A Problem in American Institutional and Intellectual Life*, 3rd edn (Chicago and London: University of Chicago Press, 1976).
Equal Justice Initiative, *Lynching in America: Confronting the Legacy of Racial Terror: Report Summary*, 2nd edn, Equal Justice Initiative, 2015, <https://lynchinginamerica.eji.org/report/> (accessed 27 November 2017).
Ewers, John Canfield, *Plains Indian History and Culture: Essays on Continuity and Change* (Norman: University of Oklahoma Press, 1997).
Fabre, Michel, *From Harlem to Paris: Black American Writers in France, 1840–1980* (Urbana and Chicago: University of Illinois Press, 1993).
Fojas, Camilla, *Border Bandits: Hollywood on the Southern Frontier* (Austin: University of Texas Press, 2008).
Fritscher, Jack, *Mapplethorpe: Assault with a Deadly Camera: A Pop Culture Memoir – An Outlaw Reminiscence* (New York: Hastings House, 1994).
Furedi, Frank, *Culture of Fear: Risk-Taking and the Morality of Low Expectation* (London and New York: Continuum, 2002).
Gates, Henry Louis Jr, 'Tarantino "unchained": Django trilogy', in Gerald Peary (ed.), *Quentin Tarantino: Interviews, Revised and Updated* (Jackson: University of Mississippi, 2013), pp. 184–98.
Gilbey, Ryan, 'Sultans of smug: the Coen brothers are the most conservative of directors', *New Statesman*, 14 February 2011, p. 42.
Gilmore, Richard, '*No Country for Old Men*: the Coens' tragic Western', in Mark T. Conard (ed.), *The Philosophy of the Coen Brothers* (Lexington: University Press of Kentucky, 2009).
Gittell, Noah, 'The Coen brothers' subtle politics', *The Atlantic*, 20 December 2013, <https://www.theatlantic.com/entertainment/archive/2013/12/the-coen-brothers-subtle-politics/282501/> (accessed 30 January 2018).
Golden Gate Bridge Highway and Transportation District, 'Construction timeline Golden Gate Bridge: December 1932 to April 1937', Golden Gate Bridge Highway and Transportation District, <http://goldengatebridge.org/research/ConstructionTimeline.php> (accessed 13 July 2018).
Gray, Richard, *After the Fall: American Literature Since 9/11* (Malden, MA, and Oxford: Wiley-Blackwell, 2011).
Grønstad, Asbjørn, *Transfigurations: Violence, Death and Masculinity in American Cinema* (Amsterdam: Amsterdam University Press, 2008).
Gunning, Tom, 'Those drawn with a very fine camel's hair brush: the origins of film genres', *Iris*, 1995, 20: 49–61.
Guru-Murthy, Krishnan, 'Tarantino uncut: when Quentin met Krishnan', *Channel 4 News*, 10 January 2013, <https://www.channel4.com/news/tarantino-uncut-when-quentin-met-krishnan-transcript> (accessed 29 April 2013).

Hagans, Dominic, *Wounded Rangers: Under Enemy Fire in Afghanistan* (Cirencester: Mereo, 2013).
Halberstam, Judith, *Female Masculinity* (Durham, NC: Duke University Press, 1998).
Hall, Stuart, 'Encoding/decoding', in Stuart Hall, Dorothy Hobson, Andrew Lowe and Paul Willis (eds), *Culture, Media, Language: Working Papers in Cultural Studies, 1972–79* (New York and London: Routledge, [1980] 2005), pp. 117–27.
Hall, Stuart, 'Race, culture, and communications: looking backward and forward at cultural studies', in Marcus E. Green (ed.), *Rethinking Gramsci* (London and New York: Routledge, 2011).
Hancock, Larry, *Surprise Attack: From Pearl Harbor to 9/11 to Benghazi* (Berkeley, CA: Counterpoint, 2016).
Hansen, Ron, *The Assassination of Jesse James by the Coward Robert Ford* (New York: Knopf Doubleday, 1983).
Harper's Weekly, 'A typical negro', *Harper's Weekly: A Journal of Civilisation*, 4 July 1863, 7(340): 429, <https://archive.org/stream/harpersweeklyv7bonn#page/428/mode/2up/search/gordon> (accessed 26 March 2018).
Herman, David (ed.), *The Cambridge Companion to Narrative* (Cambridge: Cambridge University Press, 2007).
Hesson, Ted, 'Five ways immigration system changed after 9/11,' *ABC News*, 11 September 2012, <http://abcnews.go.com/ABC_Univision/News/ways-immigration-system-changed-911/story?id=17231590> (accessed 8 November 2017).
Higbee, Will and Song Hwee Lim, 'Concepts of transnational cinema: towards a critical transnationalism in film studies', *Transnational Cinemas*, 2010, 1(1): 7–21.
Hilger, Michael, *Native Americans in the Movies: Portrayals from Silent Films to the Present* (Lanham, MD: Rowman & Littlefield, 2016).
Hiller, Jennifer, 'A 21st-century oil boom in the Lone State', *San Antonio Express-News*, 25 February 2013, <http://www.mysanantonio.com/business/article/A-21st-century-oil-boom-in-the-Lone-Star-State-4303192.php> (accessed 14 November 2017).
Hodgson, Godfrey, *The Myth of American Exceptionalism* (New Haven, CT, and London: Yale University Press, 2009).
Hooton, Christopher, 'Jamie Foxx recalling Quentin Tarantino shouting at him on the Django Unchained set doesn't go where you'd think', *Independent*, 30 May 2017, <https://www.independent.co.uk/arts-entertainment/films/news/jamie-foxx-interview-quentin-tarantino-howard-stern-django-unchained-behind-the-scenes-shouting-rant-a7762541.html> (accessed 27 April 2017).
Horn, John, 'With both barrels', *Los Angeles Times*, 2 May 2007, <http://articles.latimes.com/2007/may/02/entertainment/et-pitt2> (accessed 1 June 2014).

Horne, Thomas A., 'James Mangold's *3:10 to Yuma* and the mission in Iraq,' *Journal of Film and Video*, Fall 2013, 65(3): 40–8.

Horsley, Jason, *The Secret Life of Movies: Schizophrenic and Shamanic Journeys in America* (Jefferson, NC: McFarland, 2009).

Hunnef, Jenna, '"Fooling around with Papa's pistol": avenging patriarchy in *True Grit*', in Scott F. Stoddart (ed.), *The New Westerns: Critical Essays on the Genre Since 9/11* (Jefferson, NC: McFarland, 2016), pp. 40–61.

Jackson, Cassandra, 'Visualizing slavery: photography and the disabled subject in the art of Carrie Mae Weems', in Christopher M. Bell (ed.), *Blackness and Disability: Critical Examinations and Cultural Interventions* (Münster: LIT Verlag, 2011).

Jaggi, Maya, 'The last word', *The Guardian*, 21 December 2001, <https://www.theguardian.com/education/2001/dec/21/artsandhumanities.highereducation> (accessed 22 March 2018).

Jameson, Fredric, 'Postmodernism and consumer society', in Hal Foster (ed.), *Postmodern Culture* (London: Pluto Press, 1985).

Jamieson, Amie, Hyon B. Shin and Jennifer Day, 'Voting and registration in the election of November 2000', US Census Bureau, *Current Population Reports*, February 2002, <https://www.census.gov/prod/2002pubs/p20-542.pdf> (accessed 6 June 2018).

Jeffery, Renée (ed.), *Confronting Evil in International Relations: Ethical Responses to Problems of Moral Agency* (Basingstoke and New York: Palgrave Macmillan, 2008).

Jenkins, Philip, *A History of the United States*, 3rd edn (Basingstoke and New York: Palgrave MacMillan, 2007).

Jones, Reece, 'Death in the sands: the horror of the US-Mexico border', *The Guardian*, 4 October 2016, <https://www.theguardian.com/us-news/2016/oct/04/us-mexico-border-patrol-trump-beautiful-wall> (accessed 8 November 2017).

Katz, Mark N., *Leaving Without Losing: The War on Terror After Iraq and Afghanistan* (Baltimore: Johns Hopkins University Press, 2012).

Kellermann, Arthur L. and Philip J. Cook, 'Armed and dangerous: guns in American homes', in Michael A. Bellesiles (ed.), *Lethal Imagination: Violence and Brutality in American History* (New York and London: New York University Press, 1999).

Kellner, Douglas M., *Cinema Wars: Hollywood Film and Politics in the Bush-Cheney Era* (Oxford and Malden, MA: John Wiley, 2010).

Keresztesi, Rita, 'Cowboys and West Indians: decolonizing the Western and Perry Henzall's *The Harder They Come*', in MaryEllen Higgins, Rita Keresztesi and Dayna Oscherwitz (eds), *The Western in the Global South* (New York and London: Routledge, 2015).

Kerner, Aaron Michael, *Torture Porn in the Wake of 9/11: Horror, Exploitation, and the Cinema of Sensation* (New Brunswick, NJ: Rutgers University Press, 2015).

Khatchadourian, Raffi, 'The Kill Company: did a colonel's fiery rhetoric set the conditions for a massacre?', *The New Yorker*, 6 and 13 July 2009, <http://

www.newyorker.com/magazine/2009/07/06/the-kill-company> (accessed 6 June 2017).

Kirchmeier, Jeffrey L., *Imprisoned by the Past: Warren McCleskey and the American Death Penalty* (Oxford: Oxford University Press, 2015).

Kit, Borys, 'Lone Ranger budget back up to $250 million', *The Hollywood Reporter*, 22 June 2012, <http://www.hollywoodreporter.com/heat-vision/lone-ranger-budget-johnny-depp-336526> (accessed 1 October 2017).

Klein, Michael, 'Historical memory, film, and the Vietnam era', in Linda Dittmar and Gene Michaud (eds), *From Hanoi to Hollywood: The Vietnam War in American Film* (New Brunswick, NJ, and London: Rutgers University Press, 1990), pp. 19–40.

Knowlton, Christopher, *Cattle Kingdom: The Hidden History of the Cowboy West* (Boston, MA: Eamon Dolan/Houghton Mifflin Harcourt, 2017).

Kollin, Susan, *Captivating Westerns: The Middle East in the American West* (Lincoln and London: University of Nebraska Press, 2015).

Korte, Gregory, 'Mexican slur has long history in politics', *USA Today*, 29 March 2013, <https://www.usatoday.com/story/news/politics/2013/03/29/mexican-immigration-slur-history/2036329/> (accessed 7 November 2017).

Krogstad, Jens, Jefferey S. Passel and D'Vera Cohn, 'Five facts about illegal immigration in the U.S.', Pew Research Center, 27 April 2017, <http://www.pewresearch.org/fact-tank/2017/04/27/5-facts-about-illegal-immigration-in-the-u-s/> (accessed 7 November 2017).

Kuška, Martin, 'New sources of fear in a late modern society: the globalization of risk', in Radek Trnka, Karel Balcar and Martin Kuška (eds), *Re-Constructing Emotional Spaces: From Experience to Regulation* (Prague: Prague College of Psychosocial Studies Press, 2011), pp. 105–19.

Laclau, Ernesto and Chantal Mouffe, 'Post-Marxism without apologies', *New Left Review*, 1987, 1(166): 79–108.

Landry, Clay, 'The real story of Hugh Glass – sources', Museum of the Mountain Man, Pinedale, Wyoming, <http://hughglass.org/sources/> (accessed 2 December 2017).

Langman, Larry and David Ebner (eds), *Hollywood's Image of the South: A Century of Southern Films* (Westport, CT, and London: Greenwood Press, 2001).

LaPierre, Wayne, *Guns, Crime and Freedom* (Washington, DC: Regnery, 1994).

LaPierre, Wayne, *Guns, Freedom and Terrorism* (Nashville, TN: WND Books, 2003).

Lawson, George, 'Introduction: the 'what', 'when' and 'where' of the global 1989', in George Lawson, Chris Armbruster and Michael Cox (eds), *The Global 1989: Continuity and Change in World Politics* (Cambridge: Cambridge University Press, 2010).

Leal, David L. and Nestor P. Rodriguez (eds), *Migration in an Era of Restriction and Recession: Sending and Receiving Nations in a Changing Global Environment* (New York: Springer, 2016).

Leeming, David and Jake Page, *Myths, Legends and Folktales of America: An Anthology* (Oxford and New York: Oxford University Press, 1999).

Leonard, David J., 'Django blues: whiteness and Hollywood's continued failures', in Oliver C. Speck (ed.), *Quentin Tarantino's Django Unchained: The Continuation of Metacinema* (New York and London: Bloomsbury, 2014), pp. 269–86.

Lewis, Hilary, 'Natalie Portman on *Jane Got a Gun* off-camera woes: "It gives you the feeling that you can do anything"', *The Hollywood Reporter*, 28 January 2016, <http://www.hollywoodreporter.com/news/jane-got-a-gun-natalie-860212> (accessed 5 June 2017).

Limon, John, *Writing after War: American War Fiction from Realism to Postmodernism* (Oxford: Oxford University Press, 1993).

Lions Clubs International, 'Purpose and ethics', Lions Clubs International, <http://www.lionsclubs.org/EN/who-we-are/mission-and-history/purpose-and-ethics.php> (accessed 6 November 2017).

Locke, John, *Second Treatise on Civil Government: An Essay Concerning the True Original, Extent and End of Civil Government* (Wheeling, IL: Harlan Davidson, 1982).

Lowenstein, Adam, 'Spectacle horror and *Hostel*: why 'torture porn' does not exist', *Critical Quarterly*, 2011, 53(1): 42–60.

Lowenstein, Adam, 'Transforming horror: David Cronenberg's cinematic gestures after 9/11', in Aviva Briefel and Sam J. Miller (eds), *Horror after 9/11: World of Fear, Cinema of Terror* (Austin: University of Texas Press, 2011).

Lusted, David, *The Western* (Harlow: Pearson Education, 2003).

McCune, Brent G. and Dennis L. Soden, 'Regulating the push and pull of migration in the post-9/11 era on the southern border', in Matthew J. Morgan (ed.), *The Impact of 9/11 and the New Legal Landscape: The Day That Changed Everything?* (New York: Palgrave Macmillan, 2009).

McGilvray, James, *Chomsky: Language, Mind, Politics*, 2nd edn (Cambridge and Malden, MA: Polity, 2014).

McSweeney, Terence, *The 'War on Terror' and American Film: 9/11 Frames Per Second* (Edinburgh: Edinburgh University Press, 2014), pp. 119–22.

McVeigh, Stephen, *The American Western* (Edinburgh: Edinburgh University Press, 2007).

Manikkalingam, Ram, 'Foreword', in Bradley Jay Strawser (ed.), *Opposing Perspectives on the Drone Debate* (New York: Palgrave Macmillan, 2014).

Mapplethorpe, Robert, *Black Book* (New York: St Martin's Press, 1988).

Massumi, Brian, 'The autonomy of affect', *Cultural Critique*, 1995, 31: 83–109.

Massumi, Brian, 'Notes on the translation and Acknowledgements', in Gilles Deleuze and Félix Guattari, *A Thousand Plateaus: Capitalism and Schizophrenia* (London and New York: Continuum, [1987] 2004), pp. xvii–xx.

Massumi, Brian, 'The future birth of the affective fact: the political ontology of threat', in Melissa Gregg and Gregory J. Seigworth (eds), *The Affect Theory Reader* (Durham, NC, and London: Duke University Press, 2010), pp. 52–70.

Mepham, John, 'The theory of ideology in *Capital*', *Radical Philosophy*, Summer 1972, 2: 12–19.

Mercer, Kobena, *Welcome to the Jungle: New Positions in Black Cultural Studies* (New York and London: Routledge, 1994).

Mexal, Stephen, 'Two ways to Yuma: Locke, liberalism, and western masculinity in *3:10 to Yuma*', in Jennifer L. McMahon and B. Steve Csaki (eds), *The Philosophy of the Western* (Lexington: University of Kentucky Press, 2010).

Moerk, Christian, 'An actor, a writer and the silent border between them', *New York Times*, 11 December 2005, <http://www.nytimes.com/2005/12/11/movies/an-actor-a-writer-and-the-silent-border-between-them.html> (accessed 15 November 2017).

Morris, Gregory L., *Talking Up a Storm: Voices of the New West* (Lincoln: University of Nebraska Press, 1995).

Moses, Wilson Jeremiah, *Black Messiahs and Uncle Toms: Social and Literary Manipulations of a Religious Myth* (University Park: Pennsylvania State University Press, 1994).

Moss, Andrew, 'Schizophrenia and postmodernism: *Raising Arizona*, *Barton Fink*, and "The Coen Brothers"', *Post Script: Essays in Film and the Humanities*, 2008, 27(2): 23–37.

Mountz, Alison, 'The Other', in Carolyn Gallaher, Carl Dahlman, Mary Gilmartin, Alison Mountz and Peter Shirlow, *Key Concepts in Political Geography* (London and Los Angeles: Sage, 2009).

MovieManiacs, 'Django Unchained: meet the press', MovieManiacs, 2013, <https://www.youtube.com/watch?v=-1QpScB-HJg> (accessed 29 April 2018).

Mythen, Gabe and Sandra Walklate, 'Communicating the terrorist risk: harnessing a culture of fear?', *Crime Media Culture*, 2006, 2(2): 123–42.

National Park Service, Fort Smith, 'Men executed at Fort Smith: 1873 to 1896', <https://www.nps.gov/fosm/learn/historyculture/executions-at-fort-smith-1873-to-1896.htm> (accessed 16 January 2018).

Nelson, Andrew Patrick (ed.), *Contemporary Westerns: Film and Television Since 1990* (Lanham, MD: Scarecrow Press, 2013).

Nelson, Andrew Patrick, *Still in the Saddle: The Hollywood Western, 1969–1980* (Norman: University of Oklahoma Press, 2015).

Noble, Marianne, 'The ecstasies of sentimental wounding in *Uncle Tom's Cabin*', *Yale Journal of Criticism*, Fall 1997, 10(2): 295–320.

Obama, Barack, *Public Papers of the Presidents of the United States 2010*, Book 1 – January 1 to June 30, 2010 (Washington: United States Government), <https://www.gpo.gov/fdsys/pkg/PPP-2010-book1/pdf/PPP-2010-book1-Doc-pg597.pdf> (accessed 27 July 2017).

Obama, Barack, 'Address to the nation on foreign and domestic counter-terrorism strategies', 6 December 2015, *American Rhetoric: Online Speech Bank*, <http://www.americanrhetoric.com/speeches/barackobama/barackobamaforeigndomesticterrorismresponseovaloffice.htm> (accessed 15 August 2018).

O'Brien, Daniel, *Black Masculinity on Film: Native Sons and White Lies* (London: Palgrave Macmillan, 2017).
Office of Homeland Security, *National Strategy for Homeland Security*, Office of Homeland Security, July 2002, <https://www.dhs.gov/sites/default/files/publications/nat-strat-hls-2002.pdf> (accessed 16 June 2017).
O'Neill, Robert, *The Operator: Firing the Shots that Killed Osama bin Laden and My Years as a SEAL Team Warrior* (New York: Simon & Schuster, 2017).
Orr, Christopher, '30 years of Coens: true grit', *The Atlantic*, 26 September 2014, <https://www.theatlantic.com/entertainment/archive/2014/09/30-years-of-coens-true-grit/380776/> (accessed 8 January 2018).
Ortega, Frank, 'What's wrong with "wetback"?: What a Congressman's slur reveals', *Racism Review*, 11 April 2013, <http://www.racismreview.com/blog/2013/04/11/whats-wrong-with-wetback-what-a-congressmans-slur-reveals/> (accessed 6 November 2013).
O'Sullivan, John, 'Annexation', *United States Magazine and Democratic Review*, 1845, 17(1): 5–10, <https://pdcrodas.webs.ull.es/anglo/OSullivanAnnexation.pdf> (accessed 25 July 2018).
Owens, Ron, *Oklahoma Heroes: The Oklahoma Peace Officers Memorial* (Nashville, TN: Turner Publishing, 2000).
Palmer, R. Barton, *Joel and Ethan Coen* (Urbana: University of Illinois Press, 2004).
Parrish, Susan Scott, '*As I Lay Dying* and the modern aesthetics of ecological crisis', in John T. Matthews, *The New Cambridge Companion to William Faulkner* (Cambridge: Cambridge University Press, 2015).
Perry, Samuel P., 'Chained to it: the recurrence of the frontier hero in the films of Quentin Tarantino', in Oliver C. Speck (ed.), *Quentin Tarantino's Django Unchained: The Continuation of Metacinema* (New York and London: Bloomsbury, 2014), pp. 205–26.
Pilger, John, 'The invisible government', 16 June 2007, <http://johnpilger.com/articles/the-invisible-government> (accessed 30 January 2018).
Pinna, Antonio, 'Evaluation and ideology in political discourse: the use of extended units of meaning centred on modal verbs in G. W. Bush's Presidential speeches', in Giuliana Garzone and Srikant Sarangi, *Discourse, Ideology and Specialized Communication* (Peter Lang: Bern, 2007), pp. 433–50.
Pitts, Michael R., *Western Movies: A Guide to 5,105 Feature Films*, 2nd edn (Jefferson, NC: McFarland, 2013).
Portis, Charles, *True Grit* (London: Bloomsbury, 1968/2005).
Pulver, Andrew, 'Tommy Lee Jones on *The Homesman*: "It's a consideration of American imperialism"', *The Guardian*, 18 May 2014, <https://www.theguardian.com/film/2014/may/18/tommy-lee-jones-the-homesman-cannes-film-festival-hilary-swank> (accessed 15 August 2018).
Raphael, Ray, *Founding Myths: Stories That Hide Our Patriotic Past* (New York and London: New Press, 2004).

Rasmussen, Mikkel Vedby, *The Military's Business: Designing Military Power for the Future* (Cambridge: Cambridge University Press, 2015).

Rayner, Martha, 'You love the law too much', in Jonathan Hafetz (ed.), *Obama's Guantánamo: Stories from an Enduring Prison* (New York: New York University Press, 2016).

Reiss, Tom, *The Black Count: Glory, Revolution, Betrayal and the Real Count of Monte Cristo* (London: Harvill Secker, 2012).

Restad, Hilde Eliassen, *American Exceptionalism: An Idea that Made a Nation and Remade the World* (London and New York: Routledge, 2015).

Reyes, Xavier Aldana, *Body Gothic: Corporeal Transgression in Contemporary Literature and Horror Film* (Cardiff: University of Wales Press, 2014).

Rieupeyrout, Jean-Louis, *Le Western: ou, Le cinéma américain par excellence* (Paris: Éditions du Cerf, 1953).

Riofrio, John D. "Rio", *Continental Shifts: Migration, Representation, and the Struggle for Justice in Latin(o) America* (Austin: University of Texas Press, 2015).

Ritchie, David T., '"Western" notions of justice: legal outsiders in American cinema', *Suffolk University Law Review*, 2009, 42(49): 849–68, <http://suffolklawreview.org/ritchie-justice/> (accessed 15 January 2018).

Robinson, J. Dennis, *Jesse James: Legendary Rebel and Outlaw* (Minneapolis, MN: Compass Point Books, 2007).

Rueda, Carolina, 'Carlos Bolado's *Bajo California*: crossing borders and dislocating the western tradition', in MaryEllen Higgins, Rita Keresztesi and Dayna Oscherwitz (eds), *The Western in the Global South* (New York and London: Routledge, 2015).

Schouler, James, *History of the United States of America, Under the Constitution: 1801–1817; Jefferson Republicans* (New York: Dodd, Mead, 1894).

Schwartz, Harvey, *Building the Golden Gate Bridge: A Workers' Oral History* (Seattle: University of Washington Press, 2015).

Schwarzmantel, John, *Democracy and Political Violence* (Edinburgh: Edinburgh University Press, 2011).

Sebald, W. G., 'Reflections: a natural history of destruction', *The New Yorker*, 4 November 2002, pp. 66–77.

Sebald, W. G., *On the Natural History of Destruction*, trans. Anthea Bell (New York: Random House, 2003).

Seesengood, Robert Paul and Jennifer L. Koosed, *Jesse's Lineage: The Legendary Lives of David, Jesus, and Jesse James* (New York and London: Bloomsbury, 2013).

Settle, William, *Jesse James Was His Name: or, Fact and Fiction Concerning the Careers of the Notorious James Brothers of Missouri* (Lincoln: University of Nebraska Press, 1977).

Shouse, Eric, 'Feeling, emotion, affect', *M/C Journal*, 2005, 8(6), <http://journal.media-culture.org.au/0512/03-shouse.php> (accessed 23 November 2017).

Shugerman, Emily, 'Donald Trump says Mexico will pay for border wall after meeting with President Peña Nieto', *Independent*, 7 July 2017, <http://www.independent.co.uk/news/world-0/us-politics/donald-trump-mexico-pay-border-wall-meeting-president-pena-nieto-immigration-a7829266.html> (accessed 7 November 2017).

Slack, Jeremy, Daniel E. Martinez, Alison Elizabeth Lee and Scott Whiteford, 'The geography of border militarization: violence, death and health in Mexico and the United States', *Journal of Latin American Geography*, 2016, 15(1): 7–32.

Sledge, Michael, *Soldier Dead: How We Recover, Identify, Bury, and Honour Our Military Fallen* (New York: Columbia University Press, 2005).

Slotkin, Richard, *Gunfighter Nation: The Myth of the Frontier in Twentieth-Century America* (Norman: University of Oklahoma Press, 1998).

Smallman, Shawn, *Dangerous Spirits: The Windigo in Myth and History* (Victoria, BC: Heritage House, 2015).

Snyder, Timothy, *On Tyranny: Twenty Lessons From the Twentieth Century* (London: Bodley Head, 2017).

Spanos, William V., *American Exceptionalism in the Age of Globalization: The Specter of Vietnam* (Albany, NY: State University of New York Press, 2008).

Speck, Oliver C., 'Introduction: a southern state of exception', in Oliver C. Speck (ed.), *Quentin Tarantino's Django Unchained: The Continuation of Metacinema* (New York and London: Bloomsbury, 2014).

Speck, Oliver C. (ed.), *Quentin Tarantino's Django Unchained: The Continuation of Metacinema* (New York and London: Bloomsbury, 2014).

Sternheimer, Karen, *Celebrity Culture and the American Dream: Stardom and Social Mobility* (New York: Routledge, 2011).

Stiles, T. J., *Jesse James: Last Rebel of the Civil War* (London: Vintage, 2007).

Stockwell, Peter, *Cognitive Poetics: An Introduction* (London and New York: Routledge, 2002).

Stoddart, Scott F., '*Epilogue* – new visions/new vistas: Christopher Nolan's *Batman* trilogy and the New Western', in Scott F. Stoddart (ed.), *The New Westerns: Critical Essays on the Genre Since 9/11* (Jefferson, NC: McFarland, 2016).

Strang, Brent, 'Disinterring the Western in *Three Burials of Melquiades Estrada* and *No Country for Old Men*', in MaryEllen Higgins, Rita Keresztesi and Dayna Oscherwitz (eds), *The Western in the Global South* (New York and London: Routledge, 2015).

Swofford, Anthony, 'Foreword', in Iraq Veterans Against the War and Aaron Glantz, *Winter Soldier: Iraq and Afghanistan: Eyewitness Accounts of the Occupation* (Chicago, IL: Haymarket Books, 2008).

Temoney, Kate E., 'The "D" is silent, but human rights are not: *Django Unchained* as human rights discourse', in Oliver C. Speck (ed.), *Quentin Tarantino's Django Unchained: The Continuation of Metacinema* (New York and London: Bloomsbury, 2014), pp. 123–40.

Thompson, Anne, 'Alejandro G. Iñárritu on leading Oscar nominee *The Revenant*: "This was a film that easily could kill you"', *IndieWire*, 14 January 2016, <http://www.indiewire.com/2016/01/alejandro-g-inarritu-on-leading-oscar-nominee-the-revenant-this-was-a-film-that-easily-could-kill-you-175267/> (accessed 7 December 2017).

Tischler, Nancy, *Encyclopedia of Contemporary Christian Fiction: From C. S. Lewis to Left Behind* (Santa Barbara, CA: ABC-CLIO, 2009).

Tuller, Roger H., *'Let No Guilty Man Escape:' A Judicial Biography of 'Hanging Judge' Isaac C. Parker* (Norman: University of Oklahoma Press, 2001).

Turner, Ralph Lamar, '"Why do you think i am paying you if not to have my way?" Genre complications in the free-market critiques of fictional and filmed versions of *True Grit*', *Journal of Popular Culture*, 2015, 48(2): 355–70.

Urwin, Gregory J. W. (ed.), *Black Flag Over Dixie: Racial Atrocities and Reprisals in the Civil War* (Carbondale: Southern Illinois University Press, 2004).

Walker, Janet (ed.), *Westerns: Films through History* (New York and London: Routledge, 2001).

Walker, Joseph S., 'Coen, Coen on the range: Rooster Cogburn(s) and domestic space', in Scott F. Stoddart (ed.), *The New Westerns: Critical Essays on the Genre Since 9/11* (Jefferson, NC: McFarland, 2016), pp. 62–80.

Wall Street Journal, 'Reporter Daniel Pearl is dead, killed by his captors in Pakistan', *Wall Street Journal*, 24 February 2002, <https://www.wsj.com/articles/SB1014311357552611480> (accessed 14 November 2017).

Wecter, Dixon, *The Hero in America: A Chronicle of Hero-Worship* (New York: Scribner, [1941] 1963).

Welt, 'Django Unchained - Die komplette Pressekonferenz zur Deutschlandpremiere', *Welt*, 8 January 2013, <https://www.youtube.com/watch?v=hPsBl8pBEd0> (accessed 5 May 2018).

Wessells, Michael G., *Child Soldiers: From Violence to Protection* (Cambridge, MA: Harvard University Press, 2006).

White, James E., *Contemporary Moral Problems: War, Terrorism, and Torture* (Belmont, CA: Wadsworth, 2011).

White, John, *Westerns* (London and New York: Routledge, 2011).

Williams, John Hoyt, *A Great and Shining Road: The Epic Story of the Transcontinental Railroad* (Lincoln: University of Nebraska Press, 1996).

Williams, Linda, 'Film bodies: gender, genre, and excess', *Film Quarterly*, 1991, 44(4): 2–13.

Winkler, Adam, *Gunfight: The Battle Over the Right to Bear Arms in America* (New York and London: W. W. Norton, 2011).

Wishart, D. J., *The Fur Trade of the American West, 1807–1840: A Geographical Synthesis* (Lincoln: University of Nebraska Press, [1979] 1992).

Woodhall, Woody, 'Creating the sounds for *The Revenant*', *ProVideo Coalition*, 2 January 2016, <https://www.provideocoalition.com/creating-the-sounds-for-the-revenant/> (accessed 29 November 2017).

Woods, Tim, *Beginning Postmodernism* (Manchester and New York: Manchester University Press, 1999).
Žižek, Slavoj, *Welcome to the Desert of the Real: Five Essays on September 11 and Related Dates* (London and New York: Verso, 2002).
Žižek, Slavoj, *Against the Double Blackmail: Refugees, Terror and Other Troubles with the Neighbours* (London and New York: Penguin, 2017).

Index

3:10 to Yuma see Mangold, James
9/11, 1–2, 37, 99

Abrams, Dennis, 114
Addio Zio Tom/Goodbye Uncle Tom, 117
affect, 74–5, 100–1
Afghanistan, 37, 96, 97, 144
Alamo, The see Wayne, John
Altheide, David, 165, 169
American Civil War, 32, 35n, 64, 86–7, 162
   Quantrill's Raiders, 69n, 162
American Dream, 21
American exceptionalism, 99, 169
Anderson, Gary Clayton, 112
Andreas, Peter, 143
Appaloosa, 10, 16n
Aquila, Richard, 7, 36
As I Lay Dying, 144–5
Assassination of Jesse James by the Coward, Robert Ford, The see Dominik, Andrew
Auerbach, John, 66

Bad Day at Black Rock, 23
Ballad of Little Jo, The, 62–3
Band of Angels, 117
Bandy, Mary Lea and Kevin Stoehr, 9
Barber, Daniel
   Keeping Room, The, 11
Birth of a Nation, The, 111
Black Mama, White Mama, 115

blaxploitation, 114–15
Blazing Saddles, 79
body abuse, 94, 95, 97
   gore fest, 93
   pain porn, 95
   torture porn, 95–6, 105, 108n
Boetticher, Budd, 112
Bone Tomahawk see Zahler, S. Craig
borders *see* economic migration
Boss Nigger, 115
Brody, Richard, 40
Buck and the Preacher, 116
Bush, George W., 1, 2–3, 13n
Butler, Judith, 105

Cadwalladr, Carole, 95
Carter, Matthew, 7, 145, 146
Cawelti, John G., 67n
   'hero's code', 37
Charley One-Eye, 114
Chomsky, Noam, 6, 171
Christianity, 84–5
   and mysticism, 103–4
   Calvinist doctrine of the 'elect', 48
   redemption, 146
   salvation, 134–5
Civil Rights Movement, 39, 172
Cobb, Jasmine Nichole and John L. Jackson, 114
Coen, Ethan, 43

Coen, Joel and Ethan
  film style, 49–50
  No Country for Old Men, 12
  True Grit, 9, 10, 36–53
Cogburn, John Franklin, 37
Cold War, 8, 66
Corber, Robert J., 63
Corbucci, Sergio, 112, 116
Corkin, Stanley, 8, 172
Costner, Kevin, 22–3, 27
  Open Range, 9, 10, 21–35, 170–1
Cousins, Mark, 4
Cowboys & Aliens see Favreau, Jon
Csicsery-Ronay, Istvan, 78
  mutopia, 78
cultural conflict, 102–3
  and ethnic cleansing, 112
culture of fear, 160–1, 164, 165, 169
Cunningham, Hilary, 143

Darktown Strutters, 115
Defiant Ones, The, 117
democracy, 58–9, 65–6, 68n
  democratic freedoms, 29, 30, 31
Demos, Virginia, 101
Der Ring des Nibelungen (*The Ring of the Nibelung*), 118
DiCaprio, Leonardo, 101
Dirty Harry see Eastwood, Clint
distanciation *see* position of spectator
Django, 116
Django Unchained see Tarantino, Quentin
Dolin, Eric Jay, 102
Dominik, Andrew
  Assassination of Jesse James by the Coward, Robert Ford, The, 10, 47, 152–67

drone warfare, 46, 123
  and 'kill-list', 128n
Dumas, Alexandre, 118–19, 120–1, 127n
Dumas, Thomas-Alexandre, 119
Duvall, Robert, 21

Eastwood, Clint
  Dirty Harry, 68n
  Outlaw Josey Wales, The, 139
  Unforgiven, 48
Eberwein, Robert, 43
economic migration, 141–3
  and borders, 143–4, 149n
  and fur trade, 103
Edwards, Jason A. and David Weiss, 99
Edwards, John N., 161–2
Elkins, Stanley M., 124
Enlightenment, The, 82
escapism, 75
evil, 35n, 49, 64–5, 82–3, 139, 161
  good versus evil, 4
Ewers, John Canfield, 93
exceptionalism *see* American exceptionalism
executions, 30, 31, 60–1, 64

Fabre, Michel, 119
Favreau, Jon
  Cowboys & Aliens, 11
fear culture *see* culture of fear
first transcontinental railroad, 77
Fojas, Camilla, 4
Ford, John, 111–12
  Man Who Shot Liberty Valance, The, 38, 89n
  Searchers, The, 24, 52n, 55, 61, 82–3, 88–9n
foreign/Mexican 'Other'
  see economic migration

Fort Smith, 40–1, 51n
Forty Guns, 66
Furedi, Frank, 160–1

Gates Jr, Henry Louis, 110
gender, 91–2
   representation of men, 44, 57, 63–4
   representation of women, 56, 59, 61–3, 69n
Gilmore, Richard, 13
Giovanni, da Modena, 108n
Gittall, Noah, 43
Gone with the Wind, 113
Gray, Richard, 70n
Green Berets, The see Wayne, John
Grien, Hans Baldung, 107n
Grønstad, Asbjørn, 97
Guantanamo Bay, 122–3
Gulf War, 99
Gunning, Tom, 160
guns, 69n
   in the home, 32
   right to bear arms, 60
   use of guns, 28, 57
   women and guns, 38–9

Hagans, Dominic, 96
Halberstam, Judith, 63
Hall, Stuart, 98, 177n
Hancock, John Lee, 4
Hansen, Ron, 152–4
Hateful Eight, The see Tarantino, Quentin
Heaven's Gate, 26
Herman, David, 97
Hernandez, Martin, 94
Herzog, Werner, 101
Homeland Security Act, 59
Higbee, Will and Song Hwee Lim, 8
Hilger, Michael, 73

History of Violence, A, 67n
Hodgson, Godfrey, 99
home, 31–2, 55
homeland security, 59, 144
Horne, Thomas, 16n
Hostiles, 174
Hot Box, The, 115
Hunnef, Jenna, 44

ideology, 5–6, 7
   dominant ideology, 86, 170
   liberal ideology, 171–2
illegal immigrants *see* economic migration
Il grande silenzio/The Great Silence, 116
Il mercenario/The Mercenary, 116
Iñárritu, Alejandro González
   Revenant, The, 10, 91–108
Iraq, 3, 37, 97, 144

Jackson, Cassandra, 113
Jameson, Fredric, 122
Jane Got a Gun see O'Connor, Gavin
Jeffery, Renée, 67n
James, Jesse
   as Christ-like figure, 152–4
   as Satanic figure, 155–8
   historical figure, 158–9, 161–2, 164
Johnny Guitar, 63, 67n
Jones, Tommy Lee
   Homesman, The, 177n
   Three Burials of Melquiades Estrada, The, 10, 133–51, 171

Keeping Room, The see Barber, Daniel
Kellermann, Arthur L. and Philip J. Cook, 60
Kellner, Douglas, 7

Keresztesi, Rita, 4
Kerner, Aaron Michael, 95, 105
'kill-list' see drone warfare
Klein, Michael, 172
Kollin, Susan, 168–9
Kuška, Martin, 161

Laclau, Ernesto and Chantal Mouffe, 173
Laden, Osama bin, 25, 34n, 61
LaPierre, Wayne, 28
law and order, 38, 39, 60–1, 83, 85
Lawson, George, 14n
Legend of Nigger Charley, The, 115
Leonard, David, 124
Limon, John, 144
Little Big Man, 172–3
Locke, John
  Second Treatise on Civil Government, 82, 86
Lone Ranger, The see Verbinski, Gore
Lowenstein, Adam, 67n, 108n
Lusted, David, 5
lynchings, 93, 105n

McVeigh, Stephen, 5
Mandingo, 117, 126n
Mangold, James
  3:10 to Yuma, 11
manifest destiny *see* O'Sullivan, John
Manikkalingam, Ram, 123
Mapplethorpe, Robert, 114
Massumi, Brian, 74–5, 168
Meek's Cutoff see Reichardt, Kelly
Mepham, John, 6
Mercer, Kobena, 114
Mexican migrants *see* economic migration
Monument Valley, 77

Morris, Gregory, 164
Moses, Wilson Jeremiah, 117
Moss, Andrew, 50
mountain men, 98
mutopia *see* Csicsery-Ronay, Istvan
My Bondage and My Freedom, 124
Mythen, Gabe and Sandra Walklate, 164

narrative structure, 58, 80–1, 97–8
National Strategy for Homeland Security, 59–60
Nelson, Andrew Patrick, 9, 15n
Night of the Hunter, 29
No Country for Old Men see Coen, Joel and Ethan
Noble, Marianne, 113
Nolan, Christopher, 8
  Dark Knight, The, 24, 29

Obama, Barack, 14n, 54
O'Connor, Gavin, 60
  Jane Got a Gun, 10, 38, 54–70
Office of Homeland Security, 59
open range, 21, 25–6, 33
Open Range see Costner, Kevin
O'Sullivan, John
  manifest destiny, 33n
Outlaw Josey Wales, The, 24

Palmer, R. Barton, 50
Parker, Judge Isaac C., 40
Parrish, Susan Scott, 145
Pearl, Daniel, 150n
Pearl Harbor, 2
Perry, Samuel, 124
Pinna, Antonio, 13n
Pirates of the Caribbean series, 74
Pitts, Michael, 9
Pledge of Allegiance, 1
Portis, Charles, 39, 48

Portman, Natalie, 54
position of the spectator, 42, 45, 73, 74, 75, 76–7, 80–1, 86, 91, 94–5, 97, 100–1, 120, 121, 137–8, 170, 175
   distanciation, 137–8
post-marxism, 6
postmodernism, 42, 75–6, 78, 110–11, 120, 121–2

Quantrill's Raiders *see* American Civil War

Ramsay, Lynne, 68n
redemption *see* Christianity
Reichardt, Kelly
   Meek's Cutoff, 12
Restad, Hilde Eliassen, 99
Revenant, The see Iñárritu, Alejandro González
Reyes, Xavier Aldana, 101
Riofrio, John, 143
Ritchie, David T., 38
Roberts, Marguerite, 52n
Rueda, Carolina, 5
Russell, Charles Marion, 33n

salvation *see* Christianity
Scalphunters, The, 116
Schouler, James, 124
Schwarzmantel, John, 59, 68n
Searchers, The see Ford, John
Sebald, W. G. 'Max', 109–10
Second Treatise on Civil Government see Locke, John
Seesengood, Robert and Jennifer Koosed, 153–4
Settle, William, 159
Seven, 156
Seven Men From Now, 35n
Shane, 7, 25, 55, 62, 65
Shouse, Eric, 75, 100–1

Skin Game, 116
Sledge, Michael, 96
Slotkin, Richard, 45
Snyder, Timothy, 173, 177n
Soldier Blue, 172–3
Spanos, William V., 99
Speck, Oliver C., 109
spectacle, 74, 86, 121, 173
   body spectacle, 91, 95
spectator *see* position of spectator
Steele, Colonel Michael Dane, 69n
Sternheimer, Karen, 163
Stiles, T. J., 162
Stockwell, Peter, 81
Stoddart, Scott, 5, 7
Strang, Brent, 135, 140
Swofford, Anthony, 97

Tambakis, Anthony, 58
Tarantino, Quentin
   Django Unchained, 10, 109–29, 170
   Hateful Eight, The, 12
   Inglourious Basterds, 109
   Pulp Fiction, 121–2
   Reservoir Dogs, 120
Temoney, Kate, 129n
Three Burials of Melquiades Estrada, The see Jones, Tommy Lee
Tischler, Nancy, 153
torture, 34n, 61, 64, 96, 176
torture porn, 95, 101, 105, 108n
True Grit (1969), 36, 39
Trump, Donald, 43, 148n
Turner, Ralph Lamar, 4

Unforgiven see Eastwood, Clint

Verbinski, Gore
   The Lone Ranger, 10, 11, 73–90

Vietnam War, 23, 35n, 39, 43, 51n, 87, 99–100, 172–3

Walker, Janet, 5
Walker, Joseph, S., 7, 23, 44, 146
Waltz, Christoph, 109
'War on Terror', 24–5, 99–100, 169
'War on Terror' Westerns, 175–6
war veterans, 13, 24, 35n, 47, 64
Wayne, John, 36, 38, 43
  Alamo, The, 4, 55, 89n
  Green Berets, The, 43, 51–2n
Wecter, Dixon, 98
wendigo/windigo, 77, 89n

Wessells, Michael, 162
Westbound, 23
Western genre
  heroes, 45, 98
  popularity, 7
  transnational perspectives, 8, 16n
Williams, Linda, 91
Williamson, Fred, 115
Woods, Tim, 121–2

Zahler, S. Craig
  Bone Tomahawk, 12
Žižek, Slavoj, 6, 15n, 145

EU representative:
Easy Access System Europe
Mustamäe tee 50, 10621 Tallinn, Estonia
Gpsr.requests@easproject.com

www.ingramcontent.com/pod-product-compliance
Lightning Source LLC
Chambersburg PA
CBHW070824250426
43671CB00036B/2062